A Guide to the FRENCH Mediterranean PORTS including Corsica

Derek Bowskill

ADLARD COLES NAUTICAL
London

Dedication

This book is for my good friends John and Irene Coward of *Electra*. Their interest and enthusiasm, together with their humour and down-to-sea common-sense, heartened me enormously; while their realistic attitude to all things nautical did nothing but encourage me when I was in danger of becoming over anxious.

Published by Adlard Coles Nautical
an imprint of A & C Black (Publishers) Ltd
35 Bedford Row, London WC1R 4JH

Copyright © text and illustrations
Derek Bowskill 1992

First published in Great Britain by
Adlard Coles Nautical 1992

ISBN 0–7136–3565–7

A CIP catalogue record for this book is available from the British Library.

Typeset in Rockwell and printed and bound in Great Britain by Butler & Tanner Ltd, Frome and London

Contents

Preface

I have tried to write the guide that I wanted to consult when I visited these French ports for the first time from seaward. The information is neither encyclopedic nor exhaustive, but it is intended to be sufficient and necessary for a safe and anxiety-free discovery of each new port. Nor do I pretend that the comments and judgements are not partial. Many things have changed on the Mediterranean coast of France since I first arrived there over forty years ago: many of them for the better, some quite the opposite. Without being nostalgically obsessed with a world that I could never have inhabited in the first place, and without wanting to damn the French for being too far behind the times, I have written as I have found. The research was demanding (albeit pleasurably so), for, apart from the supplementary material, I have visited – and in the main enjoyed – every place of which I have written. I hope this book will tempt you to explore, to enjoy, and to compare your views with mine.

I shall be pleased to hear from anyone who cares to write: whether it be to agree, to disagree, to make a point, or just to comment; and I shall be particularly grateful to anyone who can help improve the book by informing me of any significant errors of omission or commission.

Derek Bowskill
Valcon

Acknowledgements

I would like to thank the many people who helped and prompted me during the research for this guide. In particular, I am indebted to all those kind souls at the many Capitaineries who were frequently badgered; and all those at *Motor Boats Monthly*, without whose support life would have been pretty unsupportable.

Introduction

THE GUIDE

This cruising companion/guide has two main functions: to be informative and entertaining. It is presented in three main sections: the plans, the information tables and the texts.

The plans and tables offer the basic information for approaching and entering the ports; it is presented in such a way that the facts can be quickly absorbed. With a few exceptions, the page layouts are the same for each port, thus enabling the details to be absorbed at a glance. Approach and entry are dealt with concisely in the text that follows.

The second function is that of 'appetite whetter' and 'warner-offer' of risky trifles: an aid to planning (and/or dreaming) during a bad winter. This is covered in the sections under Commentary and Remarks.

THE PLANS

The plans are, in the main, oriented northward, and have been specially drawn to facilitate an easy understanding of the nature of each port and its entry. While they are not exact to Ordnance scale, they provide a plan that is easy to follow but not inaccurate. The information given on the plans are as follows:

Information (usually the Capitainerie)
Reception quay
Anchorage
Entry marker with light, port
Entry marker with light, starboard
Sea
Sea wall
Buildings

THE TABLES

The information is laid out as shown opposite:

NAME OF PORT
LATITUDE AND LONGITUDE
ALL PORTS WORK VHF 9 UNLESS STATED OTHERWISE HERE
TELEPHONE
PORT RATING   TOWN RATING
Appeal: A – B – C
Services: 1 – 2 – 3

sea areas	*buildings*	*rocks*	*sea walls*
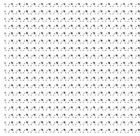	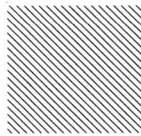	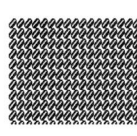	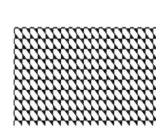

Ⱥ *Accueil Reception*

N ▲ *North*

▷ *Starboard marker Usually lit*

ⓘ *Information Capitainerie*

⚓ *Anchorage*

▯ *Port marker Usually lit*

Charts	French SHOM, ECM; British ADM
Lights	Where relevant
Marks	Where relevant
Reception	Location
Moorings	Sort and style
Draught	Maximum
Berths	Total
Fuel	Location
Weather	Sort and position
Boatyard Services	Sort and style
Shops	Sort and style

LOA Maximum

Visitors Number theoretically set aside

REMARKS Special comments qualifying any of the above.
APPROACH Notes for the outer approach.
ENTRY Notes for the inner approach and final entry.
COMMENTARY Miniature portrait of port and town.
REMARKS Additional special information where relevant.

THE ELEMENTS

Salt seas

The Mediterranean is Europe's bluest sea, its shade of artists' cobalt blue comes from the clarity of the water. However, it is not just bluer: rapid evaporation makes it more salty than the North Sea or the Atlantic. True, the mix is not as thick as Red Sea soup, but the saline effect is immediately noticeable on the boat, on the person and in the engine cooling system.

The customary winds guarantee that you can seldom cruise without taking on board a new skin before the sun is over the yard arm; and, what is more, that salt skin will carry its own impurities of dust and sand. It is possible that anything less than immediate meticulous cleansing can leave you scarred for life.

Deep waters

The Provençal coastline drops sharply into water that becomes relatively deep a short distance from the shore. From Nice to Menton the Alps plunge abruptly into the sea. For example, between Nice and Cap Ferrat the official estimates for depth indicate soundings of 1000m (3280ft) no more than 1000m offshore. For those who are used to the shoal areas of the east coast of England and the sandbanks of the Channel such an experience can come as a shock.

There are two ways of perceiving this phenomenon: no danger of grounding; what a long way down before you stop. Not only is the water deep, but it is so clear that you can see the rocks on the bottom as you enter a harbour – unnerving until you get used to the fact that you can see down for *metres* not inches as in the North Sea.

Blue skies

The atmosphere, except in high summer, is so clear that it is possible to see very distant places. Such malperceptions can cause havoc with navigation if you start to doubt radar or dead reckoning. Consequently, good binoculars are particularly advantageous. Mr Michelin says, '... outlines are sharpened and natural features acquire an architectural likeness in the clear air. The shining blue of the sea and sky blends with the green of the forest, the silver-grey of the olive trees, the red porphyry rock and the white limestone.'

Wild winds

The mistral, that classic that typically blows down the Rhône Valley, takes its name from Old Provençal: Maestral. It certainly lives up to it, being an absolute magister, master and maestro of a wind. The tramontane, also the name for the Polar Star, is a similar wind, but one that is distributed more generally over the Mediterranean, and in France tends more to the west. These winds share a number of attributes: their arrival and gusts can be forceful and unannounced, they are accompanied by fine sunny weather, they are northerlies, and they are keen like a thousand knives – cold, cutting and lethal.

My first experience was a petit mistral down the Rhône: in high summer its cool breeze, going my way, was more than welcome. The second was a young tramontane at La Ciotat. There I was well protected from the wind, although not from its unpleasantly attendant swell. The third was a combination of the two full grown, and apparently working in sympathy and harness, at Cogolin in the bay of St Tropez.

The combination of cold dry wind and hot dry sun is difficult either to believe or to endure. They say it blows for three days at a time and lasts from three to twelve. I had the three-day version: after being blown into reverse on my bike, having to remove my glasses so they were not snatched from my face, and spending one whole night tending *Valcon*'s ropes, I knew that four days would have been the end. No wonder the mistral drives people mad, can be a mitigating circumstance in a *crime passionnel,* and is cause for obsessive concern with *la meteo*. True, they can get up surprisingly fast, but attention to barometer, weather maps and forecasts usually gives a good prediction; it is only on longer passages that you are likely to be caught out.

Swell

Since there is virtually no tide in this inland sea, there is no solid moving force to organise the swell. It attacks from all quarters and its conduct and progress are difficult to predict. Weather forecasts pay little attention to it, though some local papers do their best.

Sail is not as helpful as it might be, for the winds are flukey to say the least. Fast motor cruisers cope with it very well by ignoring it at high speeds, thus adding swell to swell.

MEDITERRANEAN SEA:
French weather forecast areas

Genoa

Lyons

Provence

West Corsica

East Corsica

West Sardinia

East Sardinia

North Balearics

South Balearics

South Sardinia

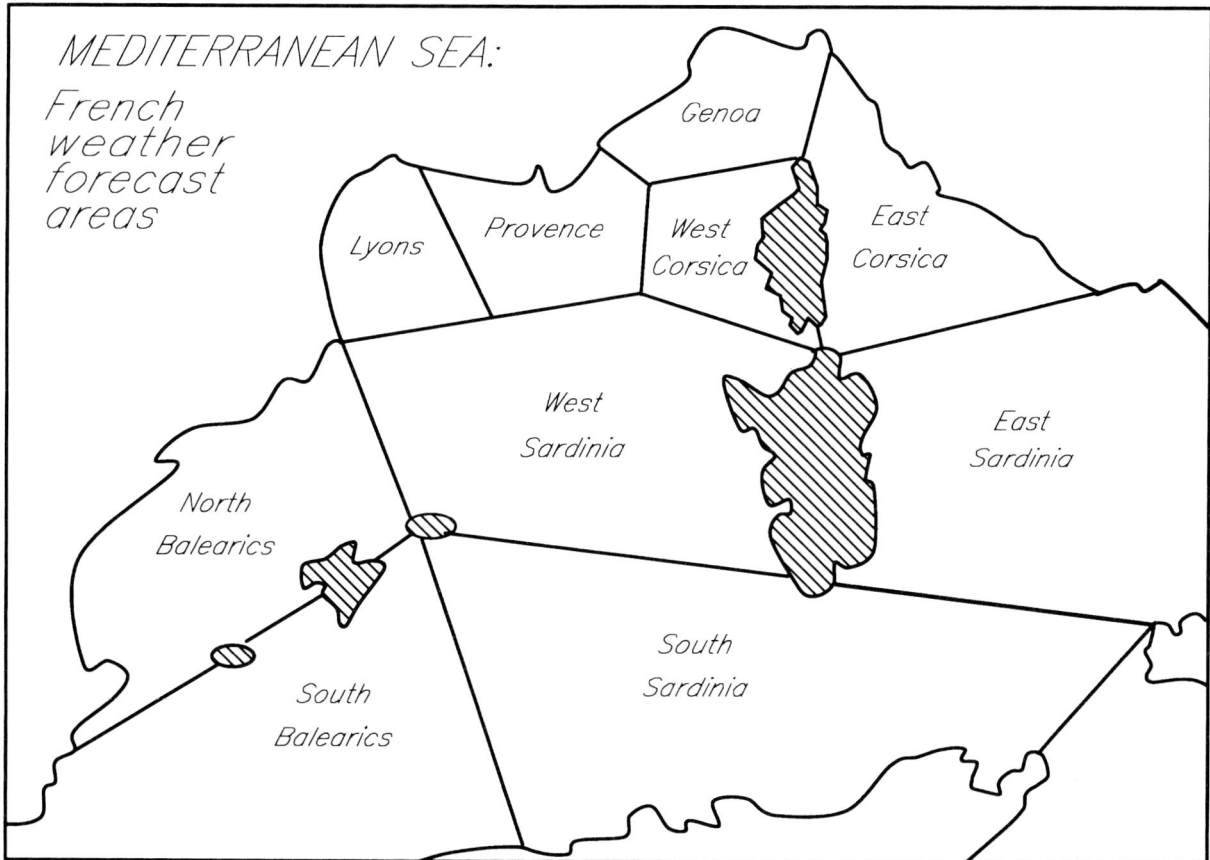

WEATHER FORECASTS

In the Mediterranean it is not easy to forecast the weather from hour to hour or dawn till dusk, let alone day to day. True, it tends to be calm first thing, to blow up during the day, and to fall off again towards evening. But that is a tendency and no more.

The choices in the Med are: setting off and hoping for the best; checking your own area forecasts regularly; and consulting all available forecasts. The latter has the drawback of being time-consuming: buying the papers, remembering the forecast times (GMT or local?), their working frequencies, the sea areas, the report format and the language to be used. There are five basic services: telephone, harbour offices, newspapers, television and radio.

Telephone services

You need a good command of the language, since they tend to be very fast. French recorded

services are very useful. The following numbers cover the main areas:

Perpignan	68 61 03 92
La Grande Motte	67 56 57 69 and 67 56 52 78
Cap d'Agde	67 26 00 21 and 67 26 00 22
Montpellier	67 65 81 81
Marseille	91 90 35 00
Marignane	42 09 09 09
Toulon	94 46 90 11 (Coastal)
	94 46 90 50 (Sea area)
St Tropez	94 97 23 57
Nice	93 83 91 12
Paris	45 55 91 36
Bastia	95 36 05 96

Harbour office services

These are usually good in France, ranging from a simple written or tape-recorded statement in French to detailed reports in French and English, sometimes with charts.

Newspapers

The two major French dailies, *Le Monde* and *Figaro,* publish comprehensive forecasts complete with 'before and after' charts.

Television

UK sets do not work in France, but for under £100 you can buy a mains/battery portable set. Monsieur Meteo (the weather man) is just as idiosyncratic as his British counterpart. He appears regularly, but not always at the advertised time. It is a good idea to tune in ten minutes early and be prepared for a twenty-minute wait.

Radio broadcasts

Public broadcasting services are very good in France, and VHF forecasts are excellent. All times are GMT/TU/UT unless otherwise indicated.

BBC Radio 4 In certain areas of the Med, depending upon exact location, time and weather conditions, BBC Radio 4 shipping bulletins can be received. Patience and good equipment are essential.

Radio France (France Inter) covers all UK sea areas as well as the western Mediterranean with two rather strange exceptions, Alboran and the South Balearics (French sea areas 511 and 512):
    on 164 kHz
    at 0645 and 2003 (after the news) Mon–Fri, local time,
    at 0655 and 2003 Sat–Sun, local time.

The broadcast in French with gale and strong winds warnings first, is extremely fast and not repeated. It can be received, depending upon conditions, from San Remo to Gibraltar and throughout Corsica and the Balearics. Radio France programmes are relayed on MW by other French stations, especially Radio Marseille on 675 kHz, and on FM from 87.8 to 100 MHz by local stations.

Radio Monte Carlo offers a similar service in French:
    on 218 and 1466 kHz
    at 0800 and 1900.
Best reception is restricted in the main to French coastal areas.

Radio France International covers the nearby Atlantic areas with many frequencies, but generally the best reception for the Med is:
    on 6175 (and occasionally on 738) kHz
    at 1140, local time.

Radio France – Nice/Côte d'Azur (General coastal forecast):
    on 103.8, 101.4 and 92.6 MHz
    at 0730/0830, 1000/1100, 1330/1400, 1500/1530, 1815/1830, local time.

Radio France – Marseille
Local forecast: Grau du Roi to La Ciotat:
    on 96.7 and 103.1 MHz
    at 0715, local time

Local forecast: Port Camargue to St Raphael
    at 1045, local time.

Radio France – Roussillon Local forecast: Roussillon
    on 92.1 MHz
    at approx 0700 Summertime only, local time.

Radio France – Herault–Montpellier Local forecast: Narbonne Plage to Port Camargue
    on 95.2/103.8 and 101.2 MHz
    at 0610 (Mon–Fri), 0715 (Sat–Sun), 1855, local time.

Radio France – Corsica General forecast
    on 101.7 MHz
    at 0728, 0840, 1155 and 1835, local time.

Radio Perpignan Local forecast: Narbonne to Cerbère
    on 92.1 MHz
    at 0700, local time.

Radio Montpellier General coastal forecast
    on 95.2, 102, 103.8 and 101.2 MHz
    at 0845 (Mon–Fri), 0755 (Sat–Sun), local time.

Radio Andorre Local forecast: Aude Roussillon, 1 May to 30 Sept
    on 702 kHz
    at 0845, 1250 and 1905, local time.

Sud Radio General coastal forecast 1 July to 8 Sept
    on 819 and 102.5 MHz
    at 0840
Also VHF 9 Canet (even hours) and Leucate (odd hours).

VHF and SSB transmissions

There is no guarantee that weather bulletins will be given at the advertised times. Occasionally, they are up to two minutes early; more frequently, though, they are up to fifteen minutes late. That is, without notice of delay being broadcast; with notice, that time can be extended to forty-five minutes – and usually without explanation. In particular, Monaco Radio is so sympathetic to its radio-telephone link call clientele that the weather broadcast can be held up for ten to fifteen minutes.

There is another hazard. The farther you are from the main station of Marseille, the more you will find weather broadcasts on VHF (especially Ch 9) and (unthinkably) also on SSB impeded and even completely disrupted by other traffic: yachtsmen and fishermen, amateurs and so-called professionals alike.

Monaco Radio – Navimet

One of the very best of the French weather forecast services is that provided by Monaco Radio on Ch 23. Known as Navimet, it is a recorded bulletin that covers the inshore area from Menton to Cannes. It is updated three times daily (when for short periods it is off the air) and is presented first in French and then in English. It is best to get to grips with the French version for two reasons. The English translation is not always exact in language or information. It comes second, and if there is not enough tape and/or time, the English bulletin comes to an abrupt end.

Coast radio stations

CROSS (Centres Regionaux Operationnels de Surveillance et de Sauvetage). They keep a 24-hour watch on VHF Ch 16, with gale warnings on reception and then every two hours. You can request a 'bulletin meteo' on Ch 16. You will then be given a working channel.

CROSSMED La Garde
Port Camargue to La Ciotat and La Ciotat to Cannes
at 0910 local time
on VHF Ch 9
Port Vendres to Menton
at 1830 local time
on VHF Ch 9

CROSSMED Agde
Cap Cerbère to Port Camargue
at 0830 local time
on VHF Ch 9

Port Vendres to Menton
at 1815 local time
on VHF Ch 9

CROSSMED Corse
Coastal areas
at 0845 and 1845 local time
on VHF Ch 9

France Telecom

All broadcasts are at 0733 and 1233 local time, preceded by an initial call on VHF Ch 16.

Marseille

Perpignan: VHF Ch	2
Sète:	25
Martigues:	28
Marseille:	26 (also try 24)
Toulon:	62

Grasse

Cavalaire:	4
Grasse:	2
Bastia:	24
Porto Vecchio:	25
Ajaccio:	24

SSB

Marseille Radio
on 1906 kHz
at 0103, 0705, 1220, 1616

Grasse Radio
on 2649 and 3722 kHz
at 0733, 1233, 1645

Monaco Radio
on 8728.2 kHz
at 0715, 1715
on 4363.6 kHz
at 0903, 1403, 1815

Monaco also broadcasts on 8743.7, 13172.1, 17251.5, 22651.8 kHz.

These services, which cover all Mediterranean sea areas, are excellent. Marseille and Grasse are in French. Each forecast and current station reports are given first at dictation speed, with each phrase repeated, followed by a repetition at normal speed. The Monaco bulletin is similar: no station reports, but with the advantage of being in French and English.

Grasse is the most locally restricted in terms of reception. With a good aerial and normal weather conditions, Marseille can be received along the whole of the French Mediterranean coast, frequently in the Balearic Islands, and from time to time on the Spanish coast. Monaco Radio can be well received from Corsica to Gibraltar, and they are always pleased to hear from listeners about local radio reception and weather conditions.

Marine Mobile

Broadcasting in English, this is Station G8 UK Maritime, with a devoted clientele somewhat charmingly known as Marine Mobile. Operating on 14.303 kHz, it goes live for a couple of hours at 0600 and 1800 GMT (or UT or TU to taste). Its prime function seems to be to keep an ever-growing family of cruising Brits, many of whom are 'live aboards', in touch with one another, as well as their loved ones back home. And if you can't get in touch direct with your contacts on the other side of the globe, there is usually someone who can help out with a relay message service.

Its daily diet consists of two main spheres of interest: the weather and news. During each broadcast, you get a run-down of the weather from more or less all the popular areas, as well as a continuing saga of cruising folk. If you listen daily, you will get to know the routines and state of health of the dedicated band that keep the station alive, and the fervent few offer much appreciated help to all those with urgent personal messages or who are just lonely on the sea. The author uses the following equipment:

Furuno SSB Transceiver FS 1550 Only moderate success: the limited number of transmission frequencies must be preset by a Furuno agent; and in spite of good antennae installations, both reception and transmission are often marred by noise and cross-station interference.

Seafarer Seavoice 550 VHF Excellent results.

Sony ICF-7600D (FM 76–108 MHz LW/MW/SW 153–29995 kHz) With top-class antennae, results are good except on long wave. When on mains and ship's batteries there is no problem, but internal battery life is ludicrous: it can be less than two hours.

Two inexpensive Philips LW/MW sets For two reasons: LW reception is better than the Sony, and battery consumption is negligible.

COST OF LIVING

Fuel

Prices are controlled by the government and are the same throughout France. Petrol costs about the same as in the UK; if anything, a little more. 'White' diesel (the only legal variety for leisure craft) tends to be much more expensive but, since prices to boats vary so much in the UK, it is difficult to give an exact comparison. In the summer of 1991 diesel was 3.60F a litre – about £2 a gallon.

Food

There is little difference in price in this area, especially if eating out in the larger towns, marina prices being, of course, sky-high world-wide. But there is a much wider choice when it comes to searching out small, back-street restaurants, where you can still eat and drink well for £7 to £8 per head.

Charcuteries and *traiteurs* are everywhere: these home-made experts constantly tempt and their food is usually excellent. However, they are expensive. Bearing in mind the splendid choice of fresh foods and the far from expensive vegetables, there is a real saving to be made by doing your own cooking.

Fees

All ports operate seasonal differentials, either two or three: summer and winter – with late spring and early autumn being optional extras. There are so many variables that it is difficult to offer reliable information. For 9–10m craft, charges range from 35F all in, to 150F for mooring fees only.

Theoretically, each port has its published rates, and the factors governing the price are the length of boat, duration of stay, and how many of the services you wish to use. Some ports offer showers, power and water all in, and some charge extra (see below). In fact the price you will be charged frequently depends more upon who is on duty, what mood he/she is in, whether or not he/she likes your boat, and how well you get on – with a most important point being how hard you try to speak to them in French. A happy preliminary chat can bring a 50 per cent reduction, or even a complimentary berth for the night.

Money

There are many ways in which the screens at cash points inform you that you are not going to get your money: 'We sincerely regret that your request cannot be met at this moment'. 'We are most sorry that your bank will not accede to your request'. 'We apologise for not being able to process your honoured application immediately'. However, some are blunt: 'Your bank would not approve this transaction'.

The most unlikely reason for failure is a shortage of funds. After all, most of us know more or less how near we are to our credit limit or overdraft facility. No, the usual reasons are technical: the individual till, the bank's system, or technical gnomes somewhere in Europe. Generally, from Monday evening to Friday afternoon, the system works well and bank notes with timed receipts, placed and dated, appear after only a few keyboard entries and few seconds' wait. However, from Friday evening (or at best Saturday noon) to Monday afternoon, the chance of failure is high.

The Monday morning syndrome is international, and in this particular it expresses itself through clogged telephone lines. This graspable explanation has been given to me by a number of banks, but none has been able to explain the too frequent failure at the weekends. Many people accept it as just foreign fate, bad luck or their ineptitude in using the keyboard, but this is not the case: cards and tills that work perfectly well before and after, frequently fail at weekends. There is a theory that it is a regular cross Channel shutdown to limit fraud, but no bank is as yet willing to confess. To guard against all this it is a good idea to open an account with a French bank and obtain a Carte Bleu from them.

EQUIPMENT

Sun and wind

A strong awning and internal and external blinds are important shields from heat, bright light and gritty winds. Neither a refrigerator nor a freezer should be deemed a luxury. However, it is not necessary to spend a fortune on so-called specialised Mediterranean equipment: my standard UK Electrolux models worked extremely well, even in temperatures above 30°C. Another way of fighting the heat is to install a barbecue outside and a microwave cooker inside – thus providing the luxury of hot food without cooking the chef. Portable electric fans (AC and DC) are indispensable.

Mains power and water supplies

Almost every port of call uses a different type of electric cable plug and/or water hose connector. Even if the actual electric plug appears to be the same, you may find it will still not work, since some have complex innards and are wired quite differently. In the immediate environs of St Tropez, you will need five different connectors for electrics and three for water.

For up-to-date marinas that pride themselves on offering you telephone, telex, fax and satellite TV in addition to your mooring, such an inane system would seem to be prompted by a lack of intelligence or an attack of wilful perversity. However, experience suggests a more compelling motive: profit. In order to survive you must purchase, hire by the day or, in a few strange cases, borrow against the deposit of your passport, ship's papers or a sum of anything up to £50, the appropriate connection for the port.

If you intend to cruise regularly in a specific area the way round the problem is to make up short lengths of cable with a plug for each known socket at one end and a connector for your long standard boat cable at the other. On the other hand, if you are planning a cruise into previously unvisited territory, it is a good idea also to carry a short lead with bare ends so that you are ready to connect with whatever gadget the next port may favour.

Some ports include electricity and water in the general mooring fee; some charge an extra flat fee for electricity, another flat fee for water, or one for both. Others charge for both on meters. However, not all guarantee that your particular post or station will carry a live socket, so carry enough cable extensions to defeat their shortcomings, at least 50m.

Gas

Camping Gaz is everywhere, but it is also expensive. If gas is of major importance on your boat, it is best to wait until you get to France and then buy one of the standard proprietary French bottles of butane: Primagaz, Totalgaz, Butagaz, Elfgaz and so on. They are inexpensive and readily available.

MOORING

More and more, the French are installing finger pontoons; but it is still usual to moor stern or bows to a quay, which may be solid terra firma concrete or a floating pontoon. In unknown territory (the inner recesses or lower depths of some ports for example) a bows-to mooring avoids the risk of any unnecessary unpleasant grounding.

Since the French have not fully mastered the art of building sea walls and breakwaters in quite the right places (or perhaps just not making

them long enough) many ports are subject to
extremely unpleasant swells and surges. Thus
strong mooring lines, chains and anti-snubbing
devices are essential.

It is a good idea to wait until you arrive in a
French port with a well-equipped chandlery and
a co-operative staff. You will then be able to get
a whole mooring set made up by those who know
exactly what wear and tear is to be expected on
a boat like yours. That said, good chandlery
stores are not all that frequent.

CUSTOMS (DOUANES)

The situation tends to be complicated, but it is
neither intimidating nor dismaying unless you
are fanatically devoted to sweet reason as a way
of life. Like most Frenchmen, customs officers
are garrulous – and confusing on the matter of
how long I could stay. Yes, I could stay for more
than six months; no, I could not stay for more
than six months, not without a Titre de Sejour,
that is; no, I was not an acceptable applicant for
a Titre de Sejour. In the end, I was issued one
such by an officer who said I didn't need one but
he would let me have one just in case.

This Titre de Sejour, the document that
permits a foreign boat an elongation of stay in
France without tax or confusion, was greeted
with joy mingled with surprise by later customs
officers, some of whom proceeded to ignore it,
but most of whom then treated me like a VIP.
Their visits were limited to a cursory chat until I
got within striking distance of the Spanish coast
at Port Leucate, when suspicion of trafficking
became the order of the day. I was hailed alongside at sea and visited in port usually for a short
meet with two douanes. But one night at 2200,
four of them descended with two Alsatian dogs
and took *Valcon* more or less apart for four
hours. After that, in spite of having jaunted in
and out of Spain, I was left alone – even waved
at.

In port offices, curious rites of passage may
reveal themselves. This is a selection:

Show your passport
Show your ship's papers
Hand in your passport
Hand in your ship's papers
Fill in 1/2/3 form(s) in du/tri/quadru/plicate
Deposit 500F against hasty departure.

Not quite an infinite variety, but more than
enough to keep anyone from going stale.

Part One

MENTON TO ST TROPEZ

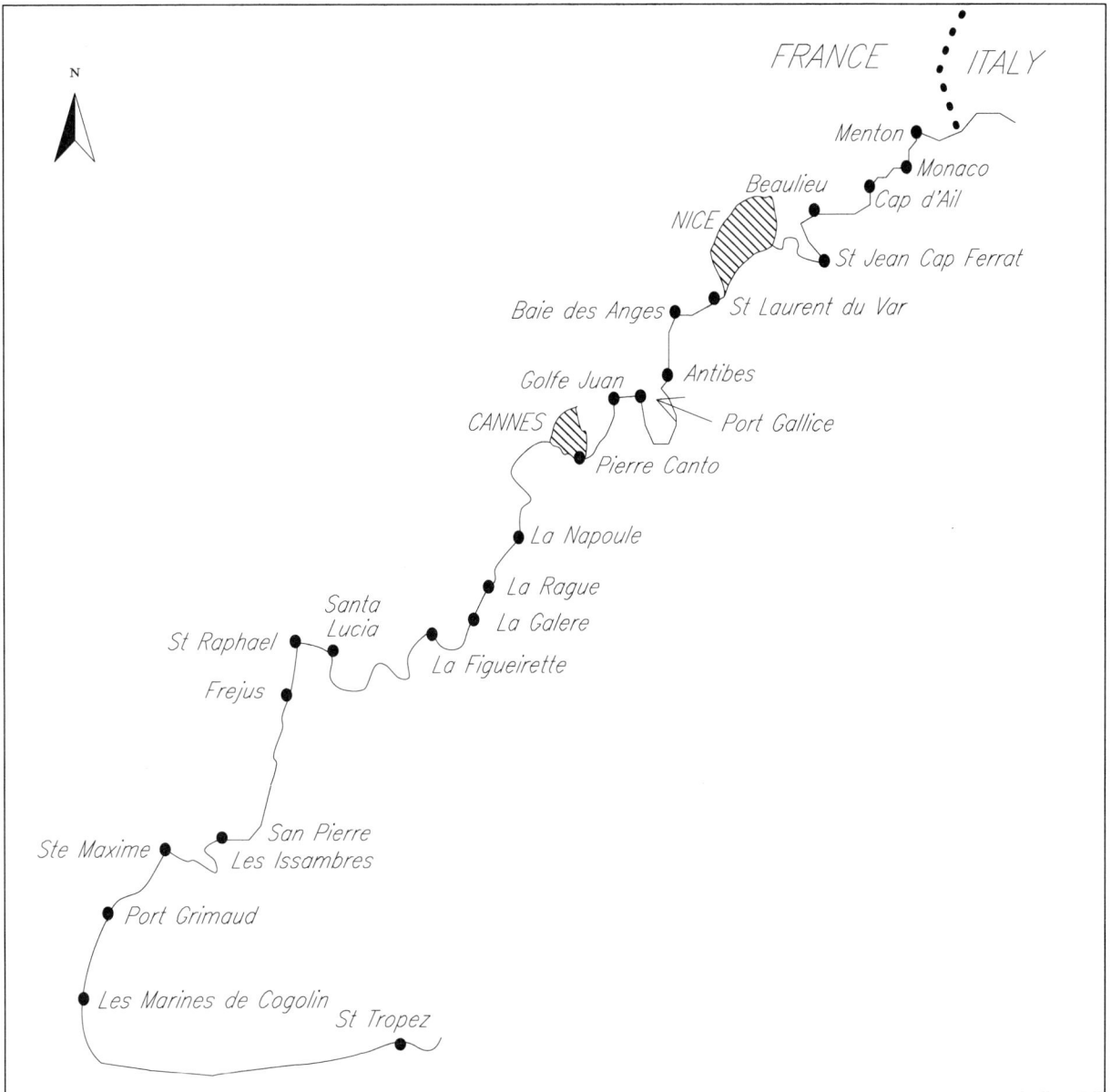

FRANCE   ITALY

Menton

Monaco

Beaulieu   Cap d'Ail

NICE

St Jean Cap Ferrat

Baie des Anges   St Laurent du Var

Golfe Juan   Antibes

CANNES   Port Gallice

Pierre Canto

La Napoule

La Rague

Santa   La Galere
Lucia

St Raphael   La Figueirette

Frejus

San Pierre

Ste Maxime   Les Issambres

Port Grimaud

Les Marines de Cogolin

St Tropez

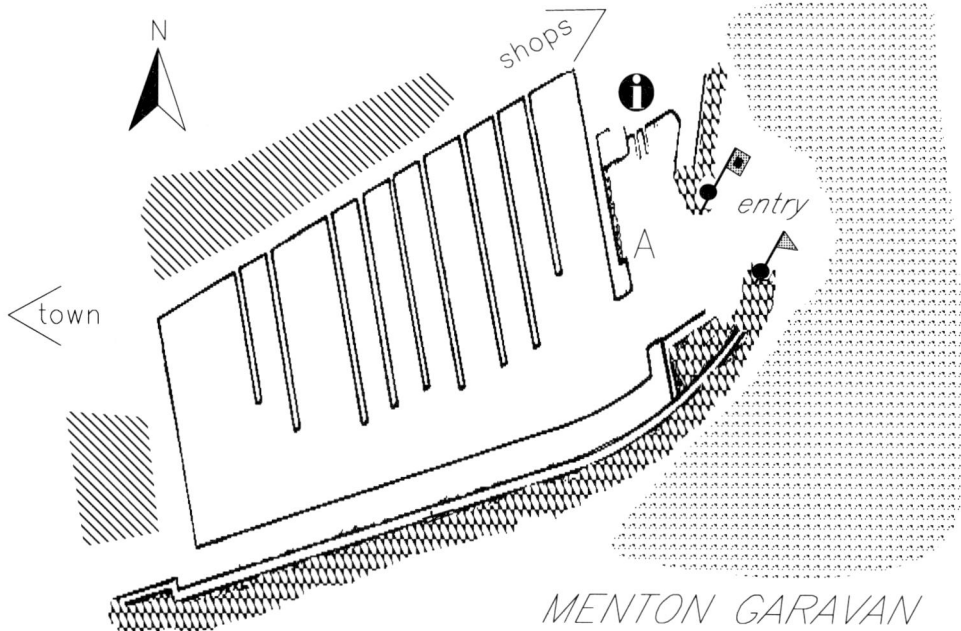

MENTON GARAVAN

Charts	SHOM 5347, 5208 ECM 500 ADM 2167
Lights	S Breakwater Fl(2)R 6s 11m 10M W/R Tower N Jetty Fl G 4s 3m 2M G/W Base
Marks	One mile to the west of Port Garavan, the church of St Michel, high in the old town of Menton, makes an unmistakable landmark by day or by night, when it is strikingly lit.
Reception	Just inside the harbour to starboard at the fuel quay.
Moorings	Quay: to laid chain.
Draught	4.5m **LOA** 40m
Berths	800 **Visitors** 144
Fuel	Reception quay.
Weather	Large automatic column TV screen next to the Capitainerie.
Boatyard Services	Comprehensive.
Shops	Codec supermarket on site; general grocery just across the road with a cafe and paper shop next door. Town shops are comprehensive: good cheese, poor charcuterie. There is a covered market by the old port, good for meat; and an open one by the railway station, good for country fruit and vegetables.

REMARKS

Toilets outstandingly good – clean and fresh with plenty of usable loo paper; and the showers, delicate delights, can be used ad infinitum.

APPROACH

Menton lies midway in the bay formed by Cap Martin and Capo Mortalo (marked by a YB Cardinal), but does not come into view from the west until Cap Martin has been rounded into 030°. Then it is unmistakable even from a distance because of the St Michel clock tower in old Menton, just to the west of Menton Garavan.

You will soon know if you have overshot Garavan and sailed into Italian waters because the coastline presents you with a new phenomenon: rows of slender parallel greenhouses clinging to the steep sides of the mountains, glinting from above the ribbon-fringe of the developed beach strip far below them.

ENTRY

The entrance is marked by a red-topped white tower. Having turned in to port, you will see the green and white light structure on the north jetty, in front of the Capitainerie tower block. The reception and fuel quay is then dead ahead. Radar alerts the Capitainerie in their eyrie of all entries and exits.

Winds from the south and east can make entry difficult, especially because of the configuration of the coast on the Italian side. Once inside, however, the port is well protected from the mistral and all easterlies.

COMMENTARY

This marina, with its many services and its agreeable climate, is a favourite stopping-off place and wintering hole for Italians and Brits alike. It is difficult to get a place even for a few days, let alone the winter.

Menton's situation is paramount. Citrus fruits are on the trees all the year round in Menton but, somewhat surprisingly since it is so close, no such claim can be made for the Italian Riviera. Protected by the Alps, Menton enjoys an exceptional climate, claiming 300 days of sunshine out of 365. I was there on one 6 November to enjoy the fourth day of rain that year! Lemon, lime and orange trees flourish in the marina, symbols of the delights of the famous February Lemon Festival.

If further proof were needed it can be found at the Tropical Garden, just off the Promenade de la Mer. The Villa Val Rameh has a terraced garden with over 700 species of Mediterranean tropical and sub-tropical flora, all fully acclimatised to Menton. In the midst of the citrus groves you will come across passiflora, guava and avocado, and find the lotus flourishing in a large pool. From here you also get a good view of the old town and the bay.

Local legend has it that when Adam and Eve were invited to leave the Garden of Eden, Eve managed to smuggle out a lemon. After years of melancholy wandering they found some high wooded slopes by the sea, where it was always spring. Eve took the lemon (unwithered from being kept on her breast), kissed its glowing skin and planted it. The slopes were soon covered with beautiful scented trees.

Such was the romantic legendary beginning of the earthly paradise today known as Menton. Certainly the facts are that the oldest known inhabitant of the Riviera lived here some 30 000 years ago, leaving his skull behind to prove it. It can now be seen at Menton's Municipal Museum. Its owner has come to be known as the Grimaldi Man, since his remains were found in Les Rochers Rouge just below the little village of Grimaldi at the Italian border. After that, all was silence until the 13th century.

Menton is no more than 500m from the Italian border, halfway between Rome and Paris, and is the first and last staging post of the French Riviera. While there is still argument as to where the Côte d'Azur ends, there is none whatsoever about where it begins. Here at Menton: as they say, the doorway to France. There is a local stopping train service between Vintimille in Italy and St Raphael. Menton is the first stop on the French coastline.

REMARKS

Shopping is easy at the local supermarket, but both the old and new towns alike are best investigated. In the main, the place is given over to tourist trappings; however, careful exploration exposes a number of dedicated artisans, particularly for cheese and wine. Olive bread is extremely good here.

There are extensive facilities for boat works and chandlery alongside the marina, parallel to the main road. There are also some domestic services, in particular a good laundry and dry cleaning service. The post office (noted for the irregularity of its hours and staff) is close to the supermarket. ■

MENTON VIEUX PORT
43.47.00 N 07.31.00 E
VHF 16,9
Tel. 93 35 80 56
Port C3   Town B1

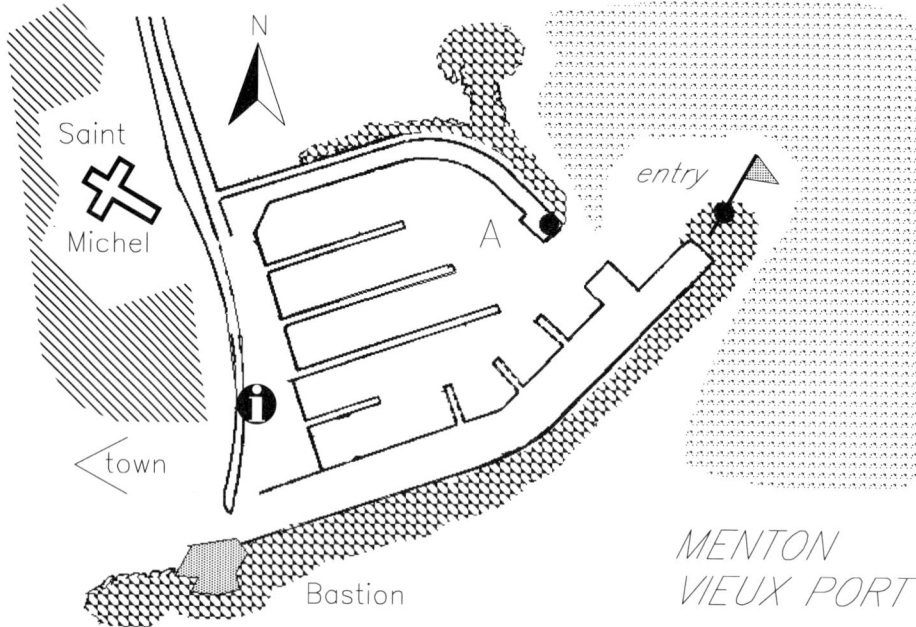

Charts	SHOM 5347, 5208, 1821 ECM 500 ADM 2167
Lights	S Jetty VQ(4)R 3s 16m 10M W Tower
Marks	The church of St Michel is unmistakable, and is strikingly lit at night. At the actual entrance there is no starboard light; instead you need to watch out for the statue of the saint on the starboard hand at the end of the jetty. Your final allocated berth may be just behind him.
Reception	There is no reception quay as such. However, you will probably be accosted by means of a loud hailer from the south quay – that is, immediately to port after you enter.
Moorings	Quay: probably on the jetty by the entrance, stern to with buoys, or you may have to use your anchor. There are some floating pontoons.
Draught	5m
LOA	25m
Berths	440
Visitors	50 (Their published figures are optimistic and guile may be required for hassle-free berthing.)
Fuel	At Menton Garavan.
Weather	Large outdoor TV screen at Garavan Capitainerie.
Boatyard Services	In conjunction with Garavan, comprehensive.
Shops	Market and town shops immediately accessible from the quay. For additional comment, please see Menton Garavan.

APPROACH

As for Menton Garavan, with the St Michel clock tower standing out clearly above the port. The final approach is quite stunning, with beaches, villas and minarets overlooked and dominated by the baroque cemetery, perched up on high.

ENTRY

There is the usual white tower with red top, but where you would normally expect to find a starboard hand green light, you are presented with Volti's eye-catching sculpture of St Michel looking more like a severe Amazonian warrior maiden. To erect such a piece of sculpture instead of the standard tower seems a most fitting tribute to a port that is almost the HQ of homage to Jean Cocteau.

Winds from the east and south east can cause difficulties in the 40m entrance; and when they get above 5–6, east winds create a really unpleasant swell, undercurrents and surges, making life generally unpleasant for those craft at visitors' berths, but extremely so for those vessels moored on the inner pontoons to the west.

COMMENTARY

The old town of Menton, with its intriguing Kasbah that is unique in Europe, is up the hills and almost far away; but it is well worth the long haul – if only for the burial ground which is on the site of the old feudal castle. Guy de Maupassant called it 'the aristocratic cemetery of Europe' because there were so many titled corpses interred there.

Dead bodies are also to be found, but in less profusion, on the fishermen's stalls on the quay; but you need to get there early if you are to be offered much more than lean pickings. Some French fishermen seem to be able to make a living from selling no more than a couple of kilos a day. Nearby, just over the wall, are other bodies, not at all fish-like, laid out on the gently sloping sandy beach.

The run-down, fly-blown offices of the Capitainerie are situated on the Quai Gordon Bennett. Paradoxically, it takes its name from the American millionaire who owned the *New York Herald* and whose world renowned hotel has a commanding position over Beaulieu Bay.

Another exile, the Spanish novelist Vicente Blasco (Blood and Sand) Ibanez, made his home in the Villa Fontana Rosa. In 1968 Graham Sutherland was made an honorary citizen of Menton. He did the drawings for the Coventry Cathedral tapestry in a garage in the port. Indeed, Menton has been a haunt of writers and royalty for many years. Katharine Mansfield lived in the Villa Isola Bella close by, and there is an avenue that bears her name. No doubt specially for dyed in the wool ex-pats, Queen Victoria's coat of arms stands in monumental stone not far away.

However, it is to Jean Cocteau that the crown must go: the 17th-century Bastion, built by Honore II of Monaco, is in truth 'his' museum, since it not only houses his works but was also restored mainly by his own hands. On the ground floor is Salamander, a mosaic in grey and white tesserae, and the famous tapestry of Judith and Holofernes, while upstairs is an amazing collection of paintings, pastels, drawing and ceramics – the most unusual of which are those of animals, and the most famous perhaps is the Innamorati.

The somewhat rundown red and ochre Town Hall is renowned for its Salles de Mariages, which was decorated by Cocteau in 1957. The fisherman, with a fish for an eye (a repeating whim of Cocteau), wears local headgear and the girl wears a Nice bonnet. Orpheus and Eurydice adorn one wall, while a traditional wedding is celebrated on the other. The ceiling has Poetry riding Pegasus. Always one for style, Cocteau finished this one with a lashing of gilt and velvet, and adorned it with two extravagant mirrors, well engraved.

If you walk to Volti's sculpture at the end of the Empress Eugenie jetty by the harbour entrance you are rewarded with a stunning view of the old town against the backdrop of the mountains, and a fine panorama from Cap Martin to Bordighera in Italy. The harbour is well placed for the town shops, and in particular for the nearby cheese cave, which also has a very good line in frozen snails à la bourguignon. Here, the largest are the best.

Towering above the port is the old fortress of Roquebrune (rocca bruna), built in the 10th century by Conrad, Count of Ventimiglia. It was in the hands of the Grimaldis for 500 years from 1350, but was bought for the municipality in 1911 by a well-wishing Englishman, Sir William Ingram. Roquebrune's other famous visitors were Churchill, van Meegeren (the Dutch forger), and Le Corbusier, who drowned at Cap Martin. ■

MONACO (MONTE CARLO)
43.44.10 N 07.25.50 E
VHF 16, 12, 6
Tel. 93 30 19 21
Port C1   Town B1

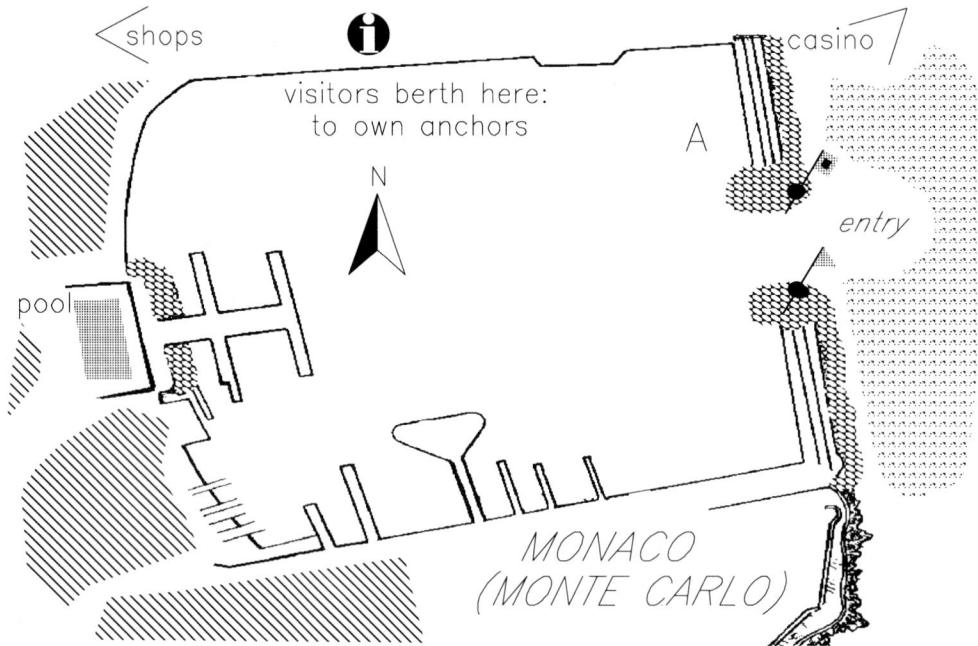

shops

visitors berth here:
to own anchors

casino

A

entry

N

pool

MONACO
(MONTE CARLO)

Charts	SHOM 6881, 6863, 6952 ECM 500 ADM 2167, 149
Lights	S Jetty Oc R 4s 16m 11M W/R Tower
	N Jetty Oc G 4s 16m 11M G/W Base
Marks	The Rock, Le Tête de Chien, the Oceanographic Museum, and the skyscrapers are all famous and unmistakable.
Reception	Inner wall of east jetty, immediately to starboard upon entry. Surprisingly, it is large enough only for craft up to 15m.
Moorings	Quay: stern to with anchor.
Draught	5–30m **LOA** 140m
Berths	700 **Visitors** 60
Fuel	Central pontoons.
Weather	Tape outside the office of the Capitainerie on the Quai des États Unis.
Boatyard Services	Comprehensive.
Shops	With the exception of the Codec supermarket, very close to the harbour, ordinary shopping is something of a disaster, because the few dedicated artisans are difficult to locate in this temple devoted to the wealthy and the sybaritic.

REMARKS

True, the harbour is open to weather and swell, but the mooring fees are appealingly low. Visitors usually berth on the northerly Quai des États Unis, which is very exposed to easterly weather, while the most amenable berths are to be found on the inner wall of the north jetty itself, immediately off it. However, no matter the position, preferential treatment has always been given to the luxurious yachts of the rich and beautiful – no less than appropriate for what was originally the dream port and total responsibility of its initiator, Prince Albert I. Prince Rainier added the Olympic swimming pool.

APPROACH

The port lies midway between the two unmistakable headlands of Cap Ferrat to the south west and Cap Martin to the north east. But the Port of Monaco does not appear until you are close and turn to approach it from the east. One mile to the west of the port is the strange natural mountain phenomenon known as the Tête de Chien and its man made white radar dome and structures. The great Rock of Monaco itself is also a major landmark, as are the Prince's palace, and the truly amazing sight of conglomerated skyscrapers. From the west you will probably be accompanied by helicopters zooming in and out of the heliport at Cap d'Ail. This stretch of coast, in the Baie de Rocco, is a prohibited zone and is designated as such by Cardinal marks. It is followed by the standard red-topped white tower that marks the entrance to the port of Fontvieille. The Oceanographic Museum, just to the south of the port, dominates from its cliffside eyrie.

However, all this may change, for there are plans for great alterations to take place over the next twenty years. With typical Gallic optimism, the Monagesques have in mind a vast man made lagoon, known as Project Augusta, consisting of a stabilised floating city using offshore oil technology and space age architecture. A smaller improvement also under consideration is the installation of a breakwater to protect the present harbour from its inclement swells.

ENTRY

The entry is straightforward, marked by the two white towers on the jetties, although it tends to be extremely busy with various waterborne items: anything from vast cruisers to windsurfers. The reception quay is tucked away behind the starboard tower.

COMMENTARY

On my first visit, the Principality was en fête for the Prince's birthday. It was a poor introduction to Monaco's much vaunted addiction to style, epitomised by the uniforms of the police and the palace guards. The quayside fair was chocolate-box, and the uniforms chocolate soldier. However, the senior officer who called on me late one night owed nothing to light opera: he was an expert in cold, menacing grilling, and demanded to see every piece of documentation there was on board.

Had I been there for a Grand Prix, either ashore or afloat, or indeed any one of the many starred events of the high season, I doubt I would have found a place. That is, unless I had been able to find a Mr Brit Fixit and pay a lot for him to do it for me in advance. Monaco's many amazingly locomotive speed events must be deemed to be somewhat 'loco' in their own right, but in spite of the continuing toll of lives and limbs they continue to fascinate, profit and proliferate.

The tiny state, known to the Romans as Portus Monoeci, the Port of Hercules, was in the 1850s, (like Caesar's Gaul) divided into three parts: Monaco was a village of no more than 2000 souls; La Condamine had one house; and Monte Carlo itself was a bare stony patch except for a few olive trees. It is now a veritable miniature Manhattan, thanks to Prince Charles III. Facing bankruptcy, he enlisted the aid of the ex-waiter François Blanc to develop the Casino. Blanc died a millionaire three times over and the Prince did away with taxation. In 1887 many of the crowned heads of Europe called on the Prince. Two famed visitors did not: Queen Victoria, who did not approve of gambling, and Charles Wells who certainly did, being the original 'man who broke the bank at Monte Carlo'.

The principality (a mere 375 acres) worked for its living: Monaco, on The Rock, for history and culture (Diaghilev's *Ballets Russe de Monte Carlo,* for example); Monte Carlo for la dolce vita; and La Condamine, on the isthmus between, for commerce. It has cruelly been described as 'unrestrained urbanisation'.

The Oceanographic Museum (Jacques Cousteau), the Palace, and the Cathedral (all choice relics funded by the Casino's vast profits) are not to be missed. Neither is the Casino, since all streets seem to lead to it. ∎

FONTVIEILLE
43.43.70 N 07.25.40 E
Tel. 93 50 03 73
Port B1   Town C3

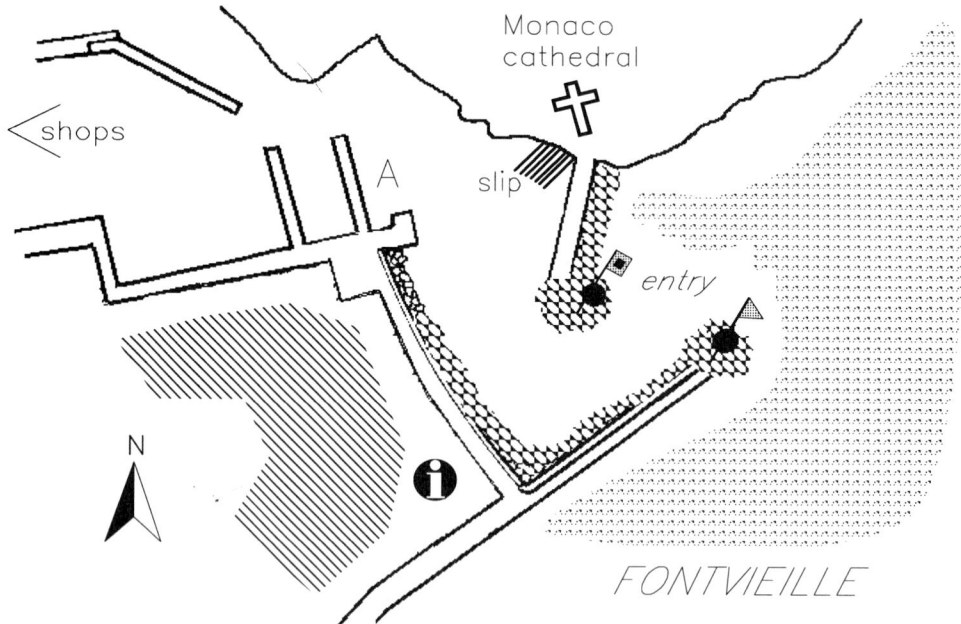

Charts	SHOM 6881, 6863, 6952 ECM 500 ADM 2167, 149				
Lights	Cap Ferrat	Fl 3s	69m	25M	W	Tower
	Fontvieille	Oc(2)R 6s	10m	10M	W/R Tower
	N Jetty	Fl G 4s	5m	7M	G	Base
	S Jetty	Fl R 4s	3m	4M	W/R Tower

Marks   The Rock, Le Tête de Chien, and Monaco's Oceanographic Museum and skyscrapers are all conspicuous.

Reception   The port jetties after the two breakwaters and before the inner basin.

Moorings   Floating pontoons and catways; and to anchor and chain.

Draught 11m   **LOA** 35m

Berths 170   **Visitors** 10

Fuel   Monaco and Cap d'Ail.

Weather   Teletape: 93.30.13.13.

Boatyard Services   Poor.

Shops   While there are some shops within reach, shopping is insubstantial and of a scrappy nature, and very poor for all but low grade comestibles. Although many improvements have been promised, it will probably be best to shop at nearby Monte Carlo for some time to come.

APPROACH

Landmarks are the mountainous Tête de Chien with the white radar dome and structures that are poised at the summit, and the famous Rock of Monaco. The Oceanographic Museum, just to the east of the port, dominates from its cliffside eyrie. (See also the approach for Monaco.)

ENTRY

While the marina itself is fully protected from all winds and weather, the actual entry can be hazardous with winds from the east, through south to the south west – namely, anything with any seaward in it.

The final approach entry is impressive and romantic: under the puissant cliffs and dominant edifice of the Oceanographic Museum to the east. The inner route is formed by the protective dog leg: first turn at the white tower with a red top, second at the green pillar, and finally to port round the third unlit jetty into the sanctum of the basin itself. There is a small jetty at the very far end of the basin and it carries a red light, but the area shallows to just over a metre.

COMMENTARY

Fontvieille enjoys a beautiful and naturally concealed position under the sheltering patronage of its natural cliffs. Moreover, it is additionally well protected by its recently constructed artificial jetties and counter jetties. Originally it was a small fishing port, but those days are gone for ever; it has now been enlarged and dredged to 10m or more and fishing boats are no longer part of its existence. Its sheltered life, in every way, is due in no small part to the fact that it is also part of the Principality of Monaco.

Other forms of protection and patronage are to be found in the huge blocks of flats, one of which sports a mock English pub sign: The Ship and Castle. Rolls Royce cars, among which will be the near obligatory Corniche, loiter at the quayside, and sometimes the assembly is so huge that even they find themselves double rafted. One would not think it possible to find space on which to build more flats, high-rise or otherwise, but development is still taking place. It comes as something of a surprise to leave behind the expensive ambience, attributes and grand style of the marina to discover that the heart of Fontvieille lies in heavy trade and that most of its scant square metres are being devoted to light industry. To accommodate this progress and the heady plans for extension, a man made peninsula is slowly but surely emerging off Fontvieille's coast.

As yet, there is little that can rival the Louis II stadium, that world-famous sports complex designed by a certain Monsieur Pottier to withstand earth tremors. Unless, that is, you happen to be keen on plants. In which case the magnificent Tropical Gardens which cascade down a steep rock face magnificently show off 6000 specimens of semi-desert flora, including the unforgettably named 'mother-in-law cushions'. Opening off the garden are caves in dolomitic limestone which have produced artefacts of human existence dating back some 200 000 years.

Fontvieille Park with its international collection of plants will also delight. Nearby, the Princess Grace rose garden is planted with nearly 4000 varieties, many of which are specially bred and generated by world-famous gardeners. The controversial statue of Princess Grace erected in 1983 was created by Kees Verkade.

From the marina it is easy to visit Monaco's Prince's Palace, the Cathedral and the Oceanographic Museum, which was founded by Prince Albert I in 1910.

The Palace square boasts the well-kept cannon given by Louis XIV, and affords a splendid view – if you can manage to glimpse it between the ice cream cones. The oldest parts of the palace date back to the 13th century, while the south side, in Italian Renaissance style, are 15th and 16th century. The Cathedral was built between 1875 and 1903 of white stone from La Turbie on the ruins of the old church of St Nicolas. It is a vivid, awe inspiring technicolour experience.

But for sheer electric captivation, there is little to compete with the Oceanographic Museum. It consists of a basement aquarium of ninety separate basins of tropical and Mediterranean fauna; a ground-floor exhibition area with underwater craft and a zoology hall to the left; and the first floor is devoted to the exploits of the founding Prince's voyages and an exhibition of open shells and stuffed specimens. From the second floor terrace you get a panorama of the coast from Esterel to the Italian Riviera and inland to the Tête de Chien.

The trip from the marina is exhausting to undertake in one day, but it is by far the most rewarding part of the Principality of Monaco to explore. ■

CAP D'AIL
43.43.50 N 07.25.00 E
Tel. 93 78 28 46
Port C2   Town Monaco

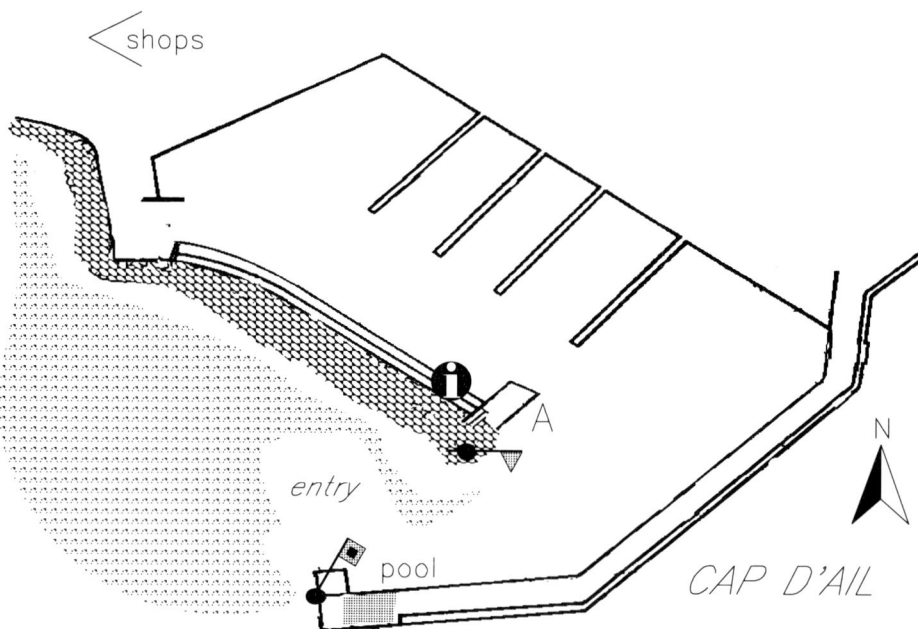

Charts	SHOM 6952, 6863 ECM 500 ADM 2167, 149					
Lights	Cap Ferrat	Fl 3s	69m	25M	W	Tower
	Cap d'Ail	Fl G 4s	11m	10M	W/G	Tower
	SW Jetty	Fl G 4s	7m	6M	G	Structure
	N Jetty	Fl R 4s	4m	5M	R	Structure

Marks Cap Ferrat lighthouse is prominent 5 miles to the south west. Nearer, the peak of Tête de Chien, the Monaco skyscrapers, and the Oceanographic Museum are all conspicuous.

Reception By the Capitainerie and fuel station on the port jetty.

Moorings Quay: stern to, requiring lines15m + the length of your craft secured to two chains at the bows.

Draught	20m	**LOA**	80m
Berths	253	**Visitors**	53

Fuel By the Capitainerie.

Weather Posted daily at the Capitainerie.

Boatyard Services Comprehensive.

Shops While most visitors' basic needs can be met in the not inexpensive shops of the local Galerie, it is better to go to Monaco where the Codec supermarket offers much better value and far greater choice.

REMARKS

Because of its proximity to Monaco, and with the favoured Côte d'Azur climate, the marina is extremely popular – and usually packed. To avoid disappointment, visitors should phone in advance to reserve a berth.

APPROACH

The Tête de Chien is right above the port, which lies halfway between Cap Ferrat and Cap Martin, and is easy to distinguish both from east and west. It has additional special features: a heliport that will no doubt provide you with entertaining non-stop traffic as you make your final approach; a positive bastion of a concrete blockhouse at the end of the outer sea wall; and the rose-tinted edifice of the Leopold Stadium.

ENTRY

The entrance is distinguished by a long line of yellow and black buoys marking the prohibited zone immediately to seaward of the breakwater alongside the heliport. It is worth noting that the beach to port (Plage Marquet) very quickly shallows and is protected by an underwater jetty: keep close to the entrance in 10m.

Entry is problem free except when strong winds are between east and west through south. Under such conditions a heavy sea with swell and surf builds up around the outer jetty, and skill is needed in boat handling to effect a safe entry. Under such circumstances it is perhaps better for a visitor to make for Monaco, where the entrance will probably be more amenable.

COMMENTARY

Its setting, at the foot of a superb mountain backdrop, is even more dramatic than that of its neighbour – Fontvieille; it is just as popular, but without such upper crust leanings, and tends towards a more sardine-tin style and character. Its prime berths are, in the main, occupied by extra large luxury cruisers, many flying the red ensign. These are to be found immediately along the inner side of the sea wall to starboard upon entry.

The jetty walls with their rock-strewn fortifications and the massive Capitainerie office have been described as bearing more resemblance to a dangerously exposed North Sea harbour than a Riviera marina. However, it is welcome if somewhat surprising to find that the extremely solid and exclusively utilitarian-looking Fort Blockhouse by the entrance is actually furnished with a clubhouse and an Olympic-size swimming pool.

One expects something rustic from a marina with a name like Cap d'Ail, especially as the true community numbers only just over 4000, but it is an entirely man made effort with an eye to self-advertisement: 'Here prestigious apartments'. Sadly, the huge development operation does nothing to add charm to what is already a fairly charmless spot. However, the pretty little church of St Nicolas makes amends, as do some of the stylish shops which constitute a veritable catacomb in the modern apartment block known as the Galerie Princess Stephanie. In addition, Cap d'Ail itself forms the lower fingers of the Tête de Chien as they reach towards the sea. With its pines, its palms, its cypress trees and its elegant and luxurious villas, it forms a magnificent spectacle.

There is a spectacular walk along the Cap d'Ail coastal path. You take the flight of steps down by La Pinède restaurant and descend to the sea. To the west are Beaulieu and Cap Ferrat. The path goes east at the foot of Cap d'Ail and gradually shows Monaco Rock, ending at Marquet Beach, where you take the road into Monaco.

Not far inland is the historical village of La Turbie, originally built in a pass on either side of the Roman Via Julia which connected Genoa and Cimiez. In the year 5 BC, the Roman Emperor Augustus put up the great monument known today as the Trophy of Augustus (or the Alpine Trophy) to commemorate the subjugation of the local rebels, mainly Ligurian mountaineers. Originally 150ft tall on a base 120ft square, it had become a heap of ruins by 1705. It had been partly wrecked by St Honorat when he found people worshipping it; further damaged by barbarians; quarried for local building in the village; turned into a fort; and finally destroyed by the French at the time they were blowing up Savoyard castles. But the rich American Edward Tuck came to the rescue and rebuilt it to its present 100ft. Another monument to man's endeavours is to be found farther up Mont Agel: the golf course laid in 1920 by Monsieur Blanc (see Monaco) at a reputed cost of £100 000. There are great views of the coast, especially at night, of the lights of Monte Carlo and Monaco. ■

BEAULIEU SUR MER
43.42.50 N 07.20.30 E
Tel. 93 01 10 49
Port A1   Town A1

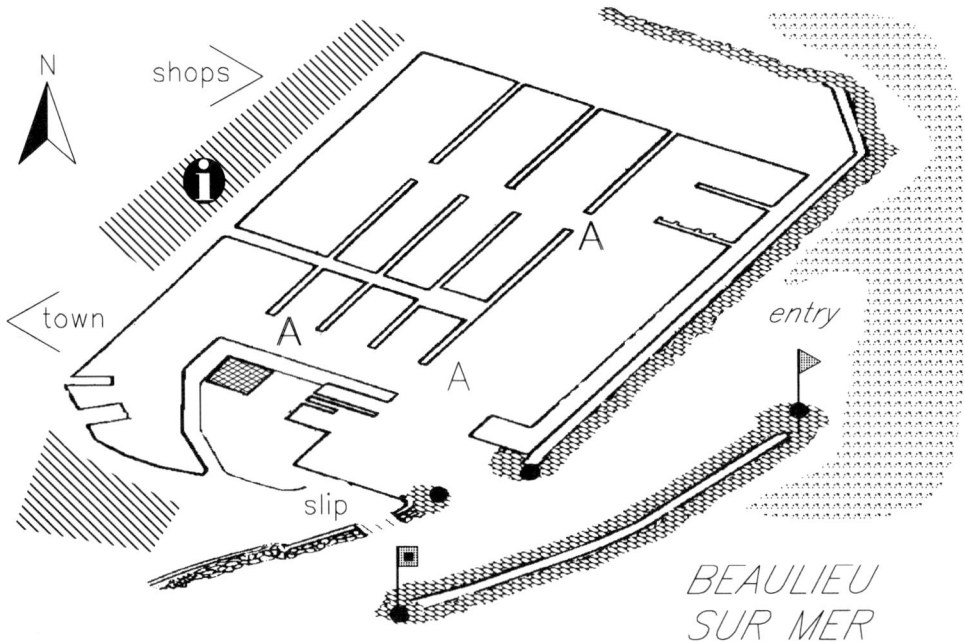

Charts	SHOM 5176, 6952, 6863 ECM 500 ADM 2167
Lights	Cap Ferrat Fl 3s 69m 25M W Tower
	Outer N Jetty Q R 7m 10M W/R Tower
	Outer S Jetty Iso G 4s 7m 8M W/G Tower
	Inner S Jetty Fl R 4s
	Inner N Jetty Fl G 4s
Reception	Either wait at the fuel station immediately inside to starboard (jill around, expecting to be loud hailed from the pontoons opposite) or try for a vacant berth on the quayside, immediately inside, to port.
Moorings	Quay: stern to with laid chains.
Draught	4.5m **LOA** 30m
Berths	776 **Visitors** 152
Fuel	At the entrance, immediately to starboard.
Weather	Teletape: 93.83.91.12. Aeroport: 93.83.05.07. Port: 93.01.10.49. Also daily bulletins at the Capitainerie.
Boatyard Services	Comprehensive. The RYS yard caters for all kinds of craft – from gentlemen's classic wooden yachts to *Virgin Atlantic Challenger II*.
Shopping	On site: tabac and expensive corner shop; a boulangerie across the main road; and in the town is a comprehensive range of domestics and comestibles, with a first-rate market.

REMARKS

Beaulieu possesses what are probably the most powerful showers on the Mediterranean coast of France. They really hurt: there is certainly no need for Swedish pine needle treatment. Here also is another first; what must be the most expensive loo paper: 10F for a few sheets of insubstantial stuff.

APPROACH

The approach is open from the east with the conspicuous headland of Cap Ferrat marking the southern end of the Baie de Beaulieu. This headland must be rounded by the Pointe de la Hospice before the port can be seen tucked away on a course of 150°M.

If for any reason you find it difficult to see the marina from the west, the old town of Eze to the east is something to spot: standing out like the peak of a mountain, the old medieval village makes a dramatic landmark.

ENTRY

The entry is straightforward, and there is a choice: smaller craft (less than 3m draught and 18m LOA) can proceed through the secondary approach channel to the south marked by a white tower with red top. Within the breakwater, there are unlit red marker buoys. The principal approach is through the north passage, turning to port after its conspicuous white tower; if conditions are poor, it is prudent to use this channel. The only threat to entry comes with bad weather and sea from east to south.

COMMENTARY

For those tempted to join the permanent lotus-eating clan of Beaulieu Brits, the news is of a disastrously long waiting list that has to be measured in years. It is not even easy to gain a place for a few days anywhere within a month of the high season, and even in winter you need to use charm to gain the consent of the harbour staff to your delicately phrased request for a berth for 'just a couple of weeks'. It is wise to telephone days ahead just for a place for a day. If not, then certainly call well ahead on the day of your proposed visit on VHF 9.

The city fathers were not slow to name their eastern region 'Little Africa' because of its climate, eg four days of frost in fifteen years. All this is thanks to the half circle of small mountains that protect the town from the ravages of the north winds. So much so, that one converted Brit told me, 'We actually like the mistral to blow. It clears the skies, brings us the sun, and we seldom feel a breath of it.' For decades it has been a favourite wintering spot, and time has only increased its popularity.

Beaulieu is a splendid place for food and drink, be it for eating in or out. On the marina front, there is a great array of restaurants varying from the African Queen (obligatory pics of Bogart, but good) at one extreme to the east, and Le Portofino at the other to the west: the former is large and swish, with lots of panache and hectic staff, while the latter is altogether more relaxed and informal, a more native treat.

Nearby are two more contrasts: Le Marrakech, a Moroccan restaurant where a regal welcome awaits you; and only just across the road from it, the world famous hotel, La Reserve, founded by Gordon Bennett, the eccentric owner of the *New York Herald*. It seems only fair to the African spirit of Beaulieu that it was actually Bennett who sent Stanley to the dark continent in the first place.

Beaulieu was an old fishing village, and one corner of the harbour still has a foot in the past, complete with fish stalls on the quay at contemporary prices. The town market has only fish and veg during the week, but a full display on Saturdays. In the square there is a mouth-watering deli, expensive but sumptuous.

You can take a pleasing walk round Cap Ferrat, and this provides a real contrast with Beaulieu's boast about its envious position on the Lower Corniche. Not a vehicle, not even a Rolls, is in sight. You start the journey at the boundary of St Jean Cap Ferrat, where there is a large map with legend for guidance.

Opposite the start of the walk there is an antiques establishment where it is a delight to browse. From here, you can see the small port of Fourmis in its pretty eponymous bay, with the Villa Kerylos built in Greek style by archaeologist Theodore Reinach, who left it to the French Institute in 1928. It is a Sybaritic edifice, fabricated inside with Carrara marble, biblical woods and actual alabaster, and furnished in ivories, bronze and leather. There are original mosaics and amphoras all round. Situated near the Casino and Bridge Club, the Villa Kerylos is now the site of Showbiz Son et Lumière. At the other end of the bay there is a tiny pebbled beach. ∎

ST JEAN CAP FERRAT
43.41.40 N 07.20.10 E
Tel. 93 76 04 56
Port B2   Town B2

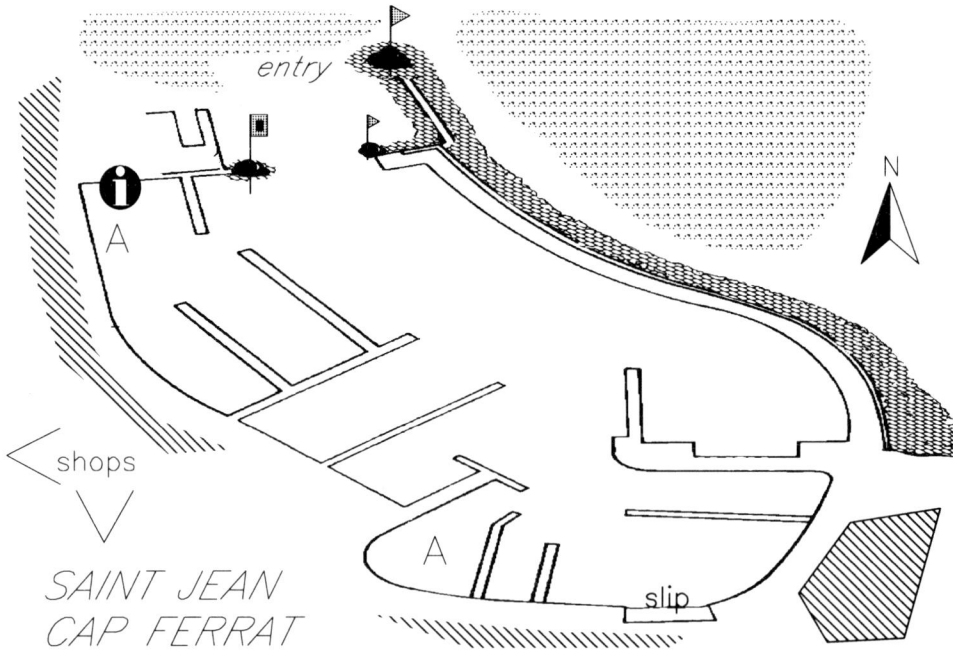

Charts	SHOM 4708, 5176, 6863, 6952	ECM 500	ADM 2167		
Lights	Cap Ferrat Light	Fl 3s	69m	25M	W Tower
	Harbour	Fl(4)R 12s	9m	9M	W/R Tower
	Inner Easy Head	F R		1M	Strip
	Inner West Head	Iso 4s		1M	Strip

Marks   Cap Ferrat lighthouse is prominent.

Reception   To starboard after the first pontoon; facing the shops.

Moorings   Quay: to laid chain.

Draught   2.5m   **LOA**   30m

Berths   560   **Visitors**   30

Fuel   To starboard immediately in the entrance. Take care to avoid the rocks around the west end jetty knuckle.

Weather   Teletape: 93.83.05.70. Posted daily by the Capitainerie.

Boatyard Services   Average.

Shops   Experimental. The shops are there, but it takes time to find them and then to assess them properly. Many are much better inside than they appear at a first glance at their exteriors; by the same perverse token, some disappoint, so it pays to be attentive, with caution being the watchword on the first day.

APPROACH

Cap Ferrat, with its signal station towering into the heavens, stands out from whichever direction you approach. From the east you go straight into the bay, and from the west you round the headland with the conspicuous hotel, and then continue to round the Pointe de St Hospice until the entrance becomes plain.

There is a pleasing anchorage just offshore in the Rade de St Hospice. There are two factors to note: take care not to encroach with your anchor into the prohibited area marked by buoys to the north east of the port; and secondly, while it is a sheltered spot in westerly weather, it is ill advised in easterlies.

ENTRY

The entrance is problem free except when there is weather from the east, when a nasty sea makes any attempt at entry unpleasant at best and hazardous otherwise. At all times it is best to open up the entrance slowly before trying to make your way in, since there is an unexpected half circle turn needed from the south.

COMMENTARY

It is impossible to consider St Jean Cap Ferrat without giving some thought to its anchorages. They rival the more celebrated one of Villefranche round the corner, but on a more modest scale. There are three. The Anse de la Scaletta is close by St Jean, looking across to Beaulieu. It is hollowed into the north face of the Presqu'ile de St Hospice, where the hills are covered in beautiful trees and lavish vegetation among which are enshrined the estates of some of the wealthiest residences in France.

The other two, the Anse de Lilong and the Anse des Fosses,on the south face of the Presqu'ile de St Hospice, are separated by only a small headland. Each has a vista of rocky hills to which cling most attractive houses set in multiflowered gardens. A high rocky bottom surrounds the area close in, and it is best to anchor off in no less than 6m, or farther out in 12m. Because of their exposed situation they are usable only in settled weather, and in season they are crowded.

Back ashore in St Jean, to landward, the marina is fenced off by a vast array of restaurants and ship's business dealers – so many that it is difficult to imagine that they are able to make a living since they seem entirely disproportionate to the number of boats or berths.

Away from the marina, in the modest town that still has the air of the small untamed fishing village that it once was, there are even more restaurants and marine traders. However, there is the bonus of back streets clinging to the steep hillside, each with its own variety of small shops and citrus trees; and there is hardly a garden to be found bare of citrus. This aspect can best be seen on the Boulevard de la Liberation, where the corner shop stands next to a small vegetable allotment and an attractive citrus orchard. All in all, such charms go to make the shoreside aspects more pleasing than the marina. The uneven stepped paving to the south of this Boulevard affords a gorgeous vista of Eze, Mount Angel and Tête de Chien. What is more, the Alps on the Franco Italian border can be seen to splendid advantage.

The resort possesses a miniature beach immediately next to the marina; and there is an extremely pleasant walk from it to Beaulieu along the coastline. If you want to tackle the 164 steps to the top of the Cap Ferrat lighthouse, there is a quite unforgettable panorama ranging from Bordighera Point in Italy to the Esterel Heights and the Alps. Nearby, the Sun Beach swimming pool has been hollowed out of the rocks.

An important landmark is the Villa des Cedres, former residence of King Leopold II of the Belgians, and now the home of M Marnier-Lapostolle of Grand Marnier fame. From 1927 to 1965, Somerset Maugham lived nearby in the Villa La Mauresque. Not far away are the museum and gardens of the Villa Ephrussi de Rothschild, the foundation that was given to the French Institute on behalf of the Academy of Fine Arts in 1934 by the Baroness. In her famous Musée de l'Ile de France (an Italianate villa built soon after 1900 not as an ordinary villa, but specially to house her Paris collection of priceless works of art) there are myriad treasures: marble columns, an 18th-century Savonnerie carpet, Flemish tapestries, terracottas and bronzes. There are many fine examples of porcelain: Vincennes, Sèvres, Dresden; and the quaint Monkey Room adds an eccentric touch. In addition to the many paintings, there is an Impressionists Gallery with works by Monet, Renoir and Sisley. It is a quite outstanding monument to the lengths that humans can go to fill a void.

In general, Cap Ferrat can be said to possess some of the most beautiful and luxurious villas and gardens of the Côte d'Azur. ∎

VILLEFRANCHE SUR MER
43.42.00 N 07.18.40 E
Tel. 93 01 70 70
Port A2   Town A3

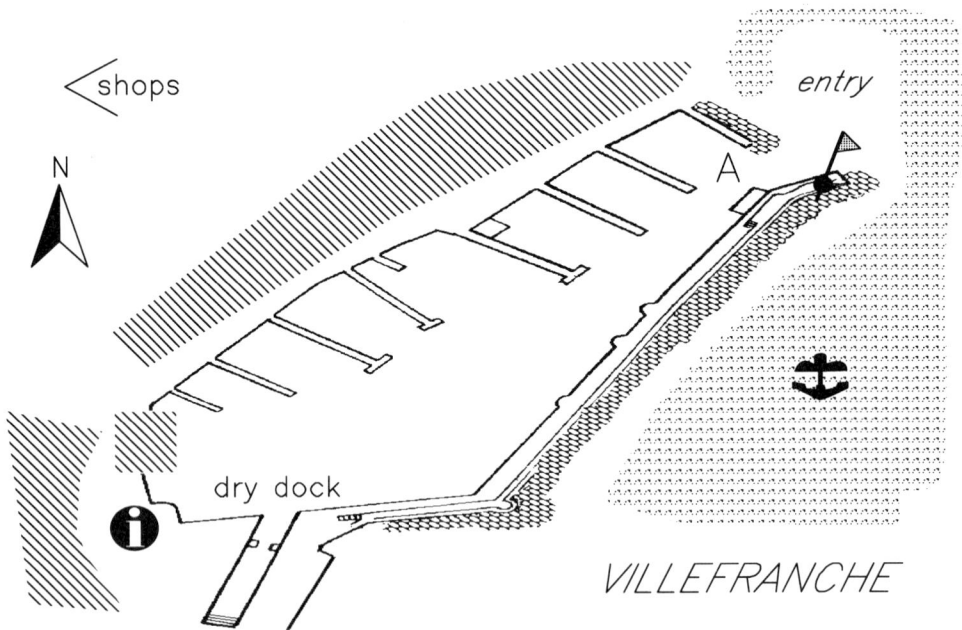

Charts	SHOM 4708, 5347 ECM 500, 501 ADM 2167, 149				
Lights	Cap Ferrat Light	Fl 3s	69m	25M	W	Tower
	Villefranche	Q WR	8m	12–8M	W/R Structure
	La Sante	Oc(2)R 6s	10m	7M	W/R Structure

Marks Cap Ferrat lighthouse: an unmistakable rounded hexagonal white tower.

Reception At the entrance: the end of the first jetty to port.

Moorings Quay and pontoons: to laid chain.

Draught	7m	**LOA**	16m
Berths	320	**Visitors**	40 (optimistic!)

Fuel In the middle of the harbour.

Weather Teletape: 93.83.91.12. Posted daily: automatic tape outside the Capitainerie.

Boatyard Services Comprehensive. Unusually, there is a large dry dock. In the main it is busy and heavily booked.

Shops The facilities, while not inferior, are not what you might expect of this mountainside fishing port and holiday resort that the nearby rich and famous have made into their exclusive 'pied-a-terre'.

16

APPROACH

From every direction, the deep inlet of the Rade de Villefranche is unmistakable and unforgettable. In addition, to the west there is the Cap de Nice with its towers, forts and domes; and to the east there is the rising hump of the headland topped by the tower of the Cap Ferrat lighthouse.

ENTRY

The entrance is on the narrow side, marked by a red light on the end of the long sea wall. This is almost met at right angles by another protecting wall to starboard as you make your final turn.

COMMENTARY

The place is called Villefranche sur Mer, but it would really be more appropriate if it were called something like Villefranche on the Mountain or Cliff Edge. The approach is splendid and dramatic whether made by boat, train, bike or bus. The favoured anchorage of both the American and French fleets lies snugly sheltered in the most attractive deep inlet, where beautifully treed cliffs drop straight down to the sea. Back in the UK, in the bays of the Wash or the Solent for example, you would be hard pressed to find any depth of water near the shore, but here you can be in 30m while no more than that distance from the shore.

What was once the naval harbour of the Dukes of Savoy is now exclusively the preserve of pleasure craft. Deservedly so, since when there is perturbation at sea, more often than not inside there is no more than a gentle swell – just enough to let you know that you are still afloat. This is because only winds from the south west can bring up a swell in the bay, and they are uncommon. It is one of the most favoured, famous and fabulous anchorages along the Mediterranean coast of France.

The train will let you alight almost at sea level, close to the Palais de la Marine of the Princes of Savoy, on the Promenade de Marinieres, while the bus stops farther up the hillside. By boat there is a choice: the marina, the anchorage in the body of the bay, or the laid buoys at its head. In addition, for very small craft, there is the extra opportunity of using the small space in the old port of La Sante (a charming miniature of a harbour) watched over by the fishermen's chapel now famous as the Cocteau museum. It is to this port, from their luxury liners lying to anchor or moored to a massive buoy, that the

rich and famous are ferried ashore. It was also from here, in 1930, that the national football team embarked to Uruguay for the first World Cup, sailing in *Le Comte Vert.*

The beach is a tiny thing: a few striking rocks catch the eye, while a thin fringe of sand awaits you after a much more substantial border of sharp shingle.

Many of its old villas are impressive: some in the classic style, complete with sculpture to match and Greek pillars and portals, stand in grounds that require the attentions of at least three men and a boy.

It is proud of its past, its frontier legend proclaiming 'Villefranche: Son Vieux Port du Guerre, Sa Citadel (AD 1557), Sa Rue Obscure [a dark tunnel from the 13th century where the village folk used to take refuge during bombardments]; Chapel St Pierre décoré par Jean Cocteau.' This chapel, completely reworked and decorated by the artist in 1957, was opened in 1964. The theme is the austere life of St Peter, relieved by scenes of Villefranche ladies and local gypsies. It makes a fitting crown for the old port, rescuing it from an otherwise sad fate of being lost among the modish restaurants (eagerly awaiting the rich tipping from the tripping rich) which stare across the bay to the hanging gardens of Cap Ferrat.

Ironically, indeed, the modern marina is surrounded by old stone buildings and walls redolent of Arabic/African influence, although behind it the anonymous high risers cling to the hillside and cover the backdrop. The marina, once a naval port where galleys were built and manned, is especially popular with beautifully maintained wooden classic sailing yachts – so much so that it would be no surprise if James Mason appeared at the wheel as the Flying Dutchman in ghostly person.

There is a splendid walk along the walls and ramparts of the Citadel. The road is cut deep into the stone but, in contrast to the hard outcrop, there were wild but gentle snapdragons blooming in the last week of November.

The Citadel, built by the Duke of Savoy, carries the legend: 'Ancien Fort St Elme 1557 – brought back to life with the inauguration of the Hotel de Ville 1981'. Its drawbridge no longer operates, but some of its great wooden and chain works are still to be seen. Its fine position commands the waters of the bay – intruders beware. The courtyard houses the works of Volti, the Italian sculptor who lived in Villefranche. ∎

NICE
43.41.50 N 07.17.10 E
VHF 16
Tel. 93 89 50 85
Port C1   Town B1

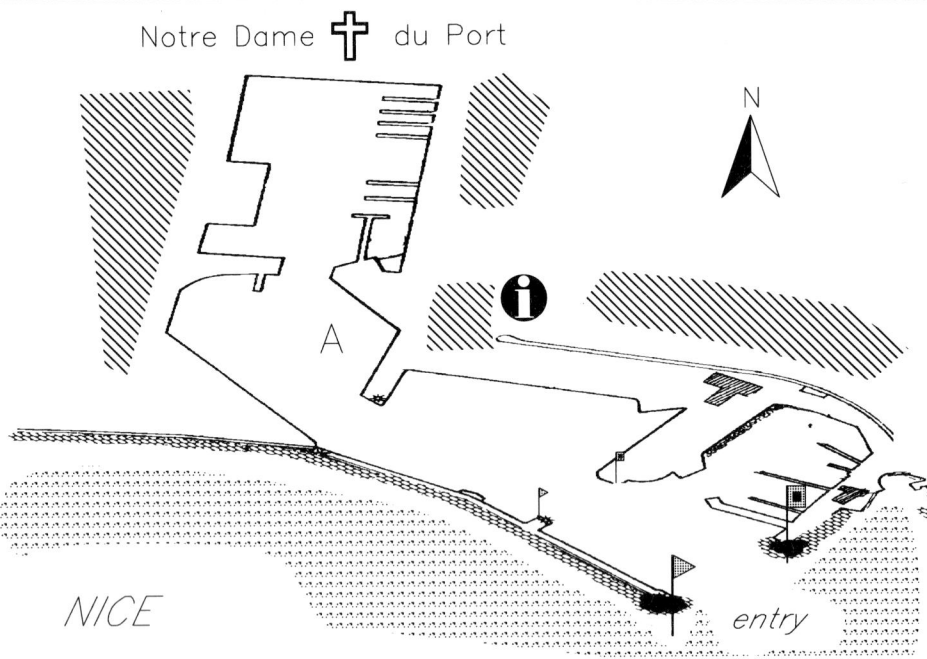

Notre Dame ✝ du Port

A

NICE

entry

Charts	SHOM 4708, 5176, 6952		ECM 500, 501		ADM 2167, 149	
Lights	Cap Ferrat	Fl 3s	69m	25M	W	Tower
	Jetty Head	Fl R 5s	21m	20M	W/R	Tower
	E Jetty Head	Fl G 4s	5m	7M	G/W	Base
	New Jetty	Fl(2)R 6s	6m	7M	W/R	Structure
	West Amiraux	Fl R 4s	6m	7M	R	Structure
	East Commerce	Fl(2)G 6s	6m	6M	W/G	Structure
	West Mole	Fl G 4s	6m	7M	W/G	Structure

Marks Cap Ferrat lighthouse.

Reception Capitainerie at the Quai Riboty, immediately to starboard in main basin.

Moorings Quay and pontoons: to laid chain; Tour Rouge (starboard by the entrance) or the Bassin Lympia (head of inner harbour).

Draught 5m   **LOA** 25m

Berths 470   **Visitors** 20

Fuel By tanker or at Villefranche.

Weather Teletape: 93.72.31.32. Posted daily every morning at the Capitainerie.

Boatyard Services Comprehensive.

Shops Comprehensive. You must diligently search if you want a touch of Niçoise individuality in anything from water to wine.

APPROACH

It is well worth a small detour to make your final approach to Nice from the south east so that you come face to face with the amazing view of the bay of Villefranche backed by its almost sheer backdrop of the Alpes Maritime. In addition, there is the splendour of the beautifully formed entrance into Nice harbour, with its dramatic carving broadcasting religious blessings over all and sundry. The alternative is the long slog past the 'Keep Out' buoys marking the seaway fringe of the airport.

ENTRY

The entrance is not easy to spot, especially from the west. The harbour wall lighthouse stands out when you are close, and the actual way in is to the north east of that mark. You skirt the end of the harbour wall, leaving the head of the Poudrière mole to starboard. Keep a lookout for the big commercial ships that regularly use the port, especially the Corsica RoRo ferries; there are blind spots on entry and near the Quai Riboty.

The reception Quai Riboty is spacious and spatial in good old stone, well hung with tractor tyres so that boats and quay are all well protected, and making it easy to berth alongside and just hop ashore. The Quai Riboty is round quite a sharp bend, and not immediately obvious, but the Capitainerie will catch your eye, or you will spot the office that stands back only a little from the quayside.

COMMENTARY

The Côte d'Azur, a name conjured up by Stephen Liégeard for a guide to the coast from Genoa to Marseille, is now agreed to start at Menton and end at Cannes (or St Raphael or Hyères, depending on how far west you live). However, there is no disagreement that its capital is Nice, named Nikêa by the Greeks who founded the colony in the 4th century BC. The River Paillon divides the city into two just as it did when the Romans arrived 200 years later. They built a large new town, Cemenelum, to the east, leaving the tiny settlement to the Greek sailors and traders. Barbarians destroyed the Roman creation, but the village survived that onslaught and all others to start a thriving life of its own in the Middle Ages. Then, for 500 years until its restoration to France in 1860, Nice was in the hands of the House of Savoy.

Like England's Great Yarmouth, Nice has outskirts named California, and, just like its colder cousin, it is a mixture of grit and grot, with the occasional pearl to rescue it. In the main, Nice is a bustling, noisy cosmopolitan city. It is proud of its international status and wants to be really on stream, which among other things means even more fast food and burger bars than usual. However, it must be said, whatever your needs (peace and quiet apart), Nice is likely to meet them – and to do so in an inimitable way, one that combines affronted pride, controlled aggression, mild amusement and sheer indifference.

While not wanting to destroy its Old Town, Nice seems not to know what to do with it. Its back streets are like a film set: attractive 'real' façades masking a mainly synthetic world selling the best of Brummagem. If you have plenty of time to explore you will find the vintage locations where, not unexpectedly, small bars and restaurants proliferate.

When it comes to the not-real-but-genuinely-old, Nice is well catered for with its museums: natural history, art and marine. There is the Matisse specialty (museum), which demonstrates his artistic development over nearly sixty years; and the Chagall Memorial with the seventeen canvases that make up the artist's now well documented and famed thirteen-year struggle to create the magnum opus known as 'The Biblical Message'. It is ironic to find, within this vast community that is devoted more than anything to the celebration of the Passing of a Fast Buck, a gallery given to displays of Naive Painting.

There is also the altogether different, but quite splendid, Place Massena where, if you don't like the Italianate architecture, you can turn your attention to the turbulence of the passing show. The harbour of Port Lympia was begun in 1750, and on the Quai Lunel is the house where Garibaldi was born in 1807. In 1822 the orange trees were killed by frost, and the English, in a rush of blood to the head, rescued the unemployed by commissioning the celebrated Promenade des Anglais.

Pan Bagna

The real thing comes from Nice. Special oil-soaked bread is used in a sandwich of raw onion, tomatoes, black olives and anchovies laced with oil and vinegar. It may be pressed. Since it takes time, the best chefs will make them only to order and serve them fresh. Don't be conned by 'I just happen to have one ...'   ∎

ST LAURENT DU VAR
43.33.00 N 07.11.00 E
VHF 16, 9
Tel. 93 07 12 70
Port B3   Town C2

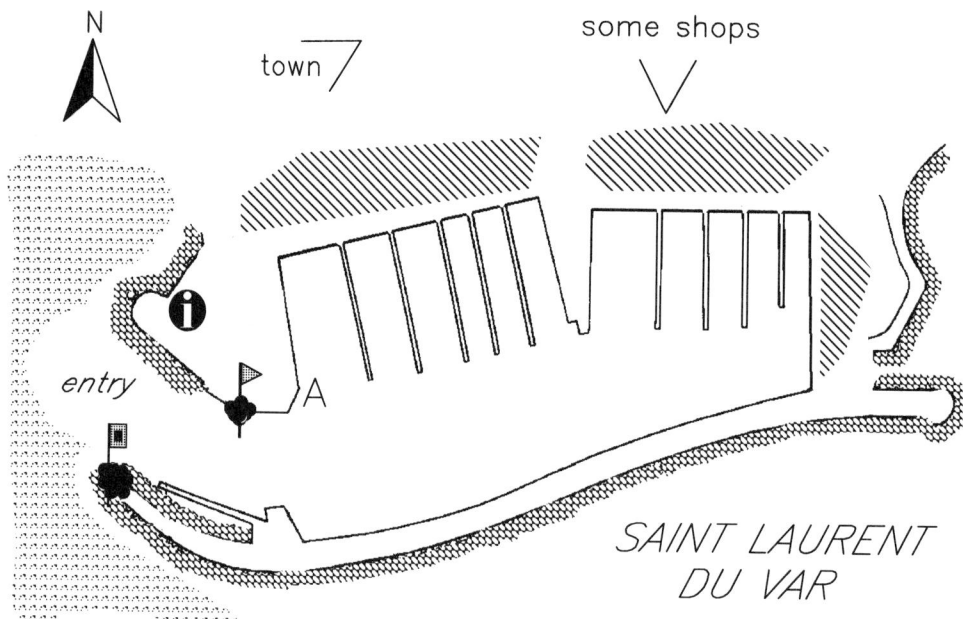

Charts	SHOM 6952, 5176 ECM 501 ADM 2167			
Lights	Head	Fl(3)WG 12s	10m	10–7M	W/G Tower
	N Inner	Iso 4s			Strip
	W Inner	Iso R 4s			Strip

Marks	Nice Airport immediately to the east.		
Reception	Capitainerie: immediately to port on entry.		
Moorings	Quay and pontoons: to laid chain.		
Draught	5m	**LOA**	23m
Berths	1063	**Visitors**	212
Fuel	Reception.		
Weather	Teletape: 93.83.91.12. Capitainerie: posted daily.		
Boatyard Services	Average.		
Shops	Immediate needs can be met in the port. The town itself is disappointingly poor, even for run-of-the-mill domestics. Any serious shopping, especially for lovers of good food, should be organised round an expedition to Nice.		

APPROACH

The port is not at all easy to spot, tucked away as it is to the side of Nice Airport and by the mouth of the famed Var river. However, those monumental edifices dedicated to leisure, the huge apartment blocks of Marina Baie des Anges, are impossible to miss only a little to the west of the port.

Do not make the mistake of confusing the entry with that for the small port of Cros de Cagnes, which is just under a mile to the west. That is accessible only for very small boats and is usually filled with fishing and leisure craft, all of these are local boats, for they are virtually the only ones who are permitted entry or made to feel welcome.

ENTRY

The most obvious mark for the straightforward entry is the substantial white tower that carries the green and white light. Do not stray towards the beach to port, with its area marked off by buoys, as it tends to shoal fairly drastically. The small red navigation mark appears only when you have rounded the outer wall and are turning to starboard for the last leg. This is where the Capitainerie, reception and fuel are situated on the port hand.

The entry is open to the mistral, but because of the protection afforded by the proximity of Cap d'Antibes, there is hardly any scope at all for a sea state to build up, let alone become particularly hazardous.

COMMENTARY

This is one of the most recent ports de plaisance on the Côte d'Azur, having been constructed in 1977. Sited at the mouth of the Var and within ear-splitting distance of Nice Airport, it is in essence a boat park for rich Varite locals and jet-setting weekenders.

Until the county of Nice became part and parcel of France in 1860, the River Var used to form the frontier with the old and then powerful kingdom of Sardinia. It is now somewhat ironic to recall that until the building of the first permanently efficient bridge, as late as 1864, all travellers had to ford the river – often one man on another man's back. That was in the pre-Corniche days. Since then, and nowadays even more so, such a form of rudimentary transport has been unthinkable in the suave and stylish district of the Var – a district that is remorselessly and regularly satirised as the home of ferocious financiers, state of the art bimbos, and young men with designer stubble, all so up and coming that they have already gone.

If neighbouring Antibes is looked on as catering especially for large expensive craft, then St Laurent du Var may fairly be said to host expensive vessels that do not quite match up to that port's large size and standards, although they could by no means be classed as modest. The port itself is expansively huge, hugely expensive and has an over-all air of humming, thriving business. There is a sophisticated commercial atmosphere all round, and the immediate environs contain a fringe of classy restaurants and smart clothes boutiques. There is also a smattering of maritime and chandlery-type boutiques.

The town of St Laurent du Var is a sorry mix of many of the worse aspects of commerce and industry. It is jumbled and extremely busy, with the port completely severed from the town and the nearby railway station by the outer circle motorway which seems to be packed non-stop with long lanes of the noisiest of thunderous French lorries, murderous motors and motorised mousquites.

First impressions, however, on going shore-side and walking towards the town along the busy and not particularly agreeable promenade that overlooks the marina, are all to do with smells. Mercifully, and quite happily in fact, these are not just – or even mainly – those of the plentiful internal combustion engines. On the whole, it is a delightful combination of natural odours that pervades. In particular, pines in abundance offer their fragrance with such extravagance that it can at times be overwhelming.

However, there is one stretch where factitious odours reign supreme: if you keep close to the edge of the promenade overlooking the marina, you pass very close to the ventilator shafts of the premises below. Most of these happen to be bars and restaurants, and from each of these great gusts are continually blasted into the atmosphere so that your senses are assaulted by a series of aromas indicating the speciality (l'arome du jour?) of the place beneath. As a gormandising pastime, it is quite intriguing, and perhaps could provide a novel form of auditioning eating houses. In *Brave New World*, Huxley introduced us to the fictional feelies and smellies, well the promenade of St Laurent du Var gets close to the real thing. ∎

BAIE DES ANGES
43.38.20 N 07.08.50 E
Tel. 93 20 01 60
Port B2   Town C3

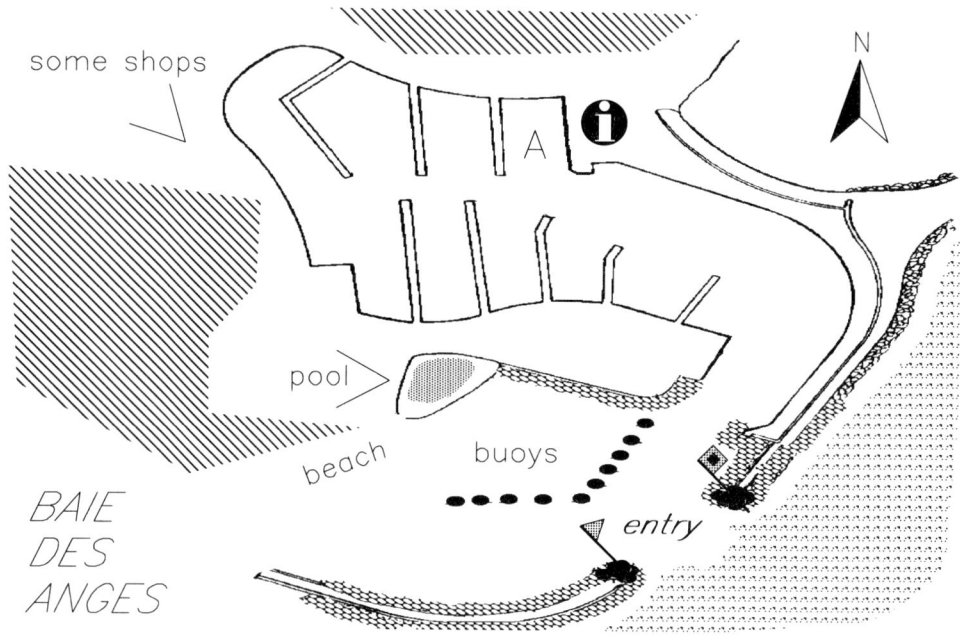

Charts	SHOM 6952, 5176 ECM 501 ADM 2167
Lights	S Breakwater Oc(2)R 6s 6m 7M Squat W/R Tower
	N Breakwater Fl G 4s 13m 9M Slender G/W Base
	Jetty F R 1M Strip light
Marks	Massive triangular blocks of flats (see below).
Reception	Capitainerie: easy to identify towards the centre of the basin.
Moorings	Quay and pontoons with laid chain to port side of berth.
Draught	4m **LOA** 30m
Berths	527 **Visitors** 60
Fuel	Capitainerie.
Weather	Teletape: 93.83.31.12. Posted twice daily at the Capitainerie, with special announcements for strong winds.
Boatyard Services	Average.
Shops	There is a first rate supermarket on site.

APPROACH

From the sea, Baie des Anges is unmistakable. The four pyramids of flats are outstanding in every way. There is nothing like them anywhere else on the Côte d'Azur. Since navigation presents no problem on the way here from either direction, it is quite amusing to pass the time by plotting planes on the radar as they come and go from Nice Airport.

ENTRY

The mistral and bad easterly weather can render the entrance difficult to unsafe. But once inside, you are protected from the worst excesses of swell by the wide spread of the protective outer sea wall.

A squat white tower carries the red light, with the green housed on a more slender one. The entrance is straightforward with a sharp turn to starboard. The Capitainerie is round the next turn to port. At the feet of the pyramids of flats, embraced as it were by the everlasting arms, the well protected marina houses a variety of craft – nothing extremely large but, on the other hand, nothing less than expensive.

COMMENTARY

It is impossible to ignore or escape from the massive and looming grandeur of the immense pyramids of apartment blocks, or the aura that they cast over the whole marina. Although they were built in the 1960s, the contours of these extraordinary apartment blocks with their stark grey/white finishes still present a futuristic aspect worthy of a film setting: a Cocteau dream sequence with *mise en scène* by Corbusier out of Bahaus.

Probably the most amazing property development on the Riviera, the whole scheme was designed by the architect André Minangoy. There are four of these seventeen-storey edifices. Each floor diminishes progressively in area towards the top, thus providing terraces at every level and ensuring that the verandah of each and every flat is optimally placed for all-round sun.

The on-site supermarket is worthy of inspection, though it may be a mite too expensive for the average cruising visitor's pocket. Its 'Special Unrepeatable Today Only' offer, when I last risked a Eurocheque by visiting, was a bottle of champagne at 120F. It is just not the kind of establishment where they would even consider common or garden coffee or vulgar washing powder as being suitable loss leaders for their clientele. It comes as something of a relief to discover that the marine shops and chandlers are well stocked with reasonably priced goods.

'Town' facilities are to all intents and purposes non-existent. As in neighbouring St Laurent, the port de plaisance itself is the haven – the remainder of the place being a ribbon development of commerce and light industry, most of it now dirty and unkempt. In addition, the busy arterial road runs very close to the marina, as do the main railway lines; however, there is the benefit that the railway station is very close.

The main complex houses an extremely attractive swimming pool. Its sophisticated decorum is in some contrast with the ambience of the nearby beach, where, on the sand-starved ribbon strip of plage, are beach attractions with names that speak for themselves: La Dolce Vita, Le Mistral and Top Fun.

The old and famous retreat village of Villeneuve Loubet is dominated by the medieval castle belonging to the Villeneuve family that goes back to the Catalans of the 13th century. The treaty of Nice was signed in the castle in 1538.

Not far away is a treat of a different kind. A Mecca for gastronomes, near the Place de la Mairie, it is the museum devoted to the life and works of Auguste Escoffier in the 1847 birthplace of this 'chef of kings and king of chefs'. One room in the house, arranged as a Provençal kitchen, contains mementoes of his time as head chef at London's Savoy and Carlton Hotels (where he created en passant the famed Peach Melba) and also showpieces of his culinary art and architecture, engineered in icing sugar and almond paste. There is also an upstairs room with an accumulation of some 15 000 menus, some of which go back to 1820. No one has seen fit to dub it the Upper Room or even to mention the Last Supper. Good cooking and eating kept Auguste Escoffier going until the age of eighty-eight. Bon appetit! ∎

ANTIBES
43.50.00 N 07.08.00 E
Tel. Port Vauban 93 34 74 00
Tel. Port de Grand Plaisance 93 34 30 30
Port B1   Town A1

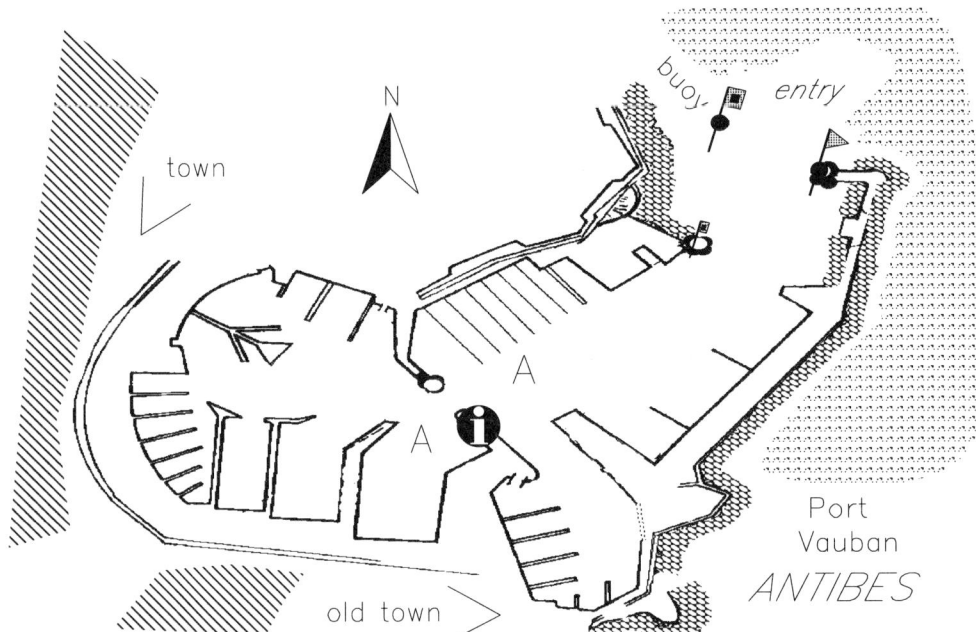

Charts	SHOM 5122, 6954, 6952, 7205 ECM 501 ADM 2167				
Lights	L'Illette	Oc(2 + 1)WRG 12s	14m	13–9M	
	La Garoupe	Fl(2)10 s	104m	31M	W. Tower
	Antibes				
	Cinq Cents	Dir Q WRG	8m	9–7M	Grey lantern
	Head	Fl(4)WR 12s	13m	16–12M	W/Y/R Tower
	Buoy	Fl(2)G 6s			G Buoy
	Jetty Head	Iso G		4M	
	Cap	F Vi		2M	W/R Tower

(The channel buoys and inner moles are also lit to standard: Red, Green and Iso White.)

Marks   The Tour du Recrutement of Fort Carré stands out remarkably with the old belfry tower immediately next door.

Reception   See opposite under Entry.

Moorings   Quay and pontoon: to laid chain.

Draught	5m	**LOA**	65m
Berths	1134	**Visitors**	170

Fuel   By Capitainerie and 'Reception' Quay.

Weather	Teletape: 93.83.31.12. and 93.83.17.24. Posted daily at the Capitainerie and elsewhere round the port.
Boatyard Services	Comprehensive: many English workers.
Town Shops	Comprehensive and choice.

APPROACH

Coming from the north east, Antibes hides its light under a bushel until you are quite close. Its low fringe developments do not reveal their high-rise potentials until the last moment. There are, however, two large markers on the skyline: one, just to the west of the port, is the signal station of La Garoupe; the other on the mountain range behind, much higher and farther inland, is a tall television mast above La Pointe des Trayas on Le Pic de l'Ours.

ENTRY

The entrance is well marked by a large white tower for the red light, and a substantial green buoy. Nearby, on the jetty of Fort Carré, is the Police du Port Reception Quay, where a sombre white-haired gentleman, garbed in apparently ancient underwear, stands rigid, his arms at strange angles as if in silent prayer.

It is important to know your place in Antibes: there are two marina facilities and two Capitaineries. The first, on the port hand, remarkable for its line of red and yellow buoys, is known as the Port or Bassin de Grande Plaisance, and can accommodate craft up to LOA 165m. It sports its own private heliport.

The second is dead ahead after this, and is the one for the majority of visitors. Soon, there should be a reception area for this one, saving congestion at the fuel quay. You are asked to call ahead on VHF 09, so that you can be received by launch and despatched with speed and courtesy to a suitable berth.

Special mention   The port is short on toilets, showers and telephones. While improvements are being made all the time, you can nevertheless be in for a long walk.

COMMENTARY

Antibes was originally a Greek colony. Facing Nice across the Baie des Anges, its name is said to stem from Antipolis, 'The City Opposite'; and indeed in most things historical, political and military the two have been class antagonists and protagonists. The early 5th century BC settlement was no more than a narrow strip where there is now a sea-front walk. In medieval times, when it was known as Antiboul, it spread to create what is now justifiably known as Old Town. There was only one gate; and insiders and outsiders so viciously distrusted one another that for years all trading took place outside the walls.

The port authorities are very proud of what they feel is its prime place on the scale of modern European marinas: 'Here, we are the largest and best of all the marinas in Europe; we take, how do you say, Les Plus Grandes Bateaux, and they are very pleased to come here. Many stay for a long time; we think it is for the tax.'

Life was not always so refined. For example, when Napoleon Bonaparte was posted here in 1794, his mother (La Madame Mère, the widow of an Ajaccio nobleman) had to wash his clothes in the local stream, while his sisters (princesses-in-waiting, as it were) stole figs and artichokes from the farmers. In fact, life and times Antibes style were pretty rough on Napoleon. After the fall of Robespierre, he was himself imprisoned in Fort Carré.

Today, Antibes cruising practice is more luxurious, although it can be a long walk round the marina to get to the particular services you require. Having the dinghy accessible can be a great help. However, the town is close by: the railway station, the post office and supermarket all within easy walking distance. Food is excellent and surprisingly inexpensive.

In complete contrast to the marina is the charming Old Town. Riddled with alleys, it is made up of small bars and artisan shops.

Also in the Old Town is the Castle of Grimaldi, built in the 12th century on foundations of the Roman castrum on the old Antipolis Acropolis. Although it was reconstructed in the 16th century, parts of the original remain, notably the Romanesque tower. In the beflowered terrace garden, Mediterranean-type statues are well laid out. The Picasso museum (he retreated here from an hotel in Golfe Juan) is also in the castle.

Antibes also has its modern and modernistic aspects, most of which are commercial and unpleasant to contemplate. These less attractive parts tend towards Juan les Pins, a resort that no longer lives up to its stylish and scandalous past.

■

GALLICE
43.33.80 N 07.07.00 E
Tel. 93 61 28 64
Port C3   Town C3

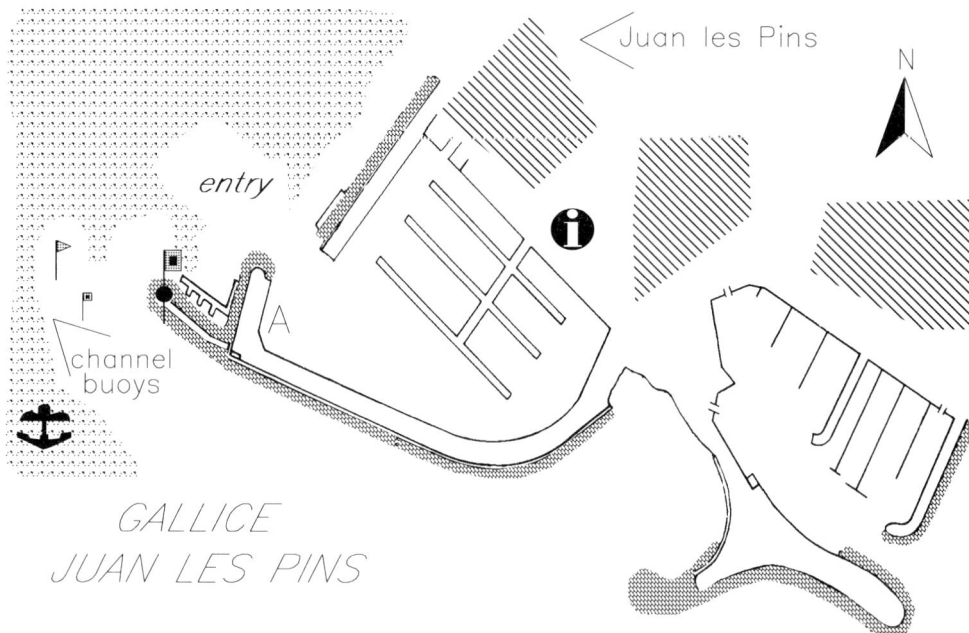

GALLICE
JUAN LES PINS

Charts	SHOM 5122, 7205, 6954 ECM 501 ADM 2167			
Lights	Vallauris Beacon	Oc(2)WRG 6s	167m	16–11M
	La Fourmigue	Fl G 4s	16m	9M
	La Garoupe	Fl(2) 10s	104m	31M
	L'Illette	Oc(2+1)WRG 12s	14m	13–9M
	Gallice W Jetty	VQ(3)G 2s	10m	9M G/W Base
	W Crouton	Q(9) 15s	4m	9M Y/B
	E Crouton	Fl(2)R 6s	1m	6M

Marks The entrance is buoyed, and the water ski ramp is marked in the summer by lights: F Bu and F Vi.

Reception This is easily seen just inside the entrance at the west counter jetty, but the Capitainerie itself is almost hidden away in the depths of the marina – a situation explained after a few moments' discussion with the authorities.

Moorings Quay and pontoons: to laid chain.

Draught 3m   **LOA** 7m (1 at 8m and 1 at 10m)

Berths 526   **Visitors** 173

Fuel Immediately on entry at the north jetty.

Weather Teletape: 93.83.31.12. Capitainerie: posted daily.

Boatyard Services Average.

Shops Mediocre – best go to Antibes where they are excellent.

APPROACH

The signal station of La Garoupe at 104m is visible for over 30 miles. At a lower level, there is the conspicuous white, black-topped tower of the Pointe de l'Illette. An unmistakable landmark closer to is Cap d'Antibes, with its forts, towers and hotels.

There are two major approaches into Golfe Juan: the east and the west. They are designated from the white tower of the major Vallauris beacon:

Lt Oc(2)WRG 6s 167m 16–11M

In addition, there is the solid green marker of La Fourmigue (Fl G 4s, 16m, 9M) more or less in the middle of Golfe Juan, which, together with its ally, Le Sécanion (red) buoy, marks the Basses de la Fourmigue. And with the islands of Marguerite and Honore marked by Les Moines Cardinal (Lt Q(6)+LFl 15s, 12m, 9M) to the south west, La Gallice could hardly be better marked.

ENTRY

Unusually, the entrance is buoyed. The final approach is quite unencumbered and the port feels fairly spacious.

COMMENTARY

Gallice is a small marina on the 'other side of the tracks' of Cap d'Antibes as it were. I had been in the HM's office no more than two minutes before I was told, very politely but even more firmly, that Gallice wanted no publicity of any kind. It had never been interested in publishing a brochure, 'like some of the bigger ports'. They advertise in none of the usual places and proudly claim to keep themselves out of the public eye. Their too-much-protested wish for a quiet life reminded me of a harbour where they used to fly their red flag at all times, described by the pilot guides as meaning 'entry dangerous', just to keep the visitors away. Perhaps Gallice's feelings may be generously represented by the name of a villa close by: Vivre en Paix.

For a marina that is the one and only leisure harbour for the famous, if not indeed infamous, Juan les Pins, Gallice sets out to keep a very low profile. It was, after all, here that the American millionaire Frank Jay Gould created, out of nothing more than silver sand and pine trees, the place that was to become an immediate living legend: one of Europe's most daring bathing resorts of the 1920s and 1930s.

Juan les Pins still has the gall and Gallic insouciance to advertise itself unashamedly as: 'an elegant winter and summer resort in a magnificent bay with a forest of pines growing down to a gently sloping one mile long beach of fine sand; well protected by sumptuous Cap d'Antibes and La Croisette Point'. True, the natural blessings are all there and the decades of civic rearrangement have done little to nullify them. True, some extremely sumptuous villas exist behind high walls and mini forests of pine trees. But when it comes to the town itself, I find it difficult to agree with any of the highly favourable brochures and guides. No more than half an hour's reconnaissance is needed to burst that bubble and expose the sordid truth that is the nature of life under the smiling superficiality and behind the fancy façade.

There is plenty of night life, with a more than average supply of restaurants, night clubs and open air cafes. Loud music-cum-muzak is very much the thing, although the World Jazz Festival has done a lot to promote better tunes and tones. An art work by Joan Miró, 'La Déese de la Mer', was anchored to the sea bottom in 1968 with a submarine support of more than 15m.

It is not far inland to Vallauris, where Picasso's Temple of Peace is situated, variously referred to as the Picasso Memorial or the Museum of Modern Art. It is a 12th-century chapel he was finally pressed into decorating after his seventieth birthday dinner. It is a windowless place in which he wanted his paintings to be lit only by live torches. Sadly, his wishes were ignored. But there is little that can affect his most famous piece,' Man with the Sheep'. Picasso took an ugly little pink villa, somewhat curiously named La Galloise (The Welshwoman), and started work at Madoura. He installed himself in a disused scent factory. He soon headed a gang of local potters, painters and hangers on.

Port du Crouton

The next door Port du Crouton is well named. It is a snug little haven of a harbour tucked in by the side of big brother Gallice, well protected from the mistral by its intelligently designed double jetty walls. It is used in the main by fishing boats, but also plays host to smaller cruising boats. It is essentially devoted to local craft. Draught and facilities are limited and space is at a premium. ∎

GOLFE JUAN (VALLAURIS)
43.34.00. N 07.04.50 E
VHF 12
Tel. 93 63 96 25
Port B2   Town A2

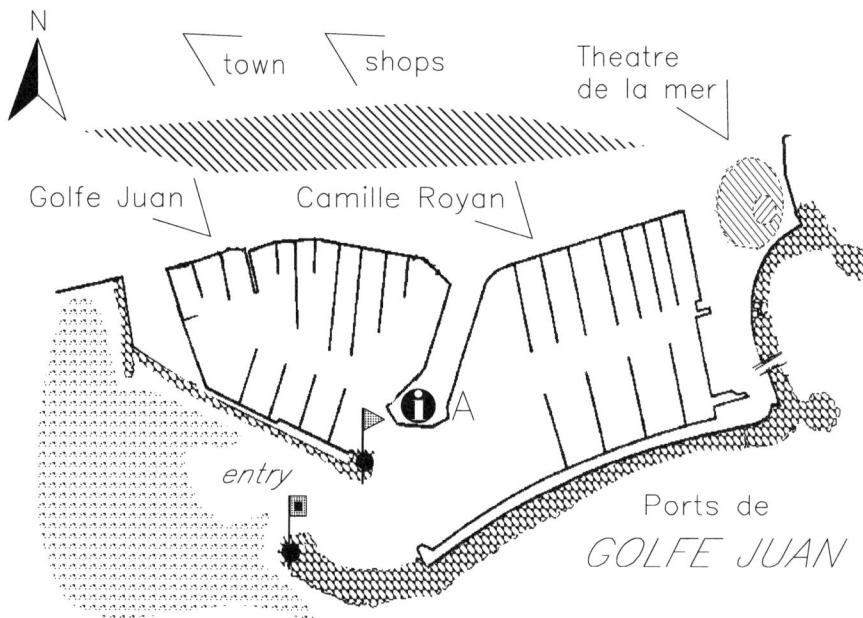

Charts	SHOM 5122, 7205, 6954 ECM 501 ADM 2167		
Lights	Vallauris Beacon	Oc(2)WRG 6s	167m	16–11M
	La Garoupe	Fl(2) 10s	104m	31M
	L'Illette	Oc(2+1)WRG 12s	14m	13–9M
	Ports de Golfe Juan:		
	S Jetty	Fl R Iso 4s	W/R Tower
	E Jetty	Fl G 5s	G/W Base
	Reception 5 luminous search lights.		
Marks	La Fourmigue Fl G 4s 16m 9M		
	Le Sécanion marked by a red buoy.		
Reception	Pontoon N, immediately to port after entry.		
Moorings	Quay and pontoons: to laid chain.		
Draught	3.5m	**LOA**	22m
Berths	847	**Visitors**	255
Fuel	Camille Royan reception quay.		
Weather	Teletape: 93.83.17.24, 93.83.91.11 and 36.65.08.09. Posted daily at 0800 at the Capitainerie.		
Boatyard Services	Average.		
Shops	Everything you need is here, but it takes a day or two to find it.		

APPROACH

Cap d'Antibes, with its forts, towers and hotels, is an unmistakable close landmark. From farther afield, the signal station of La Garoupe at 104m is visible for over 30 miles. At a lower level is the conspicuous white, black-topped tower of the Pointe de l'Illette.

There are two major approaches into Golfe Juan – the east and the west – and they are indicated from the white tower of the major Vallauris beacon. The big green beacon of La Fourmigue, more or less in the middle of Golfe Juan, and its ally, the red buoy Le Sécanion, mark the Basses de la Fourmigue. The islands of Marguerite and Honore are marked by Les Moines Cardinal to the south west. There are also yellow buoys of the Marine Reserve to be observed, a mile or so off the port in a southwesterly direction.

ENTRY

The entry is quite straightforward and, with the new extension now completed, the whole port is well protected from most bad weather. East-erlies can make entry uncomfortable or even hazardous because of the beam sea over the shallow area that extends to the south for more than half a mile.

COMMENTARY

Golfe Juan has the air of a working harbour, and is home for a collection of craft that range from quite quaint 4m GRP day cruisers with minuscule outboards to more substantial craft – though there is nothing to rival those next door at Camille. Its egalitarian atmosphere is in keeping with the PR efforts of the Tourist Board, who maximise the Republican flavour of everything bar the French onion soup.

And not without good reason, since Napoleon landed here from Elba with 1200 men in 1815. His Rule of 100 Days began with the famous notice pinned to the fishermen's huts: 'The eagle, with the national colours, will fly from steeple to steeple as far as the towers of Notre Dame.' He continued with a bivouac in a grove of olive trees while attempting to win over the garrison at Antibes. When this came to naught, he marched on Cannes and then to Grasse and onwards. The whole campaign, route and branch, is well advertised with maps and signposts; the latter, in brown and white, consist of a sculpted eagle surmounting a circle of leaves enclosing the Emperor's initial N. Chauvinistically, you are invited to foot the route of the first eight days. ▪

GOLFE JUAN (CAMILLE ROYAN)
43.34.00. N 07.04.50 E
Tel. 93 63 30 30
Port A1   Town A2

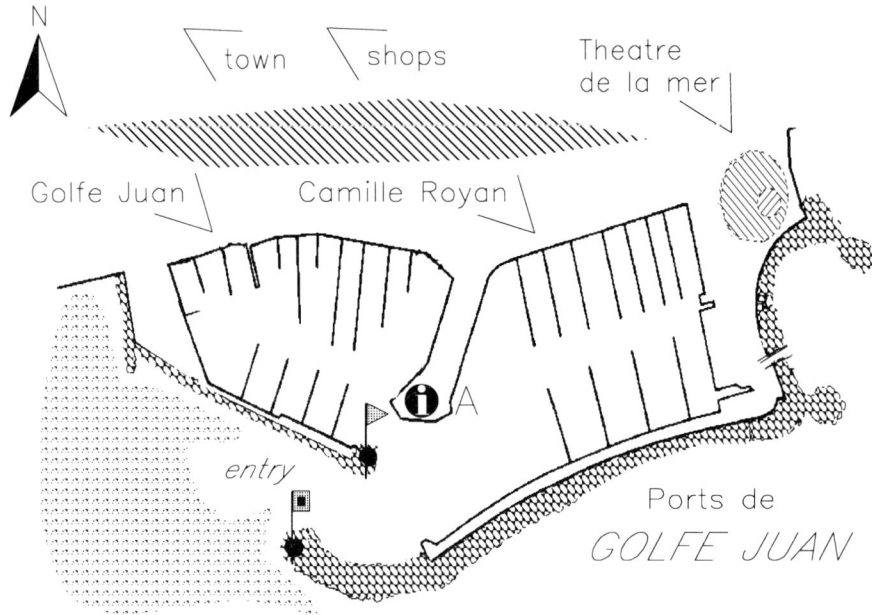

Reception	Immediately ahead upon entering.
Moorings	Concrete pontoons and floating fingers: to laid chain to be picked up on port side.

Draught	3.5m	**LOA**	22m
Berths	847	**Visitors**	250
Fuel	Reception quay.		
Boatyard Services	Good.		

COMMENTARY

The marina houses leisure craft of all kinds, ranging in size up to the very large. However, no visiting luxury liner could compete with the concrete grandeur of the new Harbour Control Office, fashioned as it is in the form a *QE2*-type wheelhouse. Between the two ports there is a good spectrum of French boating – a range not seen in every port.

Different again from many other marinas, the frontage is not a synthetic array of specially created restaurants and boutiques, but a street that really feels as if it belongs to the community. In fact, the actual town of Golfe Juan possesses an atmosphere of a small and near-isolated village with a life, style and culture all of its own. Ship chandlers and such all have their fair and necessary share, but nevertheless the general ambience is one of a small town with indigenous folk at work and play; and there is an excellent choice of cafe-bars, with no need to resort to expensive restaurants.

By the Rue des Pêcheurs and the Avenue de la Gare is the legend 'Ici commence la Route Napoleon', immediately next to the neatly juxtaposed restaurant called Le Dauphin. You may prefer to visit the Picasso shrine at Vallauris. He casually wandered into the village one day and saw the Madoura pottery of the Ramiés. He immediately set up a school; today there are said to be over 100 potteries in Vallauris, each with its own marketing front. ∎

PIERRE CANTO
43.25.00 N 07.01.50 E
Tel. 93 43 48 66
Port B3   Town A1

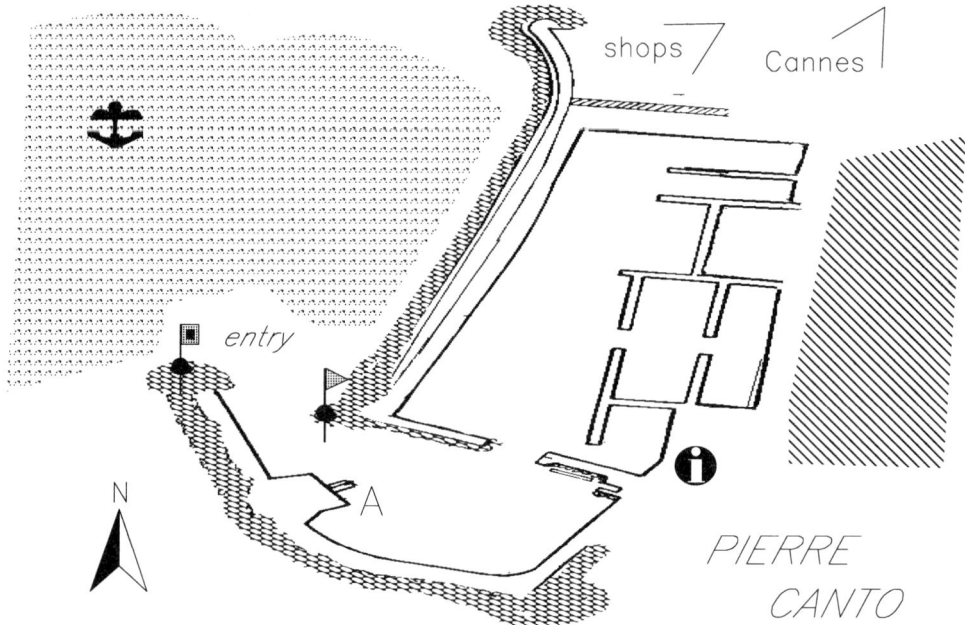

Charts	SHOM 5113, 7205, 6954 ECM 501 ADM 2167, 2166
Lights	S Jetty OcWG 4s 11m 8–12M G/W Base
	W Jetty Oc(2)R 6s 2m 6M W/R Tower
	Capitainerie: Luminous white/blue sign: 'Port P. Canto'.
Marks	The noticeable Observatoire de la Californie is directly above the entrance on a course of 035°M. The equally obvious Palm Beach Casino stands to starboard of the entrance behind the yacht harbour.
Reception	Capitainerie: straight ahead by fuel jetty.
Moorings	Quay: to laid chain.

Draught	5m	**LOA**	70m
Berths	650	**Visitors**	100

Fuel	Capitainerie.
Weather	Teletape: 93.83.91.12. Posted daily at Club House and Capitainerie, where there is also a local bulletin on tape that is updated every three hours. In addition, a 24-hour service is available on VHF 9.
Boatyard Services	Moderate.
Shops	Basic provisions can be obtained nearby, but for most things it is best to go to Cannes.

APPROACH

From the west, via the Golfe de Napoule leaving the Îles de Lerin to starboard. From the east, Cap d'Antibes direction, either round the Îles de Lerin into the Golfe de Napoule, or through one of the two shallow straits: between Ste Marguerite and St Honorat, Le Plateau du Milieu; or between Ste Marguerite and la Croisette.

ENTRY

The way in is clearly marked by the stone base of the green-topped tower. The knuckle of the second wall is marked by its red-topped white support.

COMMENTARY

You will not be able to escape the name of Pierre Canto: the man who started it all. There is no doubt that Pierre Canto perceives itself as the first not only in time but also in quality in France – if not indeed in the world. It describes itself as 'Premier port de plaisance d'Europe', challenging the claim of nearby Antibes, and setting the standard for the rest. As only fitting, Pierre Canto himself is the President Directeur General of the International Sporting Yachting Club de la Mer Port Pierre Canto.

However, in spite of its pretentious publicity material, Port Canto has none of the air of its glossy brochure, and is a most modestly welcoming marina. There is no sign of Le Snob, and the staff are all extremely helpful, efficient and friendly. It hosts a wide range of small cruising craft and fishing boats.

Palm Beach, Port Bijou and Port de Mouré Rouge

Clustered round the Point de la Croisette are three small harbours. Next door to Pierre Canto is the tiny harbour of Palm Beach (Port de la Croisette or Port Cannes II) which is host to mainly racing sailing yachts. Indeed, Palm Beach is devoted to the many popular regattas organised by its home league, the prestigious Yacht Club de Cannes. Perhaps the main concern for skippers is to avoid confusing it with the main marina when visiting for the first time.

Tucked into a small pocket of Palm Beach and one place down in the pecking order, is tiny Port Bijou, given over to small fishing craft. Round the corner, to the north west, is the shallow miniature Port de Mouré Rouge. Bijou lives up or down to its name according to your perception. Some thirty small fishing boats moor afloat while many more are just beached; this is slightly risky since the protection from the mistral is not good.

Mouré Rouge is hardly a 'port' at all. It is more of a haven, consisting of two stone jetties built round what was a summer anchorage, with its three minimal pontoons being used mainly by dinghies. Surprisingly, it has a crane and a skip capable of taking craft up to 10 tonnes.

Les Îles de Lérins

Just over 1000m from Pointe de la Croisette, the two islands of Ste Marguerite and St Honorat are usually visited by all boats cruising the two bays between La Galère and Cap d'Antibes. These two offshore islands are popular with day trippers, many in boats with glass bottoms. It is perhaps through these that the ferry skippers navigate as they speed furiously through the shallows.

Ste Marguerite island is about 2 miles by $\frac{1}{2}$ mile. It is almost all in State hands except for the Grand Jardin Domain. The island is famous for its old fort that over the centuries has housed many prisoners. The most fainthearted was perhaps Marshal Bazaine, who achieved notoriety by surrendering Metz to the Prussians in 1870. He escaped by bribing the guards to spread the rumour that he had climbed through a window about five times too small for his corpulence. The most maltreated prisoners were perhaps the six Huguenot pastors, for whom there is now a statue by Viggo Jarl in one of the cells. But the most celebrated inmate is undoubtedly the mysterious Man in the Iron Mask. Little is really known of him other than that his mask was made of velvet.

St Honorat island is even smaller (1 mile by $\frac{1}{4}$ mile) and is in the private hands of the monks who make the 'Lerina' liqueur. Walks abound and there is a terrific view from the top of the old fortified monastery.

With their pines and eucalyptus trees, their monasteries with secret liqueurs, keeps and chapels, their unimpaired shores and their generally rock encumbered situation, these islands summon up images of a Mediterranean wildlife coast that has almost disappeared.

Speed limits are in force: between Île Ste Marguerite and Pointe de la Croisette, 10 knots; and between Île Ste Marguerite and Île St Honorat, 5 knots. There are some splendid anchorages (provided you do not venture closer in than 100m) and some jetties and pontoons where moorings may be used with discretion. ■

CANNES

43.32.00 N 07.01.00 E
VHF 12
Tel. 93 39 94 24
Port B2   Town A1

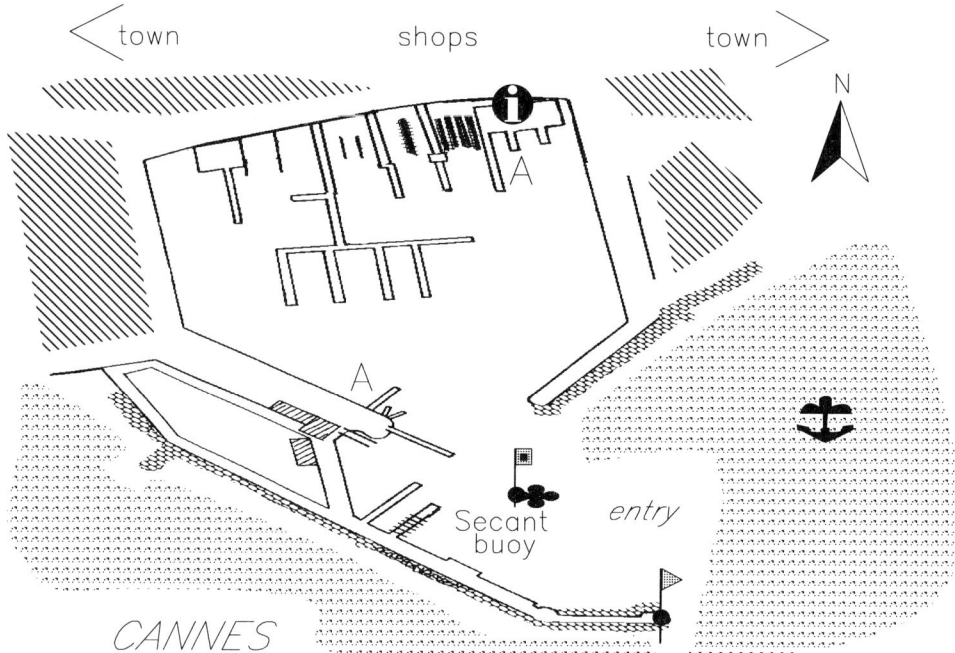

Charts	SHOM 5113, 7205, 6954 ECM 501 ADM 2166, 2167	
Lights	Jetty Head VQ(3)R 2s 22m 8M W/R Tower	
	Le Secant Fl(2)G 6s 10m 4M G/W Base	
Marks	The striking Observatoire de la Californie is poised high above the port. The hexagonal white and red tower is conspicuous.	
Reception	Difficult because of congestion, but best near the Gare Maritime, from where the vedettes leave for the islands.	
Moorings	Quay and pontoons: to laid chain.	
Draught	5m	**LOA** 60m
Berths	802	**Visitors** 240
Fuel	West jetty: outer port.	
Weather	Capitainerie: posted daily.	
Boatyard Services	Comprehensive.	
Shops	There is an excellent choice of shops just behind the front.	
Special Mention	It is possible to anchor off in the bay, except in the prohibited zone set aside for passenger ships. There are public telephones on the pontoons (coins only), but showers and toilets are in short supply.	

APPROACH

High above the port of Cannes is the noticeable Observatoire de la Californie. At sea level, the Îles de Lérins are not only conspicuous landmarks, but they form an important part of the life of the whole of the bay. The inner island, Ste Marguerite, is the larger; and the outer St Honorat possesses a noticeable château and a small collection of rocky hazards: the YB Cardinal, Les Moines, sits on some of them and is a threatening sight when the weather is inclement.

The close approach takes you past these two islands, and from here on Le Rade de Cannes begins to show itself at its most beautiful. The islands are left to starboard, although there are plenty who take the inner routes – marked on the Admiralty charts with very little water. The first sign of sophistication comes with the conspicuous Palm Beach Casino and the Port Pierre Canto yacht harbour to the east, and, very probably, parts of the US Navy to the west.

ENTRY

The entrance is clearly marked by the massive hexagonal white tower at the end of the long west jetty, which is left to port. The second white tower, Le Secant, marks the shoal areas in the outer harbour which are to be left to starboard, although many locals do anything but this.

COMMENTARY

The port of Cannes occupies a splendid position that can be seen to great advantage from the east in the early morning sun. On the other hand, its panorama comes romantically alive at night with many of its old mellowed stone buildings being warmly lit. Happily, they are not seriously jeopardised by the omnipresence of the technicolour fluorescents. In daytime, for those who want to get away, the bus journey to St Raphael along the scenic coastal route is well worth its fare.

In 1840 Cannes got its first jetty, previously having been no more than an anchorage. The first Cannes Regatta, referred to by the Prince of Wales chauvinistically as Mediterranean Cowes, was held in 1860. Guy de Maupassant's early yachting visits inspired him to describe the place as 'a dangerous port, unsheltered … where all vessels are in peril', although later he became quite addicted to the place, describing it in his story 'On the Water'. Prosper Mérimée was also smitten, as was the renowned Provençal poet Frédéric Mistral.

Today Cannes is resort of resorts and, with its many festivals, it always seems to be en fête; the most acclaimed is the International Film Festival. As the brochure says, 'In May, Cannes becomes the film capital of the world.'

Such fame and popularity was not always the case, and had it not been for an outbreak of cholera in 1834 Jean-Luc Godard might never have put in an appearance here. What happened was that the then Lord Chancellor of England, Lord Brougham, who was on his way to his lodgings in Nice, was required to remain in Cannes because of the *cordon sanitaire*. With a superb counter-attack of typically English choler, he decided to stay put and build his nest there. The English aristocracy followed him in droves to this fashionable resort, and Cannes has been in business ever since.

The marina facility faces the very front of the town, which consists of a superb range of architectural styles, with something different round almost every corner. In turn, the town turns its best front to the bay, with some remarkable feats of architecture: notably, the Carlton Hotel with a façade to rival the Grands of Eastbourne and Torquay in their prime. Virtually until after the Second World War, the season was from November until April. Today, those months are quite out of season, although, when I visited a few days after Christmas, lounging sun chairs were at the ready and the tables were laid for early lunch, quite unprotected from the elements.

Different from Nice, its rival 'queen' of the Riviera, Cannes has managed to couple a thriving 20th-century commercial existence with a discerning conservation of all that is best from the past. In particular, its old town, Le Suquet, is a paradigm of how attractive the truth can be in edifice and artifice alike.

The shops are easily accessible in the alleys and back streets just behind the main façade. In particular, food shops are worthy of close inspection – but beware, for there are really far too many temptations. Under the plane trees in the Allées de la Liberté there is a regular flower market. There is also the Sunday morning vegetable market that is first rate. Equally noteworthy and eye-catching are the arts, crafts and antiques booths along the front, where you are frequently entertained by the antics of clowns, rock'n'rollers and singing comedians manqué – all for free in a grand free-for-all. ∎

LA NAPOULE
43.05.00 N 06.56.07 E
Tel. 93 93 36 00
Port A1   Town B2

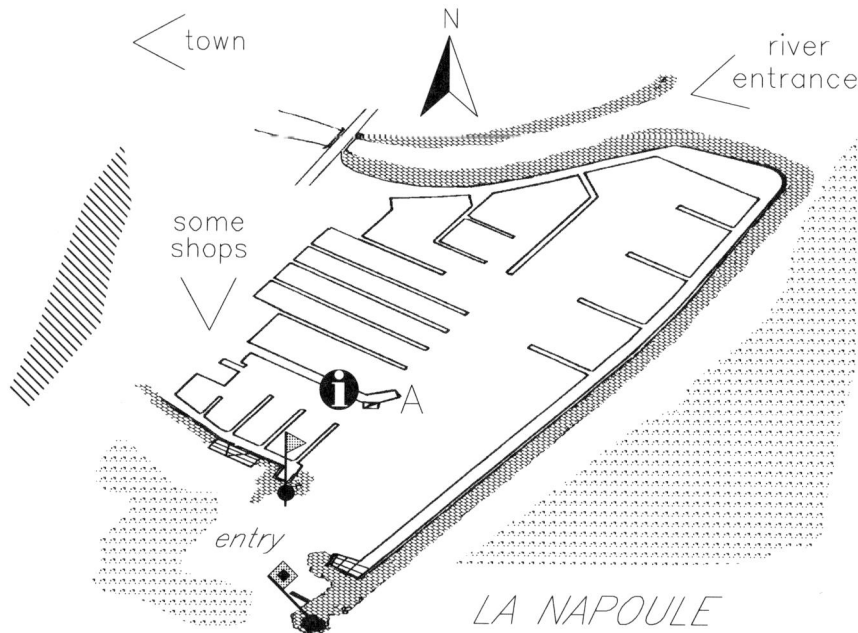

Charts	SHOM 5113, 7205, 6954 ECM 501 ADM 2166, 2167
Lights	S Breakwater Fl(3)G 12s 9m 10M G/W Base
	Inner Spur Fl G 2s 2m 2M G Structure
	Inner Jetty Oc(2)R 6s 2m 2M R Structure
Reception	Capitainerie: dead ahead after first pontoons to port.
Moorings	Quay and pontoons: to laid chain picked up to starboard.
Draught	6m **LOA** 50m
Berths	1130 **Visitors** 200
Fuel	Reception quay.
Weather	Teletape: 93.83.31.12 and 93.93.36.15. Posted daily at the Capitainerie and other places in the harbour. In addition, the port has a novel weather station: a bright LED red display under a cowl on the spur of the sea wall, just under the white tower by the HM annex.
Boatyard Services	Comprehensive.
Shops	Shopping is very limited in the immediate vicinity of the harbour and also within the nearby small community of La Napoule, but all basic needs are catered for. There is a small market on Thursdays. In addition, only a couple of miles along the main road to Cannes, there is a hypermarket with a vast range of inexpensive goods. But if you want good food, it is worth the trip to Nice.

APPROACH

There is a television mast to the south west of the Golfe de Napoule; it is nearly 60m and, standing at 500m on the Pic de l'Ours, it is conspicuous for miles around. Also easily visible is the much closer Piton de San Peyre, with the ruined buildings standing out clearly at 131m above sea level.

At a lower level and just north of the port, the white structures of Loew's Hotel and Casino cannot be mistaken. They are close to the entrance of the River Siagne; and it is worth noting that there are other inlets along this stretch of the coast.

ENTRY

The obvious close landmark is that of the conspicuous Château de la Napoule, which stands at the entrance on the port hand. The towers and gateway are all that remain of the once-proud medieval citadel of the Villeneuve. Their rich reddish-purple hues are eye-catching.

The outer sea wall is marked by a white tower with a green top; its inner spur has a small lit green structure.

COMMENTARY

Anchoring in the bay is not permitted during the season because of bathing, but (Catch 22) it can be rough out of season due to brisk easterlies. The harbour itself is well protected from such winds, although the powerful swell manages to surge quite a way through the berths – especially those backing on to the sea wall.

With its ancient castle and church overlooking a miniature sandy beach and a mellow old stone bridge, La Napoule has a most strikingly picturesque setting for its entrance. The two massive towers were restored and converted into the castle/museum in Romanesque, Gothic and Oriental by Henry Clews, perhaps the most grotesque or original of American sculptors. He was assisted by his more than capable wife.

The outer sea wall of the harbour is lit on the inside by a series of muted lamps that lend a most agreeably pleasing tone to the port. In contrast, the buildings along the front are all in the horizontal-slotted-modernistic/near Cubist style.

While there is a comprehensive service for boats (for this is the headquarters of the domain of Arie de Boom) and all the other usual services along the marina parade, there is none of the usual razzmatazz usually associated with such frontages. Indeed, this marina is a delightfully friendly, efficient, yet low key, operation. There is a very good laundrette and the harbour is positively littered with telephone kiosks.

The whole area of Mandelieu–La Napoule is given over to sport, in particular water sports and golf; indeed, many experts claim that this golf course is the most demanding on the Côte d'Azur. Rent-a-boat is very popular here, and the 1990 prices ranged from 650F to 6500F per day. Flying is also popular, and light aircraft zoom all around quite low and close from the nearby Aerodrome de Cannes Mandelieu.

One of La Napoule's nicer claims to fame is that it is the main town of the mimosa country beside the Siagne. In January and February the whole of the region, consisting of the sandy slopes behind Cannes and Mandelieu (La Croix des Gardes, La Roquette and Tanneron), become aflame with the blooms of the burnishing mimosa. Most of it, packed in wet plastics, goes to England and other northern climes to cheer and lighten dismal winter tempers, but there is also quite an export trade to Canada and the United States.

There are two kinds of mimosa, that which grows wild and the vast orchards that consist of 'grafted' plants. Cultivated mimosa is preferred by the florists, whereas the wild, because of its more powerful fragrance, is chosen by the aroma wizards who work in Grasse. This city, that owes the introduction of its scent industry to Catherine of Medici, is now acknowledged as the perfume capital of the world. A staggering fact about the area: more than 20 000 tonnes of flowers are marketed each year.

Not far from the marina are other boat homes. One is the Port du Beal. Although there are some medium-sized craft (with one catamaran called *Cat House*), this is really just a haven for tiny craft, being of no service to visitors. An altogether different kind of experience is Cannes marina; it is already vast but is still developing at a rate of knots. In addition, there is Port Inland: the River Siagne is crossed by a miniature ferry that is just large enough to transport two golf carts with drivers and staff from the nearby domain of Les Bungalows du Golf. ∎

LA RAGUE
43.31.00. N 06.56.40 E
(Also Théoule sur Mer)
Tel. 93 49 81 55
Port B3   Town Théoule

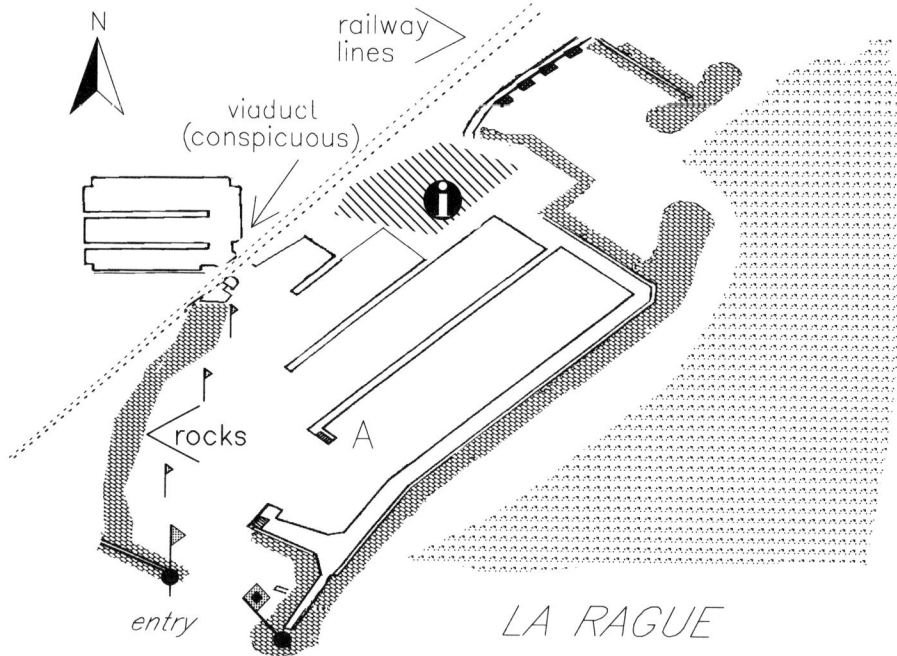

LA RAGUE

Charts	SHOM 5113, 7205, 6954 ECM 501 ADM 2167, 2166
Lights	Breakwater Head Iso G 4s 9m 10M G/W Base
	Inner Jetty Fl R 2s 4m 2M R Structure
Marks	Railway viaduct: six arches in red brick.
Reception	Dead ahead on entry: notably, a special reception quay that is obvious and easily accessible.
Moorings	Quay and pontoons: to laid chain.
Draught	8m **LOA** 30
Berths	526 **Visitors** 130
Fuel	East counter jetty immediately to port on entry.
Weather	Teletape: 93.83.31.12 and 93.72.31.32. Posted daily at the Capitainerie. Additionally, 4 Telex Meteos (3 French and 1 Italian).
Boatyard Services	Above average.
Shops	Théoule is the nearest town where a range of local goods and produce can be bought; otherwise, the choice is between the hypermarket just outside La Napoule and Cannes.

APPROACH

Just under a mile to the north, the high ground and buildings of San Peyre are outstanding. When coming from the south, the small unmarked headland of La Pointe de l'Aiguille should be left well to port; in addition, there is a shoal patch known as the Roc du Port just before this.

The final approach is dominated by the unmistakable red brick railway viaduct, usually visible for more than 2 miles. Also easy to identify are a white villa and a château-type construction that actually overlook the harbour just to port.

ENTRY

The entrance is well protected and entry is straightforward. The staff are extremely friendly, efficient and co-operative.

COMMENTARY

The railway viaduct splits the harbour into two parts, with the main and deeper part being to seaward. The inner basin, the upper room as it were, is used mainly by smaller motor cruisers and sailing craft with masts under 10m.

La Rague is one of the few French harbours that actually smells of the sea and seaweed. It is situated in a deep inlet in a gorge that gives it a powerful feeling of being not only away-from-it-all, but also cloistered in its rocky seclusion. If it were not to do it an injustice, since it is possessed of great heart and humanity missing in the other, one might describe La Rague as a miniature Fontvieille. It is extremely well surrounded and protected by the almost overpowering, vertigo-inducing rocky cliffs of the Esterel, which seem to overhang so dramatically that they must be restrained by some miraculous force. From these very cliffs there are excellent views.

The port, which currently houses a broad range of craft, is still in the process of development under the aegis of Arie de Boom. There are very reasonable facilities for boats, but there is virtually no victualling or domestic service –

the hypermarket near La Napoule or the smaller township of Théoule sur Mer being the nearest. It is one of few French marinas where there is all-round protection, good facilities for the maintenance and repair of boats; and just sufficient and necessary domestic services to sustain life within striking distance, but without the usual accompanying hysteria of marina show-biz night life. There is a small sandy beach nearby.

Port de Théoule sur Mer
43.30.50 N 06.56.40 E
Capitainerie: 93.49.97.38   VHF 16 and 9

This tiny port, less than a mile away from La Rague, is tucked away in a bay with a southern sea wall, lit from the small turret at its extremity. There is need for care since the entrance is not wide and the north quay (not lit) approaches very close (15m) to the sea wall at right angles, and with projecting low stones. This latter quay is lit by non-navigational street lamps. Approach in east to south east weather and swell is dangerous, and entry virtually impossible.

Théoule is an extremely small port originally built in the 17th century and still retaining most of its old-world charm. Its miniature Capitainerie is set into rough rock and an equally gruff weather machine seems to be suffering from some terminal illness. The tiny harbour is basically an old fishing port that has been recently, but only modestly, improved. It is essentially suitable only for small craft, there being very little space and few facilities for visitors. However, in calm settled weather, if your boat is no more than 10m and draws no more than 2m, it is worth trying to charm a berth out of the staff.

The township is charming and the people are friendly. There are basic shops near the pretty square with a modern sculpted fountain next the Mairie and La Poste. There are three small sandy beaches which are well protected by the Théoule promontory.   ∎

LA GALERE
43.30.00 N 06.57.40 E
Tel. 93 75 41 74
Port A5   Town None

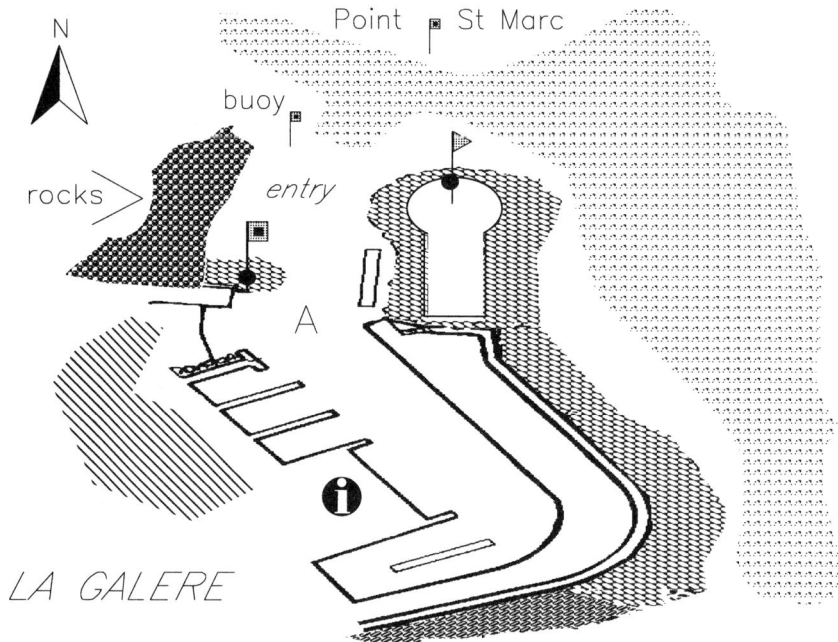

N

Point St Marc

buoy

rocks >   entry

A

LA GALERE

Charts	SHOM 5113, 7205, 6954 ECM 501 ADM 2166, 2167		
Lights	Buoy	Fl(2)G 6s	Starboard hand
	Breakwater	Q R 9m 7M	W/R Tower
	Inner	Iso W 4s	G Strip

Reception   Wait at the outer quay where there is the best water; everything is close to hand in this port.

Moorings   Quay pontoons: to laid chain.

Draught	2m	**LOA**	12m
Berths	220	**Visitors**	20 (This seems to be a theoretical

concept only. You should not rely on being permitted to stay, or even to linger. Only charm and guile in equal proportions are likely to win the day, or a berth.)

Fuel   Near entrance on the starboard hand.

Weather   Teletape: 93.83.31.12. Posted daily by the Capitainerie.

Boatyard Services   Minimal.

Shops   At Théoule, at La Napoule hypermarket, or in Cannes. However, to get to any of these there is a long climb up the hill, daunting even to hardy walkers.

APPROACH

The TV mast of Pic de l'Ours is an excellent landmark from a long distance to seaward, being just over a mile to the south of the port; closer inshore the Cardinal La Vaquette is found just off Cap de l'Esquillon and Pointe de la Paume when coming from the south.

The harbour is exceptionally striking from the sea because the pink and white villas immediately above look much more like ancient man's rough cave dwellings than contemporary man's dream houses. The scenery is also dramatic and splendid: reddish brown sandstone with rich patches of dark-hued greens makes up the mountain side. Small communities cling perilously to it, and the famous coastal railway line runs apparently hazardously below.

En route to or from St Raphael, both Cap Raise and Cap de Drammont are unmistakably mounded humps. In between is the Cardinal La Chrétienne, which marks the outlying rocks that are to be found lurking around La Boute.

ENTRY

Two green buoys mark the close local hazards of rocks just before the narrow entrance. The white tower with red top on the outer sea wall is plain to see, while the lower inner wall is marked with a noticeable green stripe. Both are lit.

COMMENTARY

A large part of the port is in fact very shallow, in spite of the depths shown on some of the charts, and care needs to be taken if you draw more than 1.5m. On this account, it is best not to venture into the depth of the port to the south; but there is no difficulty even with 3m in reaching the floating summer pontoon or the fuel quay.

The private port is defended shoresides, at the top of the hill, by impassable traffic gates and security personnel who are bright eyed and strong armed. Its approaches are stunning, by sea or land. The descent from the main road entrance becomes close to the vertiginous from a point halfway up the cliffs. The hairpin bends wander down through the architect's realised dreams of Baroque curves and honeycomb contours: perhaps the most unusual and eye-catching buildings in the Golfe de Napoule. They look their most gorgeous from seaward, when they are seen to advantage against the background of the wooded terraces on the slopes of the Esterel where it dramatically ends La Napoule bay.

The port itself is extremely modish, with the modernistic buildings sweeping down to the quay where the Capitainerie is built in the same style; and even the inside of the harbour wall, in its white worked concrete, is in keeping with the ethos. The private port houses mainly tiny craft, although there are some medium-range cruisers; but the price tags do not represent what might be expected from this very private and posh place. There are a few services but no shops. Access to the main road is tiring and, even when you get there, has little for a long way except a bus stop, which is a superb vantage point for both the man made and the natural scenic panoramas. It is a beautifully quiet and secluded spot.

All things considered, it is best to accept that La Galère is made up exclusively of summer residences, and consider it as a 'chance' summer port only. The Commandant (HM) was extremely polite when he told me La Galère was particularly reserved, in every way, for its extremely particular residents. ∎

LA FIGUEIRETTE MIRAMAR
43.29.00 N 06.56.10 E
VHF none
Tel. 93 75 41 00
Port B3   Town Théoule

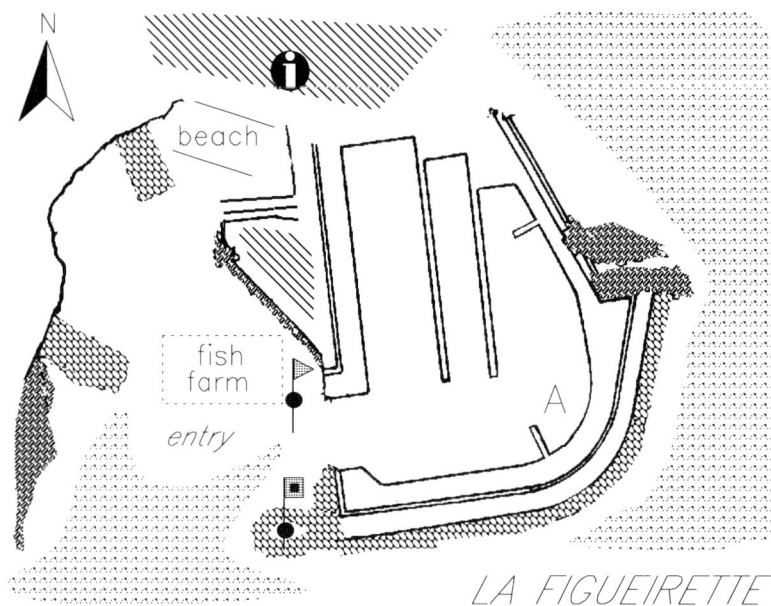

LA FIGUEIRETTE

Charts	SHOM 5113, 6954 ECM 501 ADM 2166, 2167
Lights	La Vaquette Q(3) 10s 6M BYB
	Jetty Head Fl(3)WG 12s 12m 13–10M G/W Base
	Inner Spur F R
Reception	'Blue' quay: to the west by the clubhouse.
Moorings	Quay and pontoons: to laid chain.
Draught	1.9m **LOA** 15m
Berths	235 **Visitors** 47
Fuel	North Quay.
Weather	Teletape: 93.38.95.34 or 94.46.90.11. Posted daily by the Capitainerie.
Boatyard Services	Limited.
Shops	The harbour is unfortunately out on a limb in this respect. There is a small shop within walking distance, but otherwise it is Théoule, La Napoule, Cannes or St Raphael.

APPROACH
The TV mast of Pic de l'Ours is an excellent landmark from a long way off, while closer inshore La Vaquette, an isolated rock off the Cap de l'Esquillon, is found just off Cap de l'Esquillon and Pointe de la Paume, which are immediately off the little port. The isolated danger mark for La Vaquette is not always very clear to see, being, for the French navigation authorities, a slender affair – a sort of Mediterranean withy. The sea usually marks it by breakers, but in flat calms it is not visible. There is a safe inshore passage in 10m.

Nearer to the port you are likely to see one or more of the fish farms that proliferate in the area. They are well marked by yellow buoys and afford no inconvenience for normal navigation. In the right season, you are likely to see some of these small fish farms being towed out to sea by light cruisers.

ENTRY
The modernistic white tower constructed of slender pillars with a green top at the western end of the southern sea wall marks the sharp turn to starboard that is needed to gain entry. There is no tower marking the north jetty and, since there may well be a fish farm or two parked just inside the outer entrance, extra care and a slow approach are needed. However, close in, these obstructions are marked by buoys.

Dramatically situated above the port just to the west of the entrance, as if guarding the approaches, is an unmistakable rocky headland with attractive pink and reddish buildings. In such a favoured and well-placed location, it seems certain that at some time it must have been pressed into service as a look-out post for many a romantic and profitable, if illicit, sea coming-and-going operation.

COMMENTARY
La Figueirette Miramar is an amenable little port, built in the pretty little craggy bay. For years it was a refuge for the tuna fishermen, who would stay there months at a time to repair their nets and prepare their boats while waiting for the tuna to shoal. It is still redolent of its working past, and quite lacking in the sophistication of its surroundings and the animation of the Golfe de Napoule.

It used to be a summer anchorage for leisure craft as well, but only in settled weather since winds from the south make the bay untenable. Today, entrance into Miramar is still ill advised in such conditions, although once inside there is full protection.

The harbour has no more than basic facilities with little back-up farther inland, although there is easy access to some small hotels and restaurants with good views out to sea. One small cafe sits atop a craggy pile of rocks in an idyllic position and commands a splendid view. The harbour specialises in diving, has good clean showers and toilets, and boasts one telephone. It is a quiet spot, not overcrowded and quite without pretension; altogether an intimate pleasant experience. ∎

SANTA LUCIA
43.24.70 N 06.46.90 E
Tel. 94 95 34 30
Port B1   Town B2

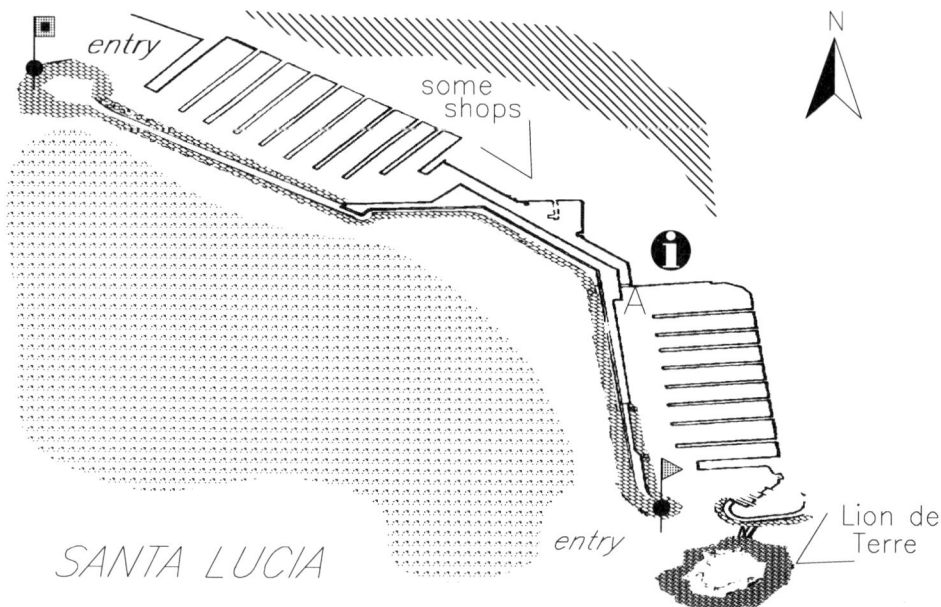

Charts	SHOM 6838, 6873 ECM 501, 502 ADM 2166				
Lights	Lion de Mer	IsoWR 4s	16m	W13M	R10M
	S Breakwater	Oc(2)WR 6s	10m	W11	R8M	R Structure
	N Breakwater	Fl G 4s	8m		9M	G Structure
	Inner Jetty	Fl R 4s				Strip light

Marks Le Lion de Mer, carrying a white structure with a red top, somewhat resembling a skeletal robot butler. At night, its light commands the whole of the bay and serves for both the old and new ports.

Reception There is no reception quay as such, though many people treat the north end of the south basin as if it is, since the Capitainerie is there.

Moorings Stern to concrete quays.

Draught	10m	**LOA**	23m
Berths	1600	**Visitors**	320

Fuel Just inside South Basin, to starboard.

Weather Teletape: 94.46.90.11, 94.46.90.50, and 93.83.31.12. Small TV in the outside entrance to the Capitainerie provides forecasts in French and English.

Boatyard Services Comprehensive.

Shops A selection in the marina, with more in St Raphael, a short walk away. Not an exciting prospect though.

APPROACH

From the east (Cap de Drammont) it can be difficult to spot the course for St Raphael, since the twin 'Lion' islands of Mer and Terre do not properly separate out until you are quite close. In addition, from time to time, there does seem to be a way in to the port, inside Le Lion de Terre, where the masts of vessels already there appear to welcome. They should be treated like the sirens that tempted Ulysses and left well alone; there is in fact a small sea wall, forming a walkway, barring the way.

If in any doubt, the cautious skipper will leave the easily spotted marker on Le Lion de Mer well to starboard until the run in is clear.

The two Lion islands, and the formation of the bay, protect the harbour areas from any big seas that might be running from the east, and that are quite hazardous even off the headland.

From the Fréjus side, the Algerian war obelisk can be difficult to pick out, standing just above the entry to the Bassin Nord for which it is a good mark. The usually obvious Lion islands do not stand out well against the headland of Cap de Drammont.

ENTRY

It is best to call the Capitainerie on VHF 9 for berthing instructions before entering. There is quite a long haul between the Bassin Nord and Bassin Sud, and choosing the wrong one in the first place could cost you the extra mile journey which means another trip out to sea.

The final entries to both basins are unencumbered, and are marked by white pillars with their respectively marked and lit tops. The Bassin Nord requires a sharp turn to starboard, leading into the area near the boatyard works to port, after which the channel weaves its way through the pontoons. The berth numbers start in the 800s and then count down. However, don't be caught out: the 900s are illogically last, near the HM and the night life.

COMMENTARY

For craft moored near the entrance, the Bassin Sud can provide a most disagreeable berth. It is extremely uncomfortable in bad weather since there is virtually no protection from swell, and even residual swell finds its way in.

The marina, a large modern operation with nearly 2000 berths, is very well run on an efficient and friendly basis. It is an extremely popular spot, partly because of this and partly due to the well-sheltered beaches at the foot of the Esterel. The idea of having a resort here is accredited to Alphonse Kerr, a pamphleteer and sometime editor of *Le Figaro*. In 1864, he wrote to a friend: 'Leave Paris, come and plant your walking stick in my garden; the next day, when you wake, you will find it has sprouted roses.' Who could resist? And, among many others, Dumas, Maupassant and Berlioz all came to stay; and Gounod composed *Romeo and Juliet* there in 1866.

It is still a fashionable host to some of Les Smart Set, but they account for no more than 10 per cent of the clientele and are not allowed to dominate the proceedings. There is a civic reception building, very modern and swish, that brings in crowds of official visitors for sumptuous buffets – usually very private, secretive, and too well guarded for gate-crashers.

Shopping in the nearby town of St Raphael is surprisingly restricted, but within the port there are laundrettes (three in fact: one run by the port, and two commercial), a small supermarket, a paper shop and a boulangerie. The port is well equipped to service and repair boats as well as provide for most needs of visiting yachtsmen. There are most maritime services and shops clustered round the berths; but there are also more yards and a chandlery in the commercial service area. There is a host of restaurants, offering perhaps the last inexpensive meals before the rash of inflation takes over to the east.

It is a pleasant walk along the beach into the town of St Raphael. One of the 'stand and stare' spots is the adventure playground where more than adventurous young people experiment on the wall of death with their skateboards.

French television and the BBC World Service are marred by poor reception; and, perhaps more importantly, the Navimet weather service on VHF 23 is also blocked by the mountains. ∎

VIEUX PORT ST RAPHAEL

(Also Port de St Aygulf)
43.25.40 N 06.45.90 E
Tel. 94 95 11 19
Port C3   Town B1

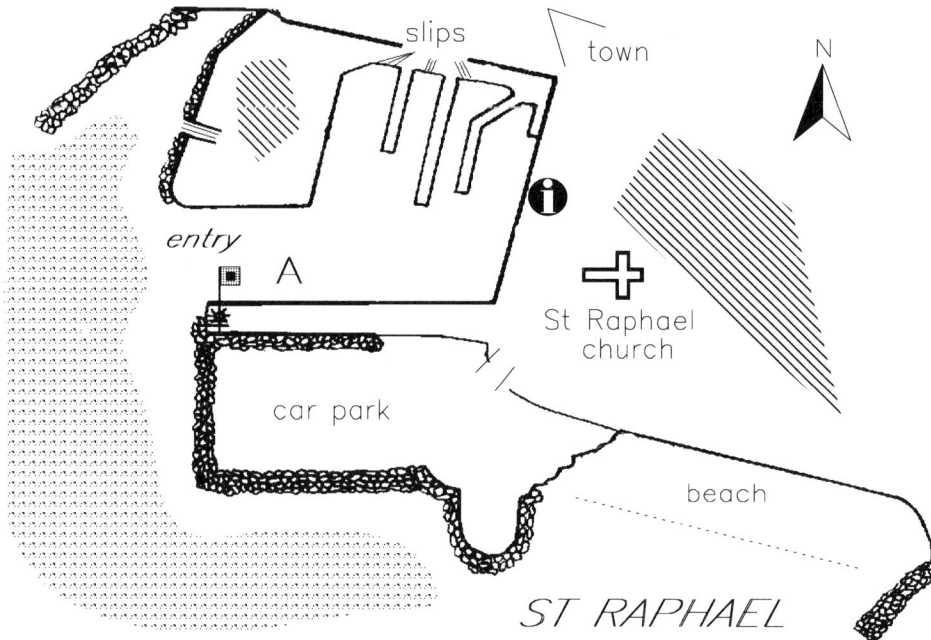

Charts	SHOM 6838, 6873 ECM 501, 502 ADM 2166
Lights	Lion de Mer Iso WR 4s 16m 13–10M W Structure
	Harbour Fl(3)G 12s 13m 14M Grey/G Top
Marks	As for Santa Lucia.
Reception	The Capitainerie is almost straight ahead. Try for a place on the Quai Kennedy (to port) or wait at the Gare Maritime (to starboard) just after the light tower. Watch out for ferries.
Moorings	Pontoons in the harbour: to laid chain; or to mooring buoys in the bay.
Draught	3m **LOA** 60m
Berths	250 **Visitors** 10
Fuel	Near the Capitainerie. It is worth noting that there is a charge of 150F for water.
Weather	Teletape: 94.46.90.11, or go to Santa Lucia.
Boatyard Services	Minimal. Go to Santa Lucia.
Shops	Shopping is not particularly rewarding: best are the Monoprix supermarket and the markets: an old one with character and a new one (open 0630) with the goods. But not far away, serving Fréjus as well, is a really excellent Casino hypermarket.

APPROACH

The dome and minarets of the tiny church can be seen rising just above the flats that otherwise mask it, and they stand immediately over the old port. An Algerian war obelisk that is difficult to isolate from its background stands to the right of St Raphael old port, and marks the Bassin Nord of Santa Lucia.

The large mooring buoys in the bay are conspicuous. There are also targets and wrecks, and naval aircraft drop various items from time to time – with and without parachutes. A proper lookout watch should be kept – for interest as well as security. On one occasion I was warned and warded off from what appeared to be experimental diving by keen naval types disguised as white Guy Couach cruising gentlemen.

ENTRY

Although the port has a large well-proportioned tower with a green top mark, it cannot be easily distinguished from its background because of the grey colour of the stone. The entry is straightforward, with the dome and a block of flats almost dead ahead.

Care is needed as the area is busy with all kinds of craft – ranging from large warships (for which the anchorage is deep enough), to ferries and fishing boats, and to tiny dinghies and windsurfing boards. Extra caution is required when rounding the knuckle of the port itself, for it is a favourite spot for local fishermen and is usually crowded with members of a not entirely co-operative local gang.

COMMENTARY

St Raphael, like its nextdoor sister Fréjus, is a daughter of Rome. In those days, just like now, it was mainly a place of leisure and a Gallo-Roman holiday resort stood on the spot presently occupied by the Casino. Terraced and decorated with mosaics, it included thermal baths and a fish reserve, for the delight of rich Romans on vacation. The villas were later plundered by the Saracens and the deserted lands were given, White Elephant like, to the Abbeys of Léran and St Victor in Marseille. In the 18th century it was inhabited by a small community of fishermen (in the present old quarters) who were so enfeebled by marsh fever that they were dubbed Pale Faces.

There was one special moment of fame and glory though. On 9 October 1799, Bonaparte landed there on his return from Egypt; and a pyramid now stands in the Avenue Commandant-Guilbaud to say so. Sadly, Napoleon returned to St Raphael in 1814, from where he set sail for Elba.

The railway station is a major one, forming the end of a link line from the Côte d'Azur to Paris, and, as the publicity people put it, the Atlantic. There is a local stopping service between this, the last stop on the coast line, and Vintimille in Italy. The journey is well worth while even if you do no more than sit and look at the scenery all the way there and back. Of equal interest is the bus journey from St Raphael to Cannes along the coast road, possessed as it is of spectacular scenery.

The harbour, which is to be found at the end of the coastal walk from Santa Lucia, is popular with the French Navy and local commercial fishing boats; but, in contrast, you are also quite likely to find a fun-fair in full swing on the quay. There is a sailing school nearby with a feverish attendance.

St Raphael, and particularly its front, is positively littered with restaurants, but a different joy is that of the Jardin Robert Marenco, where I saw a technicolour display of wallflowers and pansies at Christmas – no doubt intended to support its claim to be the very centre of the Côte d'Azur.

Port de St Aygulf
Telephone: 94 81 15 65

Just across the bay is St Aygulf, a small man made hamlet of a harbour, for small craft only, named after the Benedictine Abbot whose skull is in Grasse. Although mainly new, there are lots of old stoneworks that help to retain character. The harbour can be identified by a low white wall and large house immediately to the south. But the most outstanding landmark has to be the self-contained mini mountain in the hinterland. Snack bars and telephones abound, but other facilities are very limited; however, you can get a really edible *plat du jour* for 350F.

When there is poor weather from the east and south, cross-breaking swell on the beam makes entry to the harbour dangerous. There tends to be a sand bar just to the west of the entrance and this does nothing but worsen the situation. Under such circumstances, the water in the harbour entrance becomes a rather tricky touch-and-go 2m. ∎

FREJUS

43.25.04 N 06.45.00 E
Tel. 94 52 17 89
Port (probable) A1   Town A1

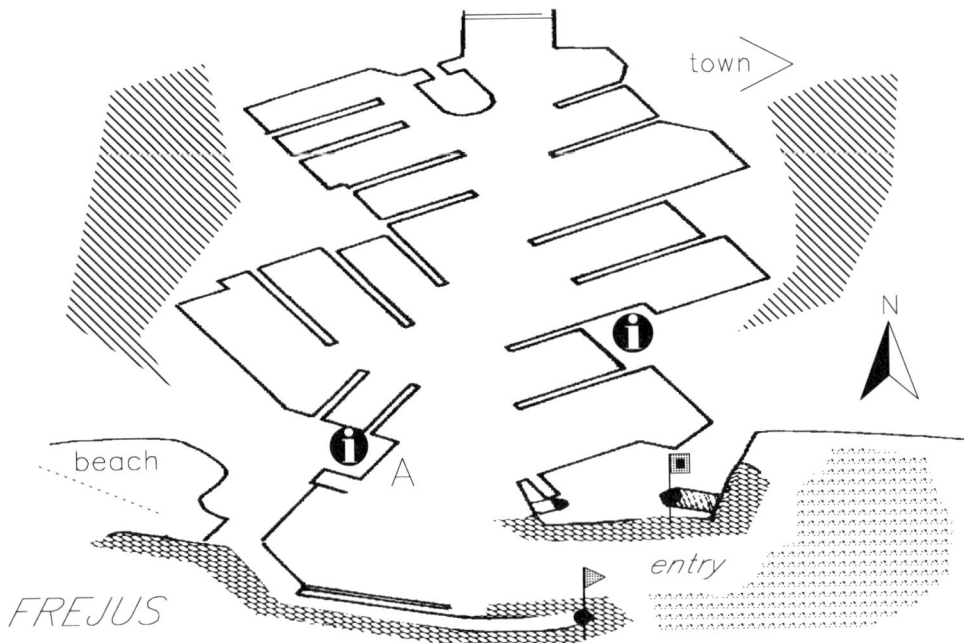

Charts	SHOM 6838, 6873 ECM 501, 502 ADM 2166				
Lights	Lion de Mer	Iso WR 4s	16m	13–10M	W	Structure
Provisional	Fréjus	Fl(4)R 15s		1.5M	W/R	Tower
		Fl G 2.5s		1M	G/W	Base

Reception	Immediately ahead to port upon entry.		
Draught	7m	**LOA**	30m
Berths	710	**Visitors**	21
Weather	Teletape: 94.46.90.11.		
Boatyard Services	To be comprehensive.		
Shopping	Excellent Casino hypermarket and boutiques nearby; a full range of shops in Fréjus; and interesting new and old markets in St Raphael.		

APPROACH

At the time of writing, the most conspicuous land-marks for the new marina village-type development are the water tower and neighbouring low works of the nearby naval airport, and the noticeably high flats to the right. In addition, set well inland, the sandstone cathedral edifice makes a good marker when approaching from Cap des Issambres.

The prohibited zone off the military airfield south of the marina is marked by four yellow buoys.

ENTRY

Wholly man made rough stone walls are marked by slender white pillars with their respective topmarks: entrance is without problem except when there is an uncommonly heavy sea in the bay from the east. Time will tell how well protected the harbour will be by a wall that at first glance does not seem high enough.

COMMENTARY

There were two Roman towns called Forum Iulii (Julius' Forum). One was in Italy, Friuli, and the other here at Fréjus. It is the oldest Roman city in Gaul, founded by Julius Caesar in 49 BC, six years after his first invasion of Britain. Augustus built up the little town into a major naval base where were built some of the ten-banked galleys that defeated Antony and Cleopatra at Actium. With some guile and foresight he left a colony of discharged but potent soldiers from his Eighth Legion (paid off with money and land) and in no time there was a population of some 40 000 souls – a figure near its present-day count.

Of that grand port, with a huge basin of 2km of quays, a major lighthouse, towers, baths, warehouses and shipyards, hardly a thing remains, for the port was long ago silted up – and then filled in by a farmer at the time of the Revolution. In its heyday there were numerous boatyards, a sports ground and a hospital – to say nothing of a fuller's earth laundry.

It seems eminently fitting therefore that 200 years on we should see Port Fréjus starting up all over again. The arena, the oldest in Gaul, is the best-known Roman ruin. It could accommodate 10 000 spectators, and now hosts summer bullfights. There are also remains of the Great Gaul's Gateway; the theatre, with its orchestra pit; the final stretch of the 25-mile long aqueduct which brought water from the Siagnole; St Antoine's Mound and Augustus' Lantern.

The area is also notable for its gnarled trees and umbrella pines. And for something quite different, just over a mile from the town centre there is the Buddhist pagoda that was built in the trees by the Vietnamese in 1919 as a memorial to all their comrades who died with the French troops in the 1914–18 war.

There is a pleasant long walk along the sea front to St Raphael and then on to Santa Lucia, with glorious sand almost all the way. Sailing and windsurfing are passionately followed in the area.

The first stage of the massive development is due for completion in six years, although the exclusive marina aspects should be fully functional by the 1992 season (but then, they were also due for 1989!). The final completion will not be achieved for at least ten years. It should not be overlooked that the main emphasis is on the housing development. ■

SAN PEIRE LES ISSAMBRES

(Also Port Ferreol and Port Tonic)

43.20.50 N 06.41.30 E

Tel. 94 81 40 29 or 94 81 40 32

Port B3   Town Ste Maxime

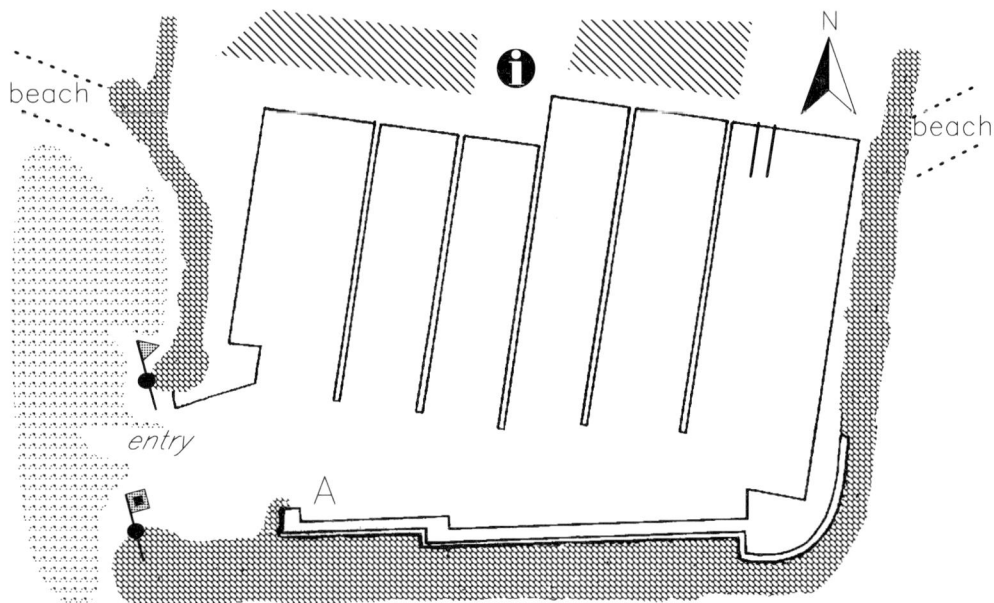

SAN PEIRE LES ISSAMBRES

Charts	SHOM 6873 ECM 502 ADM 2166
Lights	S Breakwater Oc(2)WG 6s 8m 11–8M G/W Pillar
	W Jetty Fl(2)R 6s 2M Light only
Reception	Counter jetty to port immediately inside; but also on the quay to starboard by the welcome notice and visitors' berths.
Moorings	Quay and pontoons: to laid chain.
Draught	4m **LOA** 15m
Berths	446 **Visitors** 110
Fuel	Reception quay.
Weather	Capitainerie: posted daily at 0630.
Boatyard Services	Restricted.
Shops	Locally limited, best go to Ste Maxime.

APPROACH

From the south, the rocks off the Pointe des Sardinaux are well marked by their Cardinals – of which the BYB for Les Sardinaux sits in the middle of some unpleasant hazards, rather like a spider in a web. The Pointe des Issambres is not buoyed, and its rocks reach out far enough to the east to catch out the unwary and those sailing too close.

San Peire is difficult to pick out on the busy cluttered shoreline. It lies at the junction of the lowest points of a number of the sweeping hillsides of the Massif des Maures that make for it an almost classic jigsaw backdrop. It's best to wait until the outer rocky wall and masts stand out against the dark woods.

Just next door is a shelter for small boats that should not be mistaken for the entry. An attractive but rocky bay is close by.

ENTRY

The African-style hotel, marked on the Admiralty chart, with its tall TV aerial is easy to spot. The outer sea wall is marked by a slender white tower with a green top; and the counter jetty has two miniature blockhouses, in keeping with which is the squat cube with its red light.

COMMENTARY

I have steamed past a number of times, but have still failed to identify the beacon the charts show for the Pte de la Garonne. I enquired in the office for its whereabouts and received the Gallic raised shoulder/eyebrow together with the slow extended wag of the right forefinger and the oh-so-understanding smile.

The port is wholly man made in a shallow bay, used mainly by small boats, although it does have a few medium-sized cruisers. Once inside, thanks to the miniature fortifications, you are well protected from most weathers and swells – especially from the east. A beach strip next door is, out of season, an 'island' dream; it even has its own little wooden hut with intertwined palm leaves for walls and roof. Pines abound for adequate sun protection. In season, bus transport goes from the quay to St Tropez – joining the rest of the world in mad motorised panic.

Port Ferreol
Telephone: 94 81 51 56

These tiny ports are close to San Peire. From a little way off, the entrance to Ferreol looks well-nigh impossible, nor is it indeed very wide when you actually arrive, being no more than a niche. To starboard, marking the offshore rocks, is a thin white green-topped beacon. The sea wall red mark is on a short stubby tower. A pretty little restaurant is a good landmark just to the left of the entrance.

Even once 'safely' inside there are some unmarked rocky patches to starboard. The basin is suitable only for very small boats. With no more than a slight sea from the east, it becomes a nasty spot: entry must be deemed unwise and, even inside, conditions are uncomfortable at best.

Port Ferreol is set in a pretty rocky inlet. With its cottages behind small walls, clusters of trees and bushes, and its boathouses, it is picture postcard material. Apart from the obligatory tourist watering holes, shoreside life does not exist at Ferreol or Tonic (below). There may be room for 136 boats, with a maximum LOA of 9m, but the majority of craft that use the port are no bigger than dories. There is a small slipway. It is a pleasant place to call in for a neighbourly chat in the dinghy.

Port Tonic
Telephone: 94 81 47 47

Just to the north of Ferreol is the even smaller Port Tonic; this is a man made basin in a natural inlet – just a launching pad for gadabout motorboats. Its very narrow entrance, marked by yellow buoys, is only usable in settled summer weather with a calm sea. It is unsuitable, even in an emergency, for any other craft. The tiny port is difficult to spot, huddling below the dark green treed hillside that is everywhere bespattered with the bright boxes of houses. Entry as above: from the dinghy. ∎

STE MAXIME
43.18.04 N 06.38.04 E
Tel. 94 96 74 25
Port A2   Town A2

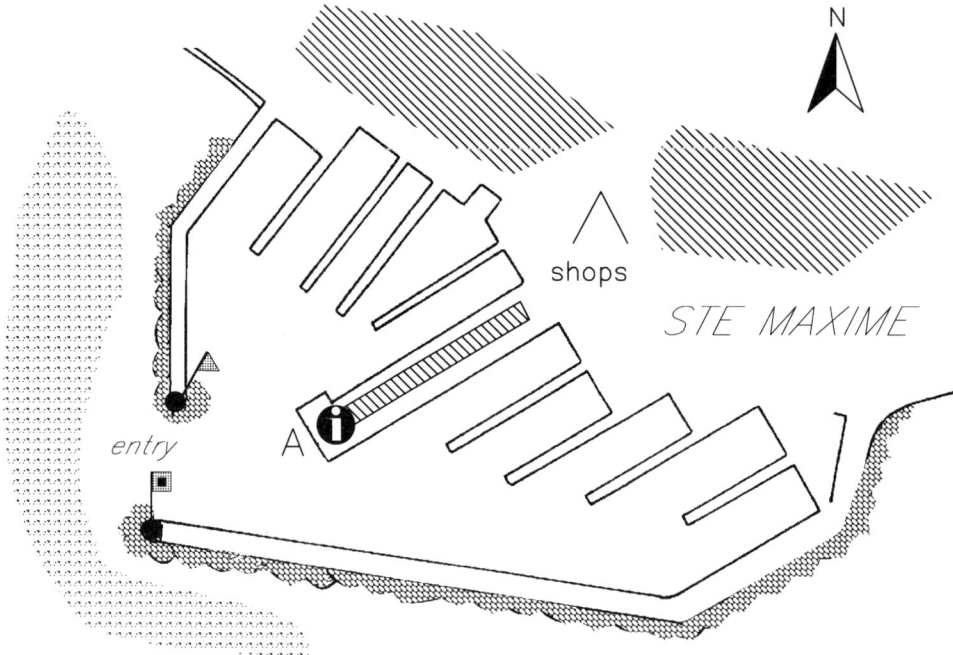

Charts	SHOM 5255, 6873 ECM 502 ADM 2166				
Lights	Sèche à l'Huile	Q 6s + LF WR	15m	9–6M	
	S Breakwater	Q(3)G 4s	8m	14M	G/W Structure
	W Breakwater	Fl R 2s	2m	2M	R Structure
	NW Quay	F W			Strip
	SE Quay	F R			Strip

Marks From the north, La Sèche à l'Huile and Les Sardinaux mark the shoals and rocks off Pointe des Sardinaux, which itself carries an old lighthouse.

From the south, you either closely cross the Golfe de St Tropez, or steam well round La Moutte which marks the shoals of the Plateau Sauvère and the rocks off the Cap de St Tropez.

Reception A spacious quay, immediately ahead upon entry.

Moorings Quay and pontoons: to laid chain. You will be given a berthing plan showing which side of the boat to take the chain.

Draught	2.5m	**LOA**	15m
Berths	764	**Visitors**	25

Fuel Reception quay.

Weather Teletape: 94.46.90.11.

Boatyard Services Reasonable.

Shops Very good selection; see following page.

APPROACH

Opinions conflict regarding the inshore passage between La Sèche à l'Huile and Les Sardinaux. While some authorities give as much as 6m on the exact north–south track, the Admiralty chart has no better than 2.6m. I found no absolutely sure and safe inshore passage to recommend either without prejudice or for all seasons. Certainly it should never be attempted except in fine settled weather.

There is also another hazard to watch out for: known as La Fourmigue, it is a rock off the coast to the east of the port. It is not marked, but is clear and plain to see, and a course half a mile off should be kept to clear it.

The major close landmark for the marina is to be seen to the north east of the entrance: a large yellow building block, solidly sombre with few windows.

ENTRY

The final entry is marked by the many horizontal window lines of the apartments to the west and the solid building to the east. But most of all perhaps, the eye is caught by the highly unusual, miniature, but nevertheless unmistakable, Brunel-type yellow bridge over the Préconcil river just behind. On close inspection, it turns out to be, disappointingly, fashioned in concrete and stucco and not the ironwork it first resembles from afar.

The Capitainerie and spacious reception quay are, for once, splendidly obvious straight ahead as you turn into the wide entrance of the port. Once inside, there is a pleasing open atmosphere and promise of well-sheltered waters – which they are, except for some swell when strong winds are in the south west.

COMMENTARY

The office of the Capitainerie lives up to the pleasant, open atmosphere in the avant port. The service is smart and the ambience friendly.

The berths within the port, especially those near the entrance, are more susceptible to swell than you would at first think. Sadly, any irritation caused by adverse conditions is exacerbated by the 'working' traffic that does not even pay lip service to the 3 knot speed limit. However, reparation comes in the form of the kindness, courtesy and friendliness of the quayside harbour staff, who try to think ahead of your needs. And full restitution is made once you have visited shoreside, when the wholly desirable aspects of the town show themselves. It must be the prime candidate for the most appealing community in the Bay of St Tropez. But for those who want to roam farther, there is a good bus service to St Tropez.

Immediately opposite the port is the church and the Carrée Tower, proud with its gleaming cannon, and now a museum of local traditions. Both are old buildings with façades of weathered stone, and both have been attractively refurbished. Facing them, the new and carefully contrived mosaic paving of the port main avenue, leading to the twin water-falling pools, provides a contrast in time and style.

In keeping with this style, the toilet and shower block, next to the Capitainerie, has been most attractively designed and appointed. Chandlery, electronics, charts and so on are to be found in the same block – together with a classy and expensive restaurant. Considering its prestigious position, and the first-rate quality of its service and facilities, the port has a high proportion of small boats.

The present-day commune of Ste Maxime grew up as a small fishing village almost as soon as it had been made safe from the corsairs by the capture of Algiers by Charles X in 1830. While it is not in any way dragging its heels, there is an atmosphere of the past that pleasantly haunts the town – in spite of the fact that it serves one of the busiest camping and general holiday areas on this stretch of the coast.

The town shops are straight across the main road from the port, situated in an attractive precinct. A choice pair are the cheese shop and the butcher: you get a varied and excellent choice in each, while both, like most of the local shop folk, go out of their way to please. Perhaps the butcher summed it up when I thanked him after a fascinating discourse on the attributes of *choucroute* – his smiling reply was 'Nous aimons les Anglais'.

Near the Lion supermarket, more of a whimper than a roar, you will find an open-air market where it seems entirely possible to unearth anything from ancient antimacassars to zany zithers. Haggling is the order of the day. ∎

PORT GRIMAUD
43.16.04 N 06.35.00 E
Tel. 94 56 29 88
Port and Town are uniquely one unit: A1

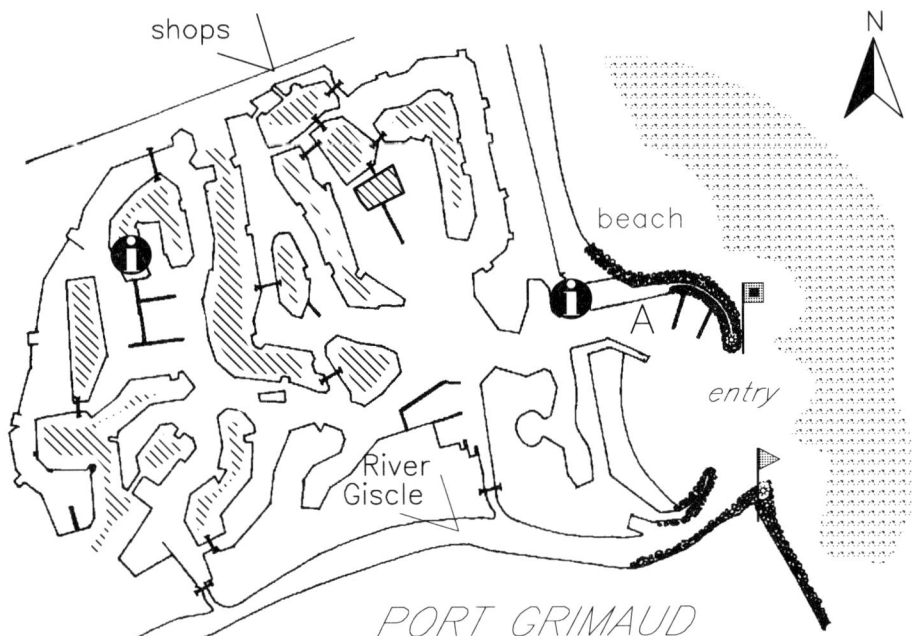

Charts	SHOM 5255, 6873	ECM 502	ADM 2166		
Lights	River Giscle	Q	6m	10M	
	Bertaud Torpedo	Iso WRG 4s		W10/G7/R7M	
	S Spur	Fl(2)R 6s	7m		W/R Tower
	N Jetty	Fl G 4s	7m	10M	G/W Base

Reception	There is a main reception quay immediately to starboard upon entry. Surprisingly run down for this extremely prestigious development, it serves all three ports.
Moorings	Various, but including quays with laid chain and pontoons with buoys.
Draught	3m **LOA** 55m
Berths	2000 **Visitors** 260
Fuel	On the quay opposite the main Capitainerie, which is itself just along the reception quay.
Weather	Teletape: 94.46.90.11. Antiope Meteo TV; also posted daily at the Capitainerie and public quay.
Boatyard Services	Comprehensive.
Shops	If not comprehensive, at least intriguing. There is a 'Giant Casino' in a vast shopping centre where you can obtain all domestics and comestibles. If you are able to take time over your shopping, however, you will be much better served in the nearby small market town of Cogolin.

APPROACH

The approach is straightforward in the Golfe de St Tropez. There are two main landmarks: the old castle in the village of Grimaud which is situated on the hills behind the marina complex, and the château to the west of the bay which is reassuringly noticeable against the attractive but busy and confused backdrop of finished and unfinished buildings.

Other than that you proceed in a mainly south-westerly direction until you reach the end of the road, where the head of the bay is formed by the vast display of the buildings of the twinned marinas of Port Grimaud and Les Marines de Cogolin. A close inspection of the chart is needed to separate the marks of one from the other; and an even closer inspection of the panorama is required to distinguish these same marks from the plethora of villas, flats, houses and general buildings behind them.

ENTRY

Once you have identified the generality of Port Grimaud in the top right hand corner as it were, the only trap to avoid is that of entering the River Giscle which is the only real separation between Grimaud and next door Cogolin. The jetties are marked and a slow approach reveals all. At the height of the summer season you just stand in line.

COMMENTARY

A trio of ports go to make up Port Grimaud, that extraordinary entirety called a marina by some but known perhaps more evocatively by others as 'Athénapolis, une cité lacustre grecque'. (No one has yet gone into print with a lack-lustre pun.) The 'lacustre' tag means a Greek city on piles or stilts. Mind you, it is not easy to see actual piles or stilts, not in the way that you can so easily in Languedoc–Roussillon, but it is clear where the idea originated. The architecture, a veritable mix, owes more to Gaudi than to Plato, for there is no sign of symmetry to be found.

None of that, however, detracts from either the achievement or the appeal, and it is possible to spend hours if not days wandering around the creation seeing something new round every corner. If you wish, you can do that by ship's tender or by making use of the taxi/tourist/sightseeing service that seems to run non stop.

Port Grimaud is sometimes referred to as a village. Never, this is a small town, with its own banks, marketplaces, *mairie* (town hall) and church; and from the tower of this last you get a brilliant view of the whole area.

The old village of Grimaud overlooks the development like a benevolent guardian. When Gibelin de Grimaldi helped William the Good drive out the Moors from the Maures, he was rewarded with a fief to which he gave his name: Grimaud. It stands on the hills behind, from where you get a good view of St Tropez Bay. There is an 11th-century Templar church and an arcaded Gothic house of the Templars in the Rue des Templiers. Here, the alleys, basalt arcades and serpentine doorways lead to the Romanesque church of St Michael. The ruins of the castle (now being restored) are most impressive and dominate what is now a nationally famous craft centre. ■

LES MARINES DE COGOLIN
43.15.09 N 06.35.03 E
Tel. 94 56 07 31
Port C2   Town B2

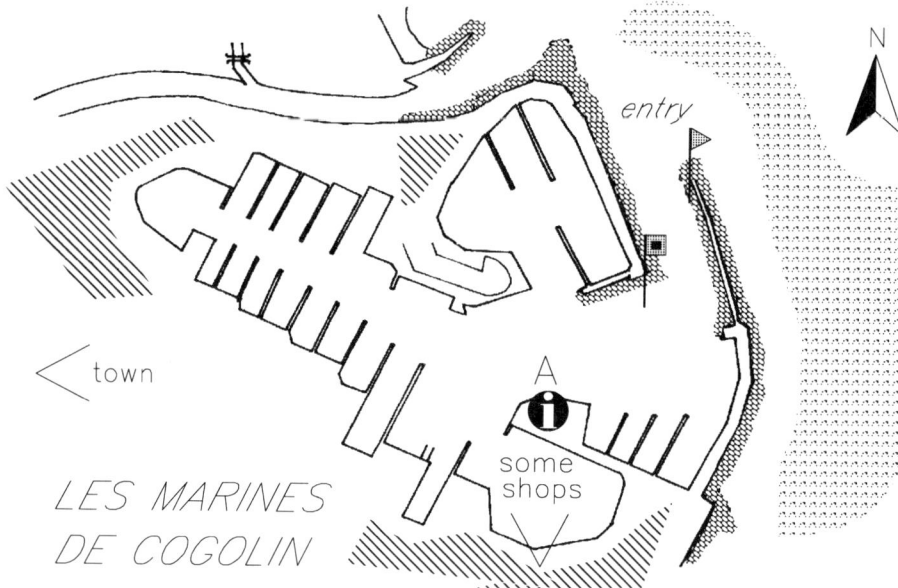

Charts	SHOM 5255, 6873 ECM 502 ADM 2166			
Lights	River Giscle	Q	6m	10M	
	Bertaud Torpedo	Iso WRG 4s		W10/G7/R7M	
	E Jetty Head	Fl(2)R 6s	8m	10M	W/R Tower
	Inner Jetty Head	Fl G 2s	2m	1M	G/W Base

Reception After the final entrance between the two walls, it is straight ahead: obvious, attractive and spacious.

Moorings Concrete quays with laid chain.

Draught 5m   **LOA** 35m

Berths 1526   **Visitors** 273

Fuel Reception quay.

Weather Teletape: 94.46.90.11. Posted at the Capitainerie in French and English, and at various other points round the marina.

Boatyard Services Comprehensive.

Shops The Casino supermarket on the main road to Ste Maxime is a first-class purveyor of all domestic needs; and there are most other general shops in its arcade.

APPROACH

The approach is straightforward in the Golfe de St Tropez. There are two main landmarks: the old castle in the village of Grimaud which is situated on the hills behind the marina complex; and the château to the west of the bay which is reassuringly noticeable against the attractive but busy and confused backdrop of finished and unfinished buildings.

Other than that, you proceed in a mainly south-westerly direction until you reach the end of the road: the vast display of buildings that form the twinned marinas of Port Grimaud and Les Marines de Cogolin. A close inspection of the chart is needed to separate the marks of one from the other; and an even closer inspection of the panorama is required to distinguish these same marks from the plethora of villas, flats, houses and general buildings behind them.

ENTRY

To port is the sinister grey aspect of the Bertaud torpedo firing range workhouse and jetty. Immediately to the left of the entrance is a detached white round tower station. The pale low hangar blocks of the large boatyard and a shocking/striking pink apartment block are good landmarks, while the entrance itself is clearly marked by a slender white pillar with red topmark. A blue and white notice, 'Marines de Cogolin', with a big arrow, hangs on the outer wall.

COMMENTARY

Les Marines de Cogolin is a vast boatpark. Holiday homes are being built and there is a move to humanise the project, but in essence a boatpark it is, and no doubt will remain. Having said that, it is a boatpark with a difference. Some of the publicity claims suggest that difference is to be found in its unique architectural style, but, apart from the occasional oddity, there is little that is even novel – nothing to compete with Grimaud next door. No, the difference is class. Finishes both inside and out are everywhere of a high order, and the staff service matches them.

It is well protected from even bad mistrals, although some of them can invade your floating privacy no matter what precautions have been taken. Swell can be a problem near the entrance.

Nearby Cogolin 'town' itself is a typical Provençal village at the bottom of foothills, picturesquely overlooked by an ancient tower and a ruined mill. For produce of a local flavour and with a touch of personal service, charismatic or otherwise, take the road to this small market town. It is best if you go by bike, so that you can keep your eyes open for all the disparate bargains that are frequently advertised on the way. Do remember that it is a working wine-growing centre, with all the talk and tasting that that inevitably means, even if you end up buying nothing at all – a most unlikely event in this eager and inexpensive domain.

Back in the town, almost every doorway opens on to some aspect of the design, manufacture, promotion and sale of carpets, pipes and bottle corks. If not, then it will open on to an activity concerned with the collecting and manipulation of reeds and canes from the local marshes. Many of them are employed in the construction of clarinets, fishing rods and furniture. Les Tapis et Tissus de Cogolin offer a tour of their workshops – workshops that are devoted to the hand weaving of furnishing fabrics and, one of their specialities, knotted, pure wool carpets.

If, after all that, your chosen special portals don't open to expose any sign of all this, then you will have selected one of the local wine caves. ∎

ST TROPEZ
43.16.04 N 06.38.04 E
Tel. 94 97 40 55
Port B1 Town B1

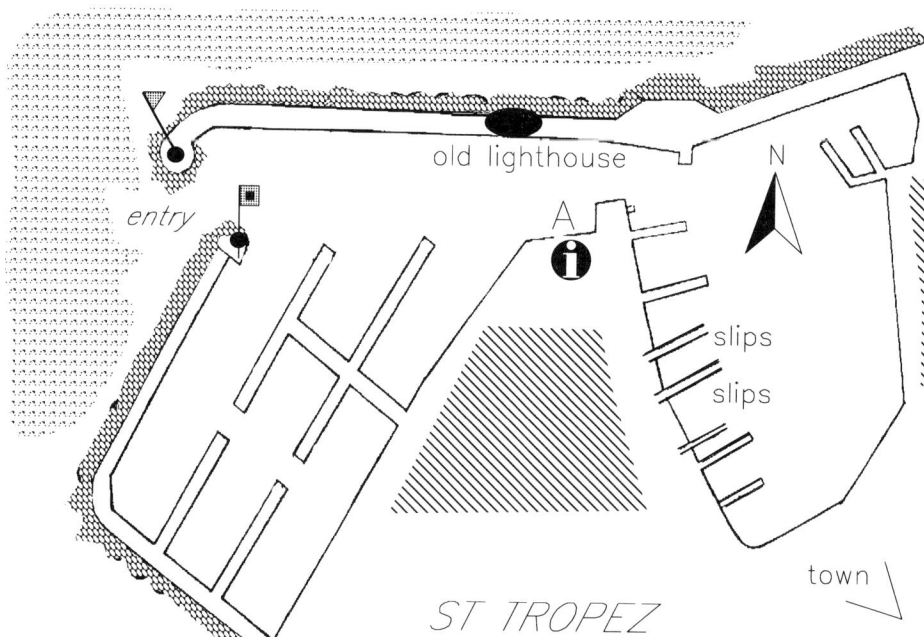

Charts	SHOM 5255, 6873/4/5 ECM 502 ADM 2166			
Lights	Bertaud Torpedo	Iso WRG 4s	W10/G7/R7M	
	N Jetty Head	Oc(2)WR 6s 8m	13—10M	Grey Tower
	S Jetty Head	Fl G 4s	7M	G/W Base

Reception   Past the first small harbour: to starboard before the entrance to the main harbour.

Moorings   Stern to quays and pontoons: to laid chain; in the old port with anchor. Out of season there are spaces alongside.

Draught	4.5m	**LOA**	15m Quai d'honneur 30m; old town quay 70m.
Berths	800	**Visitors**	150 (However, this is a quite irrelevant piece

of information at the height of the season, when you need push, pull and money just to get through the entrance.)

Fuel   Inside the starboard sea wall immediately upon entry.

Weather   Teletape: 94.46.90.11 and 94.97.23.57 for report and meteorological conditions in the Golfe. Posted twice daily by the Capitainerie.

Boatyard Services   Surprisingly, little better than modest; and, if anything, specialising in powerboats.

Shops   Very good.

APPROACH

The Golfe is entered between the Pointe des Sardines and the Cap de St Tropez. Their well-marked outlying rocks are the only natural hazards. Not at all as easy to spot are the torpedo buoys on the long central range. Great attention needs to be paid at all times, but especially at night, since many are unlit and consequently can make navigation quite problematic.

The mistral and easterlies also create difficulties here. The sea builds up very quickly, and the unpredictable swells – for it is not one entity but a conglomerate – move inexorably into the Golfe, breaking on the far shores. However, not before they have created havoc in the harbour, especially at the reception quay where they strike with unpleasant force.

ENTRY

Close to the harbour, the major landmarks are the old light and the clock tower of the church above what once were fishermen's houses in cream pink and the renowned yellow ochre. The entry poses no problem except in a bad mistral and easterly weather, with the new marina-style harbour being reached after a hairpin turn to starboard. The old port is straight ahead after the quay of the Capitainerie to starboard.

In season, it is necessary to proceed extra slowly into this foreign land, for the traffic is both heavy and busy; and, in spite of the harbour regulations, it tends also to be fast. Caution, while never the keynote of this community, must be the order of the day for any conscientious skipper. Navigating under sail is prohibited.

COMMENTARY

The Golfe de St Tropez is really worth extra special mention. It is small enough and sufficiently enclosed to be seen all round from everywhere, yet large enough (and dramatically landscaped) to be a thoroughly overwhelming experience, in particular with its own brand of miniature mountain ranges. These create a skyline that changes its aspect as you move from degree to degree. It is indeed a many faceted joy with the delights of continuing change.

When it comes to St Tropez itself, what is there left to say? So much has been written; so many have visited; and so many more have dreamed. And yet the place is fabulous; that is, a place of myth and legend – with a four-part scenario. Part one was the landfall by the dead and headless Christian centurion in AD 68; part two its dis-covery by painters in the late 1890s; part three the Bohemian development after the 1914–18 war as an international centre for the 'morally and politically unconventional', in which Colette and Cocteau played major roles; and part four, still showing non stop once a year, its growth in the 1950s into the high temple of Jet Set, Top Yacht and Haute Couture.

Some harbours in this guide have been described as 'summer port only'; St Tropez must come into the opposite category: 'summer port never'. The razzmatazz afloat, which itself is almost beyond understanding, is only marginally exceeded by that ashore. St Tropez has a population of about 6000, fewer than 250 hotel rooms, and no beach of its own; yet at high noon on Sundays, in season and in the heat, it can be hosting in excess of 50 000. Saturday morning is better, with its excellent market.

Out of season, if life doesn't actually become deadly dull, it certainly can get deathly cold. In winter, even the residents go away, for the two prevailing winds are equally unwelcome: the so-called Vent d'Italie because it brings the cold rains; and the mistral because the town, uniquely on the Côte d'Azur, faces due north.

St Tropez was, and in many ways still is, a dead end. Nobody passes through or arrives there by chance; that is just not possible. Guy de Maupassant visited the harbour in the days when it was connected with the outside world in only two primitive fashions: by an old sailing boat from St Raphael, the *Lion de Mer,* a miracle of survival; and a decrepit stagecoach that equally miraculously braved the ridges of the Maures.

There are many legends concerning the eponymous Tropez, or Torpes, the Christian centurion who was beheaded in his native Pisa at the behest of Nero. One of the most remarkable tells how his corpse, with his head beside it, was placed in an open boat together with a cock and a dog. After a nineteen-day voyage, they were miraculously landed where the town now stands. They were then afforded a decent burial by one pious lady called Celerina to whom it had all been revealed in a dream.

No one knows what happened to the cock and the dog, but it seems only fitting that Ms Bardot, who has replaced Colette as the resident femme fatale, should now have her animal protection campaign HQ here. But fashions change, and it is now typically the turn of that quirkily morose rocker Johnny Hallyday, his young but knowing wife, and his faithful Harley Davidson fans. ∎

Part Two

CAVALAIRE SUR MER TO PORT ST LOUIS DU RHONE

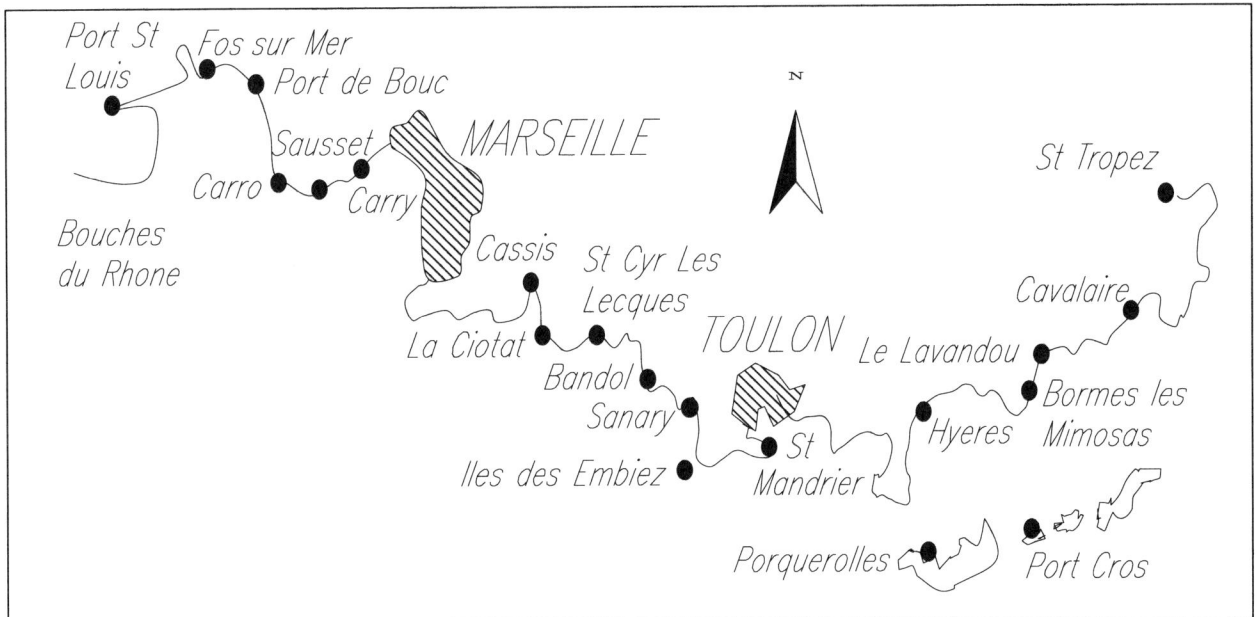

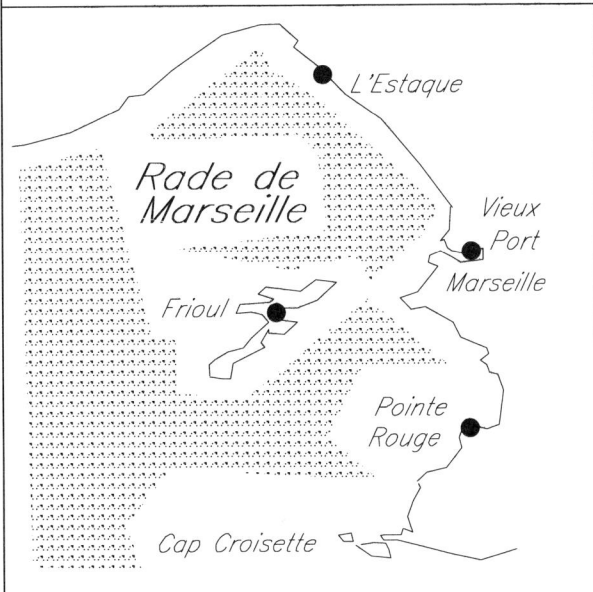

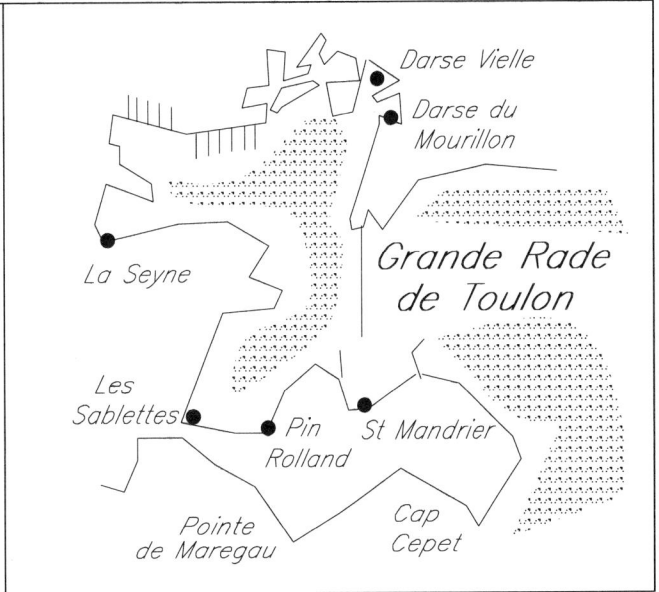

Map 1 (top):

Port St Louis · Fos sur Mer · Port de Bouc · Sausset · Carro · Carry · MARSEILLE · Cassis · St Cyr Les Lecques · La Ciotat · Bandol · Sanary · Iles des Embiez · TOULON · St Mandrier · Porquerolles · Port Cros · Hyeres · Bormes les Mimosas · Le Lavandou · Cavalaire · St Tropez · Bouches du Rhone

N

Map 2 (bottom left): Rade de Marseille

L'Estaque · Vieux Port Marseille · Frioul · Pointe Rouge · Cap Croisette

Map 3 (bottom right): Grande Rade de Toulon

Darse Vielle · Darse du Mourillon · La Seyne · Les Sablettes · Pin Rolland · St Mandrier · Pointe de Maregau · Cap Cepet

CAVALAIRE SUR MER
43.10.02 N 06.32.04 E
Tel. 94 64 12 74
Port C2   Town C2

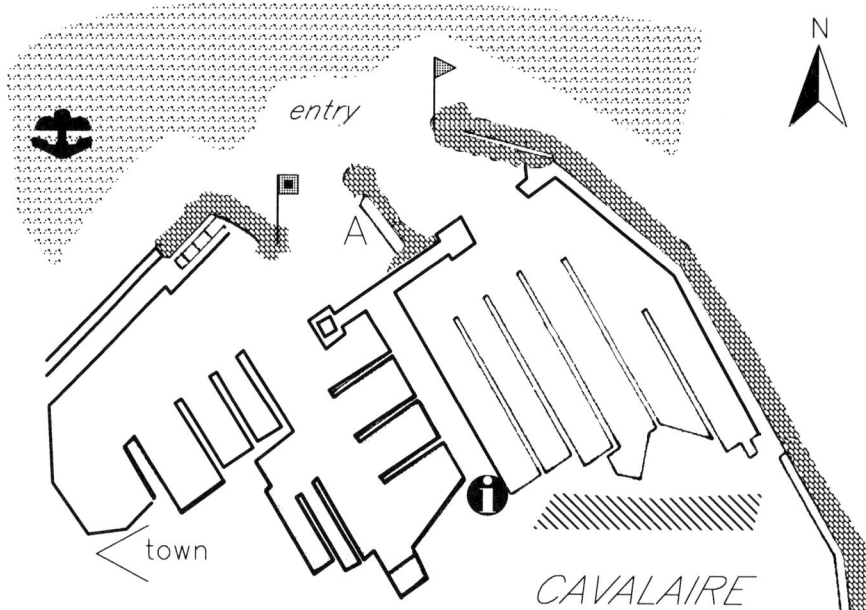

Charts	SHOM 6616, 5329 ECM 503 ADM 2165				
Lights	E Jetty Head	Fl(2)R 6s	9m	10M	W/R Tower
	Fuel Jetty	Fl R 2s	2m	2M	W/R Base
	Inner Spur	Q(3)R 6s	2m	2M	R Structure

Marks   Cap Camarrat and its square white signal station are prominent, and so are Cap Taillat and Cap Lardier. Only Camarrat is lit: Fl(4)15s 130m 26M. There is also the isolated rock of La Fourmigue, which may be safely left in any direction. It is lit: Fl(2)6s 8m 8M.

Reception   'Normally' by the fuel pontoon just to starboard, but you may have to jill around. The Capitainerie is half hidden in the depths of the marina complex. Work is still in progress, so arrangements may change.

Moorings   Concrete quays: to laid chain.

Draught 2.5m   **LOA** 15m

Berths 428   **Visitors** 60

SPECIAL NOTE: The new port is under construction: **Telephone** 94 64 16 01 **Draught** 2.5m **LOA** 15m **Berths** 579 **Visitors** 90

Fuel   Immediately to starboard on entry into the old port.

Weather   Posted three times daily by the Capitainerie; also Minitel Meteo.

Boatyard Services   Comprehensive in range and modest to fair in quality and service.

APPROACH

From the east, it is necessary to round Cap Camarrat, the major headland in the area, unmistakable with its conspicuous tower. You then follow the coast round the two smaller headlands of Taillat and Lardier, noting that the former has a close-in rock called L'Enfer. Then it is straight across the eponymous Baie de Cavalaire.

From the west, the way is clear and plain from Cap Blanc and Cap Bénat and on towards Cap Nègre, leaving to port or starboard the isolated rock of La Fourmigue. You can close the coast or make straight for Cap Cavalaire, rounding Pointe de Cavalaire and finally rounding the rocky outer sea wall of the harbour.

ENTRY

The harbour is almost completely man made and the main jetty was built out into the sea, so all that is needed is to identify its entrance tower and take the gentle turn in. Although there can be a most unpleasant swell just outside, it is not life threatening except in very bad mistrals. With the same proviso, there is also a pleasant sandy anchorage about 200m off the beach in 3–5m.

COMMENTARY

There is an agreeable stretch of beach to the west of the port and good rocky scenery to the south on the headland; this makes for enjoyable walking in either direction. This excellent beach, claimed to be one of the finest on the whole of the Mediterranean coast, situated as it is at the foot of Les Pradels mountains, is the main reason for the recent rapid growth of Cavalaire sur Mer, which was originally a fishing village and of which there is now little trace. Better than basic facilities are all available close to hand, but it cannot be said that the broadly symmetrical layout of the town, which tends to be dusty and dirty, possesses much in the way of charm or interest.

Shops are better than might be expected. The markets are not good, and certainly poor when compared with the Saturday morning operation in St Tropez. But there is a fair choice in the town shops if you hunt around.

Cavalaire sur Mer is wholly submerged in its role as a summer resort. The expanding port is similarly devoted to seasonal tourist cruising traffic. ∎

LE LAVANDOU
43.08.02 N 06.22.03 E
Tel. 94 71 08 73
Port B1   Town B2

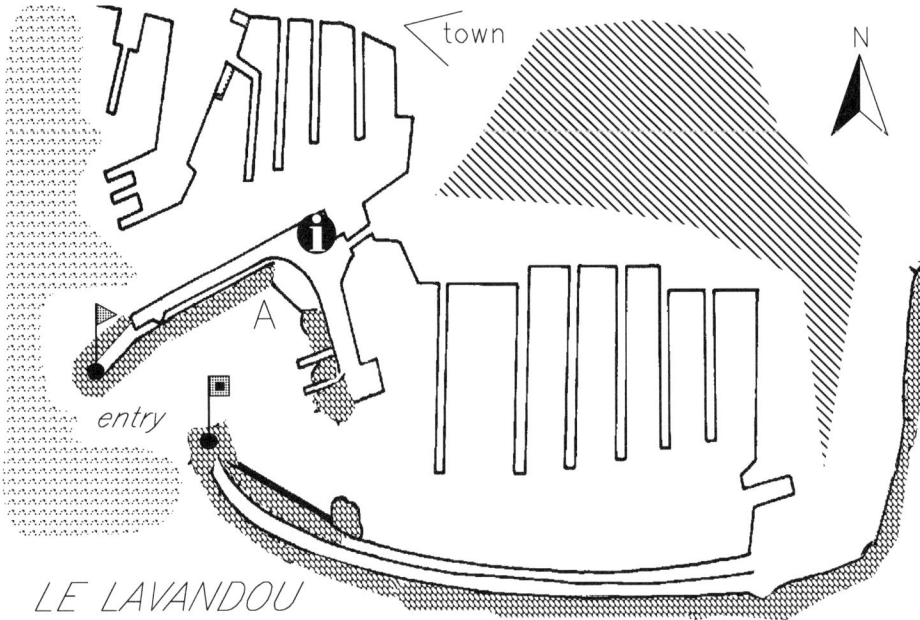

LE LAVANDOU

Charts	SHOM 6616, 5329 ECM 503 ADM 2165			
Lights	S Jetty Head	Iso WG 4s	8m	13–10M G/W Base
	Old Jetty Head	Q(9) 15s	8m	7M Y/B
	Inner Jetty Head	Fl(2) 6s		(Not visible from seaward)

Marks   Cap Blanc and Cap Bénat form the major headland from westward. It has a signal station: FlR 5s 60m 20M. Close in is the isolated hazard, îlot Christaou, marked by a beacon. There is also the isolated rock of La Fourmigue, which may be safely passed any side at 100m. It is lit: Fl(2)6s 8m 8M, and is also covered by the green section of Le Lavandou Iso WG light.

Reception   Straight ahead in the new port.

Moorings   Concrete quay: to chain in the old port; pontoons and fingers in the new port.

Draught	8m	**LOA**	23m
Berths	950	**Visitors**	100

Fuel   Immediately to port inside the old port, just after the ferry boat station.

Weather   Teletape: 94.46.90.11. And also posted daily in the Capitainerie.

Boatyard Services   Comprehensive.

Shops   Good.

APPROACH

From the east, the course is virtually due west after Cap Nègre; and from the south, virtually due north through Bormes Bay. All hazards are clear and plain to see.

ENTRY

The entry into the new harbour is unmistakable. Reception is straight ahead. Although you report initially in the new port, you are likely to be found a berth in the old harbour. There is no internal access from one to the other except for small craft that can get under the low bridge connecting the Capitainerie with the mainland.

COMMENTARY

This is a classic example of a modern marina development based on an existing small fishing port. As such, it almost rates as a case for Prince Charles, falling not into the carbuncle class but into the balloon or blister category. Although the old port is almost hemmed in by the new marina and has of necessity lost some its original character, there is little doubt that everyone seems to have gained by the completion of the project. It is a good example of how modern facilities and efficient service can still be crowned with classic Provençal style and personality.

Sheltered by the wooded slopes of neighbouring Cap Bénat, its very name recalls the lavender fields on the banks of the Batailler. While many fishermen still work out of the port, it is neither their diesel fumes nor the (in)delicate bouquet of (cooked or raw) fish that is flavour of the month. As the name suggests, there is lavender in the air; and there are working fields and scent factories nearby.

But the town's main revenue comes from the tourist industry not only ashore but also afloat; Le Lavandou is not merely a sunbathing seaside resort to rival those of the Golfe de St Tropez, it is a thriving base for the popular ferries that trip regularly to the Îles d'Hyères. The pleasing promenade, named after General de Lattre de Tassigny, evoking memories of the Allied landings in the Second World War, affords an excellent evening stroll. And for daytime exercise, there is the splendid sandy beach that sweeps round the bay almost to Bormes les Mimosas.

The town has a most attractive square, the Place Ernest-Reyer, that has been laid out as a garden. From it, there are excellent panoramas of Île du Levant and Île de Port Cros.

One shop stands out for quality and service, a delicatessen run by Jean-Marie and Nicole Pequidt at 1 Rue de la Girelle. Their gourmet products are not inexpensive, but every day there are special dishes that are guaranteed to delight. ∎

BORMES LES MIMOSAS (LA FAVIERE)
43.07.04 N 06.21.09 E
VHF 16, 9
Tel. 94 71 04 28
Port B2   Town B3

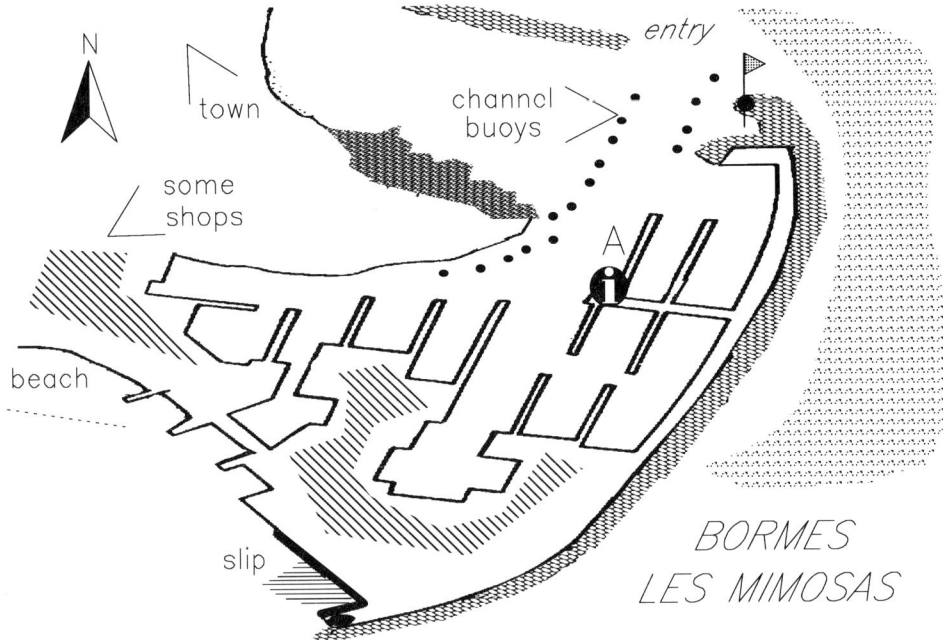

Charts	SHOM 6616, 5329 ECM 503 ADM 2165
Lights	Sea Wall Fl(2)R 6s 10m 10M W/R Tower
	South Head F V 9m 1M Tower
	Reception Fl(2)R (obscured to seaward)
	Channel Buoys No 1: Fl G 2s, No 3: Fl G(2)
Marks	Cap Blanc and Cap Bénat form the major headland from westward. It has a signal station: FlR 5s 60m 20M. Close in is the isolated hazard, îlot Christaou, marked by a beacon. There is also the isolated rock of La Fourmigue, which may be safely passed any side at 100m. It is lit: Fl(2)6s 8m 8M, and is also covered by the green section of Le Lavandou Iso WG light.
Reception	There is a spacious quay on the port hand towards the end of the buoyed channel.
Moorings	Quay: to laid chain taken to starboard.
Draught	3m **LOA** 20m
Berths	950 **Visitors** 323
Fuel	At the end of the reception quay.

Weather	Teletape: 94.46.90.11. Posted daily at 0800 at the Capitainerie; also, Meteo Minitel. A white flashing light on the roof of the Capitainerie indicates a wind of Force 6 + .
Boatyard Services	Comprehensive.
Shops	Fair to moderate in the nearby village, but chandlery is very good in the new leisure complex on site.

APPROACH

The main approaches are as for Le Lavandou. The close approach from Le Lavandou tracks you straight in. The close inshore run from Cap Bénat and the south is an unencumbered and very pretty course. The sea wall of the marina must be rounded at the north end.

ENTRY

Unusually, there is a buoyed channel. This is necessary to guide you through an entrance channel that has to be kept usable by dredging, for the whole stretch from Le Lavandou is prone to sanding and silting. This occurs severely off the starboard headland of the Pointe de Gouron. The dredging that has to take place from time to time may require access to be restricted or denied. The buoy marking is standard conical green and cylindrical red buoys, and when the channel is fully open it is wide and problem free. There is also an inner basin with access under a small low bridge.

Conditions for entry can be very bad in strong easterlies. The Capitainerie officially advises that this means Force 7 + . My own experience was that 5 + is quite enough.

COMMENTARY

The marina is a good example of reclamation and modern leisure building. Its formidable sea walls stand bravely out to sea while the sophistication of its summer accommodation contrasts with the natural surroundings ashore. Many of the marina berths are to be found in the heart of this village quarter, which in many ways is a Languedoc–Roussillon-style development in miniature.

An example of the proximity of nature to this entirely man made reclaimed facility can be seen opposite the reception quay, where the rocky headland of the old Pointe de Gouron stands out like a sentinel. It makes an agreeable change to be able to relax at your civilised berth, plugged in to all the mains, but to be able to gaze on a view that is almost as nature intended it centuries ago, owing, in fact, hardly anything to man's intervention. With its very airy and spacious, almost bracing, ambience, Bormes Favière comes as a surprising but most welcome change from most built-up marinas. Most of all, it has the air of a strikingly happy place.

The old village of Bormes is not far away on the slopes overlooking the sea. It likes to keep abreast of the times and up with the fashion, so in keeping with Juan les Pins and Hyères les Palmiers, it now designates itself Bormes les Mimosas. The recently completed marina known as Bormes Favière continues the upwardly mobile tendency.

For those interested in the history of Bormes, there is a museum at 65 Rue Carnot, which also features Brégançon Fort and La Verne Charterhouse, founded in 1170 by a spring in the Maures forest. Paintings are also on view: regional canvases from the past century; and the works of Jean-Charles Cazin, 1841–1901, who was very fond of the place. He is somewhat cavalierly described as a painter and decorator.

In the Place St François there is a statue, sombrely surrounded by dark cypress trees, to Francesca di Paola, who, according to a much believed local legend, is supposed to have saved the township from a plague in 1481. The interior of the church of St Trophyme and the flower-bedecked exterior of the castle both make enjoyable visits. What are known as the Old Streets are typically Provençal; one of them is so steep and slippery that it is known as The Neck Breaker (*rompi-cuou*).

It doesn't take long to get into open country where you will find on the steeply sloped foothills of the Dom forest that you are surrounded by lush vegetation; not only the obligatory fragrant mimosa, but also oleanders, camomile and eucalyptus. There are also three good beaches. ∎

HYERES

43.05.00 N 06.10.00 E
Tel. 94 57 58 22
Port A1   Town C3

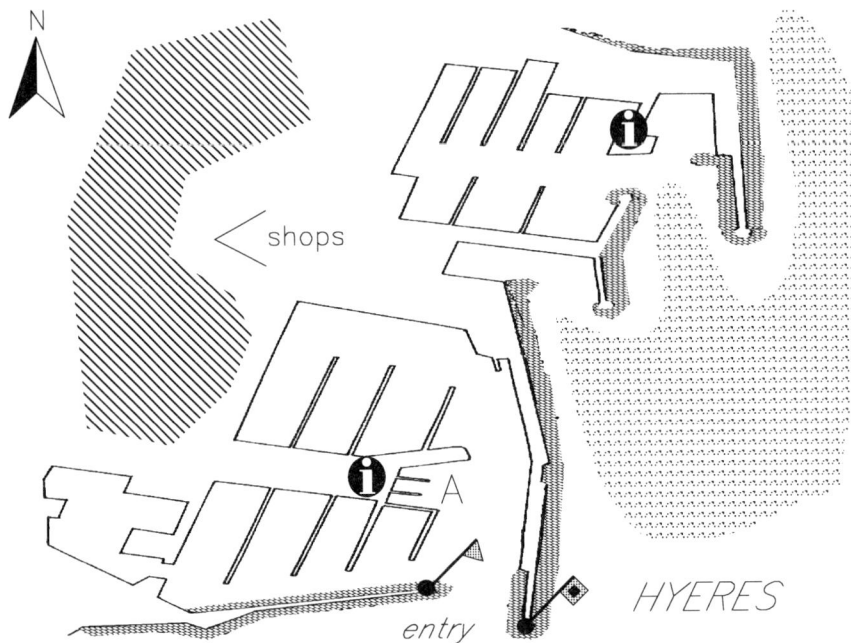

Charts	SHOM 5151, 5329, 6951 ECM 503 ADM 2165				
Lights	Cap Bénat	Fl R 5s	60m	20m	
	West Jetty	Oc R 4s	9m	8M	Metal structure with R
	NE Jetty	Fl G 4s	9m	10M	G Metal structure
	S Inner Jetty	Q(6) + LFl 15s	8m	10M	B/Y Structure
	N Inner Jetty	Fl R 5s	2m	4M	Metal structure with R
	East Jetty	Iso G 4s	8m	10M	Structure with G Top

Marks   Cap Bénat and Cap de l'Esterel are the main landmarks with flatness in between. Planes in and out of Hyères airport give some indication of the proximity.

Reception   In the south basin, it is tucked into a small bay just under halfway in on the port hand. There is very little space. Theoretically, this situation is soon to be improved. In the north basin, it is in front of the Capitainerie, which will be seen immediately ahead upon entry.

Moorings   Quay and concrete fingers, with some forty catways: to laid chain; some stern to, with bows to an easy-to-retrieve buoy.

Draught	3m	**LOA**	16m
Berths	1350	**Visitors**	120

Fuel   Next to the reception quay.

Weather	Teletape: 94.46.90.11. Daily at the Capitainerie. Also flashing white light for strong winds warning: Fl(8) 4s for Force 6–7 and Q.Fl for Force 7 + .
Boatyard Services	Comprehensive.
Shops	Domestics and provisions are not really up to standard in the shops in the immediate vicinity, but there is a handy post office in the Capitainerie. Victualling can be done with interest in the nearby town.

APPROACH

To the south are the Îles d'Hyères. Cap Blanc and Cap Bénat form the major headland from westward, while from the east the Petite Passe is negotiated and Cap de l'Esterel rounded. After that, it is a case of all eyes to the coast, for Hyères port, vast as it is, is not easy to spot from seaward. As is the case with marshes and salt pans, the coastal strip is low lying. In addition, the development of corresponding ribbons of holiday accommodation provides nothing in the way of unique or even eye-catching marks.

However, the approach is a gentle slope and without hazard. It is possible that quite a few yachts may be at anchor just to the south of the entrance and this helps identification.

ENTRY

The entry is problem free: straightforward and obvious.

COMMENTARY

Somewhat surprisingly, the ports of St Pierre de Hyères are restricted to a maximum draught of 4m. It is not unusual to find large yachts anchored to the south of the entrance. Anchoring to the north is prohibited due to the airport flight path.

Hyères, the largest, most important and prestigious leisure complex and port de plaisance in the whole area, is a modern, sophisticated and expensive experience. It is the most southerly and the oldest of the classic Riviera resorts, and, due to its climatically blessed position and the nearby airport, it is favoured by the 'nouveau riche' and 'rapide riche' alike. You will get your money's worth on the yachting and cruising fronts, but, by and large, shops, bistros, boutiques and restaurants offer only modest returns for their prices. There is plenty of scope for window shopping, especially for marine goods, and both the old and new towns are worth visiting – either for shops, gardens and history, or just gazing at the renowned palm trees that line the wide streets.

Old Hyères is now well removed from the sea, being 3 miles distant, but in the Middle Ages it was a pilgrim point of departure for the Holy Land. In 1254 St Louis landed here after the Seventh Crusade. In the 18th century it was already more than fashionable when les Anglais were discovering Nice, but lost its esteem once the heady days of Queen Victoria were over. It was much appreciated by Robert Louis Stevenson, who had been 'banished' by his doctors to the south of France and hated it. He once wrote, 'I was only happy once; that was at Hyères.'

New Hyères and its ancillaries have spread east right across the alluvial plain that borders the roadstead that bears its name.

Water sport centres have sprung up all round:

Port de Miramar la Londe:
43.07.00 N 06.14.08 E
Berths 500   LOA 9m   Draught 1.5m

Port du Ceinturon (L'Ayguade):
43.06.04 N 06.10.28 E
Berths 500   LOA 12m   Draught 1m

Port du Berriau Plage:
43.06.60 N 06.11.50 E
Berths 500   LOA 10m   Draught 1.2m

Port Pothau (Les Salines d'Hyères):
43.06.80 N 06.12.80.E
Berths 500   LOA 12m   Draught 2m

La Capte:
43.04.00 N 06.09.00 E
Berths 125   LOA 6.5m   Draught 1m

Le Niel:
43.02.02 N 06.07.07 E
Berths 127   LOA 8m   Draught 2m

Carqueiranne:
43.05.00 N 06.04.07 E
Berths 360   LOA 9m   Draught 1.2m

Les Iles D'Hyères

PORT DE PORQUEROLLES
43.00.00 N 06.12.00 E
Tel. 94 58 30 72
Port B3   Island A3

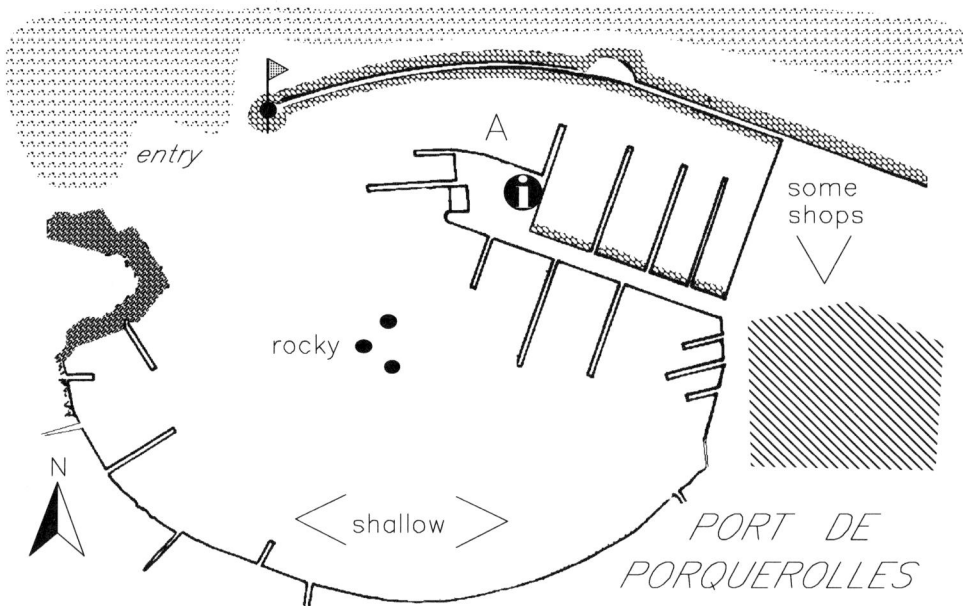

Charts	SHOM 5151, 5329, 5447, 6615 ECM 503 ADM 2165
Lights	La Jaune Garde Q WR 15m 6/3M
	Jetty Head Oc(2)WR 6s 8m 13/10M W Column
Marks	La Jaune Garde is an unmistakable large stone pillar, and the island of Grand Ribaud is opposite.
Reception	After rounding the head of the north jetty, the reception quay and Capitainerie appear to starboard.
Moorings	Quay: to laid chain.
Draught	3m **LOA** 20m
Berths	500 **Visitors** 200
Fuel	Reception quay.
Weather	Teletape: 94.46.90.11. Daily at the Capitainerie.
Boatyard Services	Modest.
Shops	Very modest.

APPROACH

From the west you use the Petite Passe, leaving the island of Grand Ribaud to port and the huge stone beacon of La Jaune Garde to starboard. Approaching from the west, by the Presqu'île de Giens, neither will separate out much from their backgrounds until you are fairly close.

After La Jaune Garde, there is no hazard within 200m of the coastline and you can follow it round until the bay opens up. Then the marks on the island will be clear to see. From the east and the north, there is no encumbrance to a straight run.

ENTRY

High above the bay to the east of the port entrance is the old fort of Ste Agathe. Halfway between the fort and the entrance to the port is the clock tower. The only complication is that of traffic – commercial, pleasure and leisure. There is only modest room to manoeuvre between the north jetty and the main quay, and the scale of operations in season is large.

COMMENTARY

Both Porquerolles and Port Cros are private property and visitors are asked to respect the no smoking and other regulations that have been practised for over sixty years to help care especially for the subtropical vegetation and protect the wildlife. Perhaps the best way to see all the islands is by dinghy, and on foot from one of the many quiet anchorages.

Porquerolles has a small reception quay and will afford you an equally small chance of obtaining a berth in the season; it is possible to anchor in the bay, although this is frequently just as busy. It is vital to keep out of the tracks of the fast ferries that seem to ply non stop.

The island consists primarily of a gorgeous nature preserve with one small village at the head of the tiny roadstead. There are very few inhabitants inland, and the island is left to the mercy of the tended vines, pines, heather, eucalyptus, arbutus and scented myrtle – a splendid *mise en scène* for *The Tempest* à Antonin Artaud.

Porquerolles village was built by the army in the 19th century and has a few cottages, a main square and a tiny church with the Stations of the Cross carved with a penknife by a soldier. The guides suggest that it looks more like a North African colonial settlement than a Provençal village. The village, consumed as it is with the sale of cheap gifts and souvenirs, is not the island's crowning feature; and such a description tends to do it more than justice. ∎

Port Cros

43.00.00 N 06.23.00 E   Tel. 94 05 90 17

Marks   Cap Bénat to the north on the mainland, Cap des Mèdes to the west on Porquerolles, and the Île du Levant to the east make for locations that should not be missed. There are two old forts high above the bay and a small haven. L'Estissac is the fort that commands the bay, L'Éminence is the other.

Approach   From the open sea there is no impediment, and from Porquerolles it is virtually easterly to the Pointe du Beau on the Île de Bagaud.

Commentary   There are small pontoons capable of taking craft not exceeding 2m draught, but most people visit the island for the scenery and an open air break and therefore tend to use the anchor – either here or in the pleasant anchorage in the bay of Port Man. This is a summer port of call and one of the most beautiful on the coast. Known as Mesé, Middle, to the Greeks, it gets its present name from the hollowed out (creux) shape of its harbour.

The Îles d'Hyères are also called the Îles d'Or, because of the yellowish rock that was at one time taken for gold ore, as in the Vallon de la Fausse Monnaie. But real are its height, its hills, its craggy rocks and its lush vegetation – entitling it to its description as the Med's Garden of Eden. Or, if you prefer to ponder on the Pointe de la Pomme d'Or, then the Garden of the Hesperides.

Île du Levant

The tiny 'port' of L'Ayguade is no more than a single landing place – the only one on the island. When the monks exclusively occupied the Levants, this island was their garden and granary. Now it is of interest, if not indeed notoriety, because it is exclusively occupied by the French Navy – except for the nudists on the west end of the island, where they have squatters' rights in the village of Heliopolis. Occasional access is permitted to the pontoon; the island is an idyllic spot for walkers. ∎

Ports in the Rade de Toulon: Darse Vieille – Port Pin Rolland – St Mandrier

(See plan on page 61)

■■■

DARSE VIEILLE: YACHT PORT DE TOULON
43.07.00 N 05.55.08 E
Tel. 94 42 27 65
Port B1   Town B1

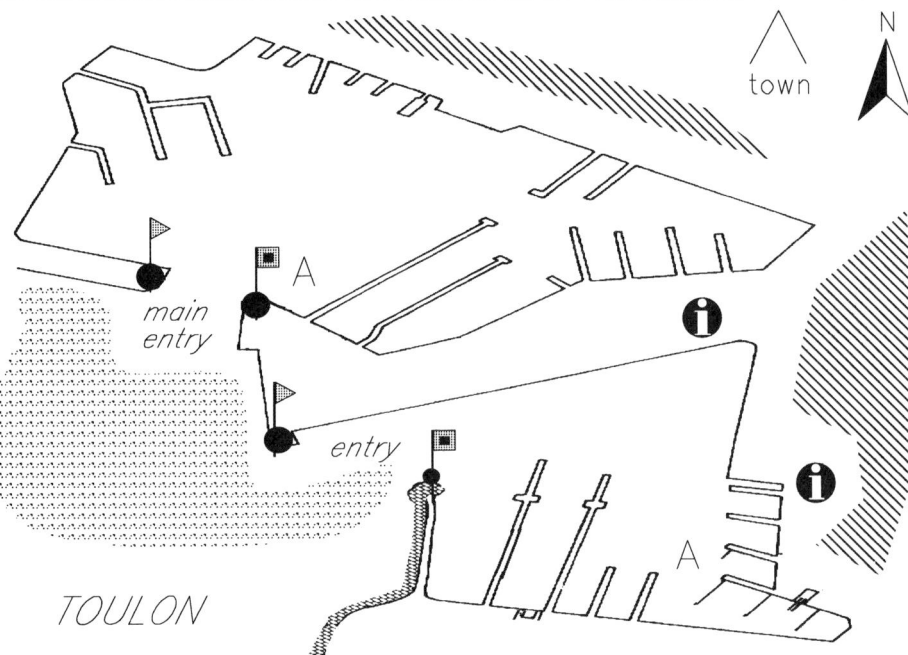

Charts	SHOM 5175, 5477, 7093 ECM 503, 504 ADM 2165, 149

Lights *Please note only those of major use to visiting yachts are included. The list is not comprehensive. Refer to ADM Chart 149.*

For the Grande Passe:

Mandrier Jetty	Fl(2)R 10s	17m	10M	W/R Tower	
La Vieille Pointe	Q R	11m	7M	W/R Tower	
Grand Jetty	Q G	13m	11M	W	Tower

To the Petite Rade:

'Gate' Buoys	Fl(2)R 6s			R	Buoy
	Fl G 4s			G	Buoy
Passe de Pipady	Iso RG 4s	21m	10M		
Banc de l'Ane	VQ(9) 10s	3m		YBY	Cardinal

Into the Darse Vieille:

Mourillon	Iso G 4s	17m	7M
Fournelle Quay	Oc(2)R 6s	7m	6M
Darse Vieille	Q R		
	Q G		

Marks Inside, from the Grande Passe, the light towers on the Grande Jetée, and the breakwater warships and light towers in the Baie de St Mandrier are unmistakable.

Reception Quay du Petit Rang, immediately to starboard after turning to starboard at the first jetty.

Moorings Quay: to laid chain.

Draught 4m **LOA** 60m

Berths 1300 **Visitors** Variable: dependent upon size of craft and proposed length of stay.

Fuel By Reception on the quai du Petit Rang.

Weather Teletape: 94.46.90.11 (coastal); 94.46.90.50 (open sea); also posted daily at the Capitainerie.

Boatyard Services Comprehensive.

Shops Comprehensive.

APPROACH

From seaward, the westward approach is from Cap Sicié and the eye catching rocks, Les Deux Frères. Then by the Presqu'île de St Mandrier, passing the miniature harbour of St Elme les Sablettes (limiting draught little more than a metre) until you round Cap Cépet. After this, it is prudent to stand well out as there are inshore hazards. For those who wish to be cautious, the track is round the red can buoy (FlR2 5s).

From the east, it is a straight run from the Petite Passe to the yellow buoy (Fl(3)Y 12s) at the entrance to the Grande Rade.

ENTRY

The major port of Toulon is protected by the vast works of the Grande Jetée. The main doorway is through the Grande Passe just to the north of Mandrier. There is another door to the north, known as the Passe de Pipady. I saw small boats using this northerly way in, but I felt it did not look the kind of healthy area I wanted to pass through; and, having approached it now a number of times from both sides, I use the longer route round the Grande Jetée.

Once through, the Baie de Lazaret (and Les Sablettes and Pin Rolland) is to the south, and the Petite Rade ahead to the north with the Baie de la Seyne in the top left hand corner to the west. As is to be expected for an area so well used by so many vessels (leisure, pleasure, commerce and combat), it is well marked and equally well patrolled by the authorities.

COMMENTARY

There are lots of berthing choices for visitors, but the one that must be the favourite is the Yacht Port de Toulon in the Darse Vieille. There is nowhere in the port where you can get away totally from the noise. It is also a major military and commercial base, and its Yacht Port suffers perhaps more than some. However, it is extremely well placed for the city, and its own facilities are not entirely second rate. Next door there is also the Darse Nord du Mourillon.

Shoresides, there are all the facilities that you expect of a major city. In the shopping arcades to the north of the Quai Stalingrad, there are delights to gladden the hearts of food devotees. Chinese Meal Makers are ethnic experts and not to be confused with the run of the soya sauce/pepper mill take-away merchants. Their wares are an array of colourful delicacies, the like of which I have not encountered anywhere else in Europe.

In a more modest manner, perhaps the best cheese shop on the Mediterranean coast is to be found behind the quiet and almost secluded front of a shop that might be devoted to almost any old boring business. Toulon is worth a few days' stay if only to be able to sample these simple pleasures. I was so tempted that, after advice, I made a selection that completely filled *Valcon*'s 3 star freezer. True, frozen isn't fresh, but little was lost and nothing was wasted.

And to while away the time between meals, there is ample on the historical front: from the

Roman passion for Toulon purple; to the obscure junior captain Bonaparte's famous legend, 'battery of fearless men', his conquest of Little Gibraltar, and his immediate elevation to Brigadier General; and the efforts of General de Lattre de Tassigny.

It is not all gorgeous heroic stuff. Louis XIV converted Toulon into the great arsenal and naval base, and it was not long after that that it achieved fame as the Devil's Island of its day. Criminals, vagabonds, Turkish prisoners and Negro vassals were forcibly sea-changed into galley slaves who lived, ate and slept chained by wrist to an oar and by ankle to the gangway. Amazingly, some men volunteered for these situations, and were rewarded by the right to wear moustaches.

Travellers used to visit the port to come sightseeing, '... to gaze at the galley slaves and visit them in their galleys. There one sees all the misery, filth, dirt, stench and diseases of humanity.' Unfortunately, not quite so amazing. ∎

PORT PIN ROLLAND
43.04.80 N 05.53.70 E
Tel. 94 94 33 00/94 94 61 24
Port C1   Town C3

Charts	ADM 149		
Lights	Buoys	Fl G2. 5s	G Buoy
		Fl(4)R 15s	R Buoy
	Le Manteau	Dir Oc(4)WRG 12s 3m 8M	
	(Jetty by the unnavigable Chenal des Sablettes)		
	Les Sablettes Q	3m 8M	
Marks	The channel is buoyed.		
Moorings	Pontoons.		
Draught	3m **LOA** 13m **Berths** 300		

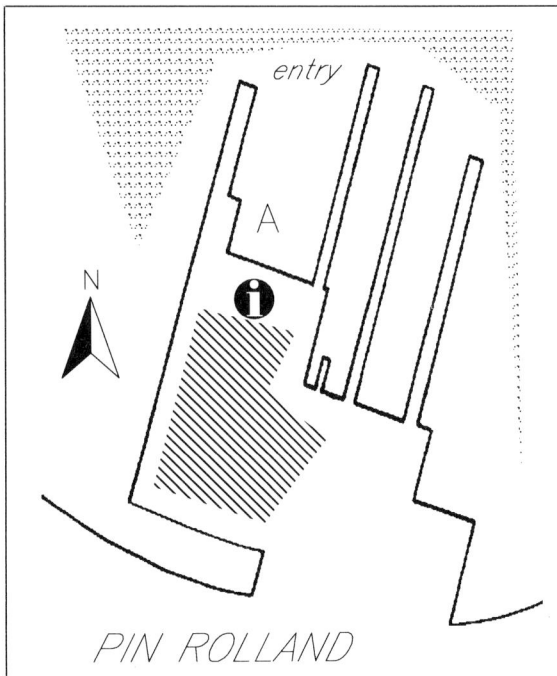

PIN ROLLAND

COMMENTARY
The buoyage marks the mussel beds and is to be strictly observed. This is not a salubrious neighbourhood by any means, but there is one of the best boatyards for leisure craft along the coast; that must perhaps be the only reason for visiting. ∎

ST MANDRIER

43.05.00 N 05.56.05 E

Tel. 94 63 97 39

Port C2   Town C2

Charts	ADM 149
Lights	Military Jetty Fl(2)G 6s 4m 5M
	Mandrier Fl G 4s 9m 5M
Marks	The outer marks and lights are described above. Mandrier has a breakwater that must be unique: it is formed by three naval warships and is situated to the north east of the entrance.
Moorings	Floating pontoons and quay: to laid chain.

Draught	2.5m	**LOA**	13m
Berths	600	**Visitors**	20

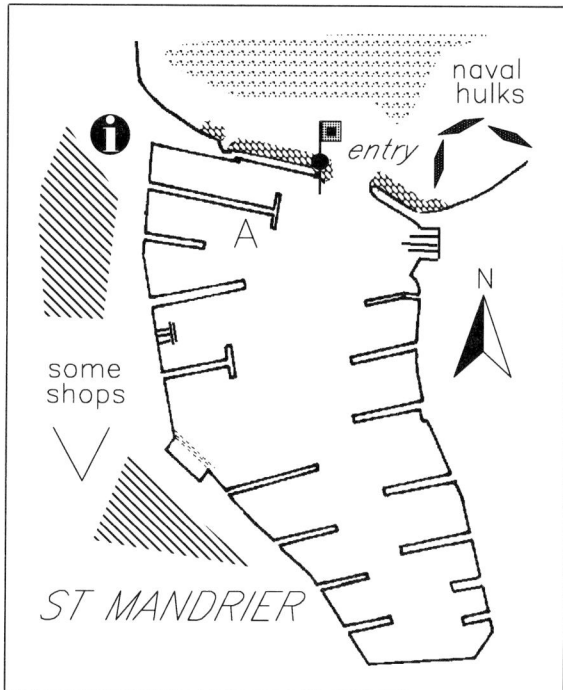

ST MANDRIER

COMMENTARY

There is little here for visitors, except as a haven if caught out on passage, as it lies midway between Porquerolles and Les Embiez. But, of all the outer ports in Toulon Roadstead, this has the greatest architectural charm and the best social and domestic facilities. It is also the one most organised to welcome visiting yachtsmen. There is a reception pontoon immediately to starboard upon entry. Pontoon Q, immediately to port upon entry, is reserved for professional yachtsmen – whatever sins are covered by that turn of phrase – and is not to be used by visitors. ∎

ST PIERRE LES EMBIEZ (ILES DES EMBIEZ)
43.04.80 N 05.47.00 E
Tel. 94 34 07 51
Port A2   Town A2

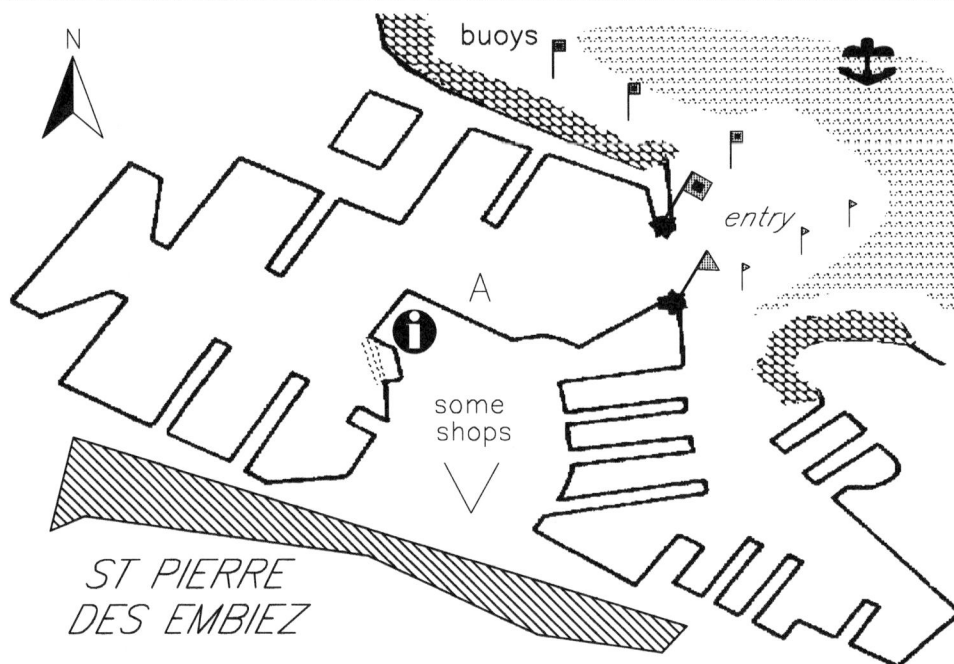

Charts	SHOM 5325, 6610 ECM 504 ADM 2164, 2165			
Lights	Cap Sicié	Fl(2) 6s	48m	9M
	Grand Rouveau	Oc(2) 6s	45m	15M
	Tour Fondue	Fl(4)WR 15s	8m	6M
	Embiez Cargo Mole	Iso R 4s		
	Port des Jeunes	Iso W 4s		
	N Jetty	Fl G 4s	4m	5M
	White Hut Leading	Oc WRG 4s		9–7M

Marks   The unmistakable Cap Sicié to the east and the two major island markers, Sèches des Magnons and La Casserlane. From the north there is a beacon off the Pointe de la Cride, and from the west you make straight for La Casserlane.

However, from all directions, the islands themselves are the main marks; and they provide the major hazards, which most people manage to avoid, as well as the traps of the apparently safe inshore passages through the rocks. Some are known as being dangerous, while some are called safe in calm weather. Visitors should take the long road round and explore the rocky minor channels in a dinghy.

Reception   Immediately ahead upon entry: obvious, well marked and usually well prepared. The Capitainerie is also there.

Moorings	Floating pontoons.		
Draught	3m	**LOA**	35m
Berths	650	**Visitors**	20
Fuel	Immediately next to the Reception Quay.		
Weather	Teletape: 94.46.90.11. Capitainerie daily.		
Boatyard Services	Reasonable.		
Shops	Modest. There is one supermarket with a strangely selected range of expensive goods and goodies. It is worth calling just to experience the unusual choice and the lay-out.		

APPROACH

The islands are well marked and all you need for a trouble-free visit is to stand well off until you are near the buoyed channel into the port.

ENTRY

The channel is dredged to 4m and buoyed in standard red and green. It begins to show itself once you have rounded La Casserlane. The buoyed channel must be observed especially to landward towards the Rade de Brusc side where the buoys are stationed close to the rocks. They will be to starboard when you are leaving, and you must stand your ground even in fast and heavy traffic or you chance finding ground in the form of a rocky bottom. There are two yellowish triangular leading marks on 206°M which take you straight to the head of the Port Embiez Cargo Mole.

COMMENTARY

One of the fine PR phrases suggests that Robinson Crusoe would have loved this location. Such a wild claim is not entirely out of keeping with the ambience of the island, although it has been almost exclusively a piece of real estate since the rich and famous Paul Ricard started his exciting and expansive operation.

There are three islands that go to make up l'Archipel des Embiez, coming from a word meaning 'passages': Tour Fondue, St Pierre and Grand Île. They have been illustriously blessed by such figures as Pope Gregory XI in 1376 and Admiral Andrea Doria in 1536. They were salt marshes for most of their days and the property of La Société des Salins d'Hyères, who abandoned them in 1940. The spirited industrialist, builder, entrepreneur and gifted amateur artist, Paul Ricard, bought it in 1958. Work started in 1959, and on 1 May 1963 it was opened under the presidency of Maréchal Juin.

The marina presents a fine view of the medieval ruins of Sabran Castle. The old naval gun site on the St Pierre promontory houses the Ricard Oceanographic Foundation. There is a museum and aquariums.

While it cannot rival the Eden of Île de Port Cros, and Crusoe would have probably detested it, it is a most pleasant spot in its own right and as a base for jilling with or without the dinghy around the islands and the nearby rocky coast. There are fine beaches, intriguing coves, and pine woods to contrast with the salt marshes – after which a visit to the vineyards for the rosé special is more than justified. It is also sited on such rich fishing banks that veritable hordes are attracted from near and far.

There is another side to the island, about which it may be said in truth from time to time, 'the isle is full of noises' albeit not 'sweet airs'. This is because such noises stem from another of Paul Ricard's interests: powerboats. The island is one of its main centres; all in keeping with his inland motor race-tracks at Le Camp du Castelet and Mas Méjanes in the Camargues.

There are two other ports nearby:

Port de la Coudouliere (Commune de Six Fours Plage)
43.05.80 N 05.48.70 E   Tel: 94 58 56 25
Buoyed berths 447   LOA 7.5m   Draught 1m

All the moorings are buoyed in the centre of the small crowded harbour which describes itself as 'port saturé'. There is little scope for visitors in any way.

Port du Brusc
43.04.60 N 05.48.20 E   Tel: 94 34 03 96
5 Visitors' berths   LOA 7.5m   Draught 1.5m
The small port is busy with ferries and there are few opportunities for visitors to berth. The approach is troubled by rocky environs and shoaling sands. The entry, to northward, is marked by a red can buoy and should be made on 150°M. ∎

SANARY
43.07.00 N 05.48.02 E
Tel. 94 74 20 95
Port A3   Town A2

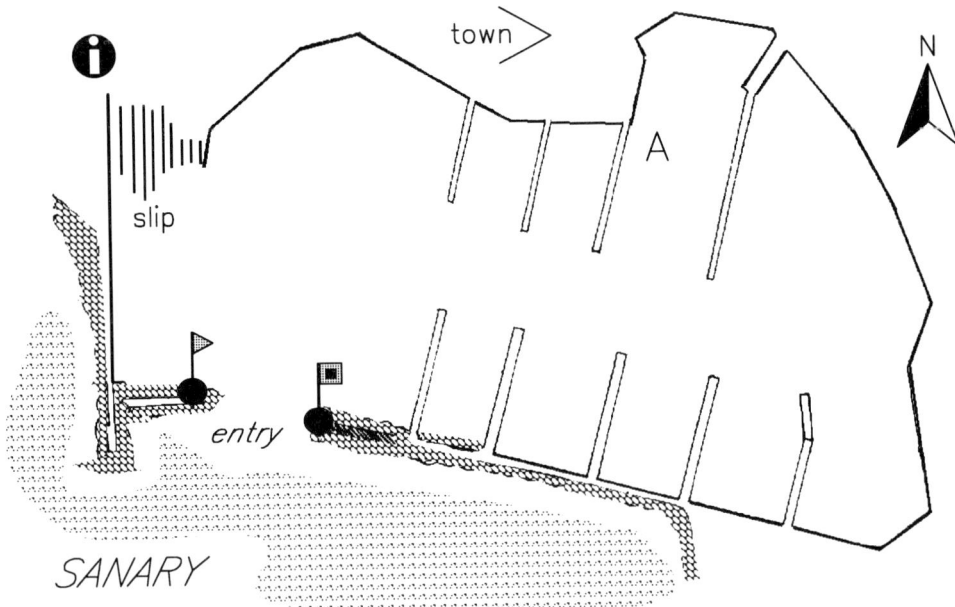

Charts	SHOM 5325, 6610 ECM 504 ADM 2164, 2165
Lights	Grand Rouveau Oc(2) 6s 45m 15M W Tower
	Bendor Oc R 7M
	W Jetty Fl R 4s 9m 10M W/R Tower

Marks The outer landmarks are the Cap de l'Aigle to the west and Cap Sicié to the east. The Baie de Sanary lies between the two headlands of Pointe Nègre to the south and Pointe de la Cride to the north. The latter is marked with a beacon. Sanary sur Mer itself is on the hinterland of its own headland, the Pointe du Bau Rouge.

The clock tower of Sanary forms a conspicuous and almost irresistible inducement as you close the harbour.

Reception There is no reception quay so you need to look out for a berthing attendant on a bicycle – and because the port is usually busy and crowded, success cannot be guaranteed. If you are left to your own devices, move slowly towards the Quai de l'Hôtel de Ville at the head, the north, of the port, looking to quay No 3 on the port hand where you may be allocated a berth. It is better not to approach any of the jetties too closely without advice. Some of them carry less water than one would expect.

Moorings Quays: to laid chains.

Draught	3.5m	**LOA**	25m
Berths	520	**Visitors**	100 (This must be treated as something of a polite fiction, for I have never visited without having had to wait in line for a long time.)

Fuel	To the north east of the port at quay No 6.
Weather	Teletape: 94.46.90.11. Capitainerie daily.
Boatyard Services	Modest.
Shops	Comprehensive and charming.

APPROACHES

From the south and Cap Sicié you round the Embiez island and, in particular, the large beacon of Sèches des Magnons. Leave the next beacon, La Casserlane, to starboard while making a northeasterly course. From the west, the approach is open. Just pick up the headland marked by La Cride and follow the coast round into the Baie de Sanary.

ENTRY

The entry is straightforward: between the jetty marked by its red and white tower and the blind green buoy that marks the sands that encroach from the beach.

COMMENTARY

Sanary, Provençal for St Nazaire, is the name of what was once a very old and tiny fishing village. It has now turned resort, but it has so turned without injury or blemish. It is an example of how the best of the past can readily coexist with the best of the present, to the mutual advantage of residents and visitors alike.

Its colour scheme, mainly pinks and white, is a dream; and the vision of the clock tower as you cruise in sets the tone for the rest of your stay. It is not a large place, neither the harbour waters or the town; nor are its boating services and facilities advanced. In spite of its popularity as a weekend spa for those who feel the need to flee Marseille, the townsfolk and shopkeepers seem to treat everyone as if they are (at warmest) close friends or (at least) distant relatives. They are all friendly and keen to be of service.

Sanary sur Mer has much to offer with its characterful houses and shops; so much, indeed, that it must draw like a magnet any skipper looking for a port of singular appeal – a place with a difference, but a difference that you dream of. A place that is, for example, halfway between a quiet anchorage and a well-run marina. Certainly the place had enough allure and presence to convince Aldous Huxley that he should install himself as a full-time resident; and he was no slouch when it came to slaughtering mediocrity.

There is no sign displayed that says 'Sanary, a fine town', but it does deserve one. It is one of the most attractive places on the French Mediterranean coast. ∎

BANDOL
43.08.00 N 05.45.05 E
VHF 16, 9
Tel. 94 29 42 64
Port B2   Town B2

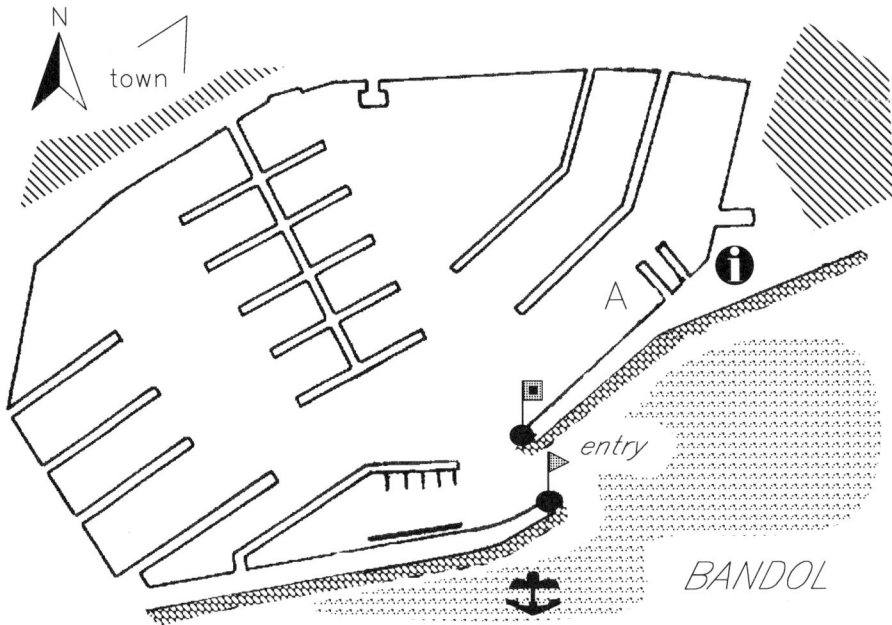

Charts	SHOM 5325, 6610 ECM 504 ADM 2164, 2165					
Lights	Grand Rouveau	Oc(2) 6s	45m	15M	W	Tower
	S Jetty Head	Oc(4)WR 12s	11m	13M	W/R	Tower
	E Jetty Head	Fl G 4s	2m	5M	G	Structure

Marks The outer landmarks are the Cap de l'Aigle to the west and Cap Sicié to the east. The Baie de Bandol lies between the Île de Bendor and the Pointe de la Cride to the south. The latter is marked with a beacon. The rock of La Fourmigue carries a BRB isolated danger mark on a large beacon.

Reception Pontoons 36 to 64.

Moorings Quay: to laid chain.

Draught	3m	**LOA**	30m
Berths	1350	**Visitors**	30

Fuel Quay by the Capitainerie.

Weather Teletape: 94.46.90.11. Capitainerie daily.

Boatyard Services Good.

Shops Good.

APPROACHES

Bendor island and the headland of La Cride can be easily seen and identified, and the mass of contemporary flats behind the port cannot be missed.

The approach to the port of Bandol is trouble free provided you take the outer route round Bendor and La Fourmigue. It is prudent not to be tempted by what look like possible passages through the gaps – although the gap between La Fourmigue and the island is safe in settled weather if you keep absolutely central.

ENTRY

Leave the island and La Fourmigue well to port, after which the entrance to Bandol becomes clear ahead. Follow the south sea wall to the end, rounding it when the entrance opens up.

COMMENTARY

Once upon a time Bandol was a small Provençal fishing village just like neighbouring Sanary, but, unlike Sanary, Bandol did not stop when it had grown into a pleasant resort. It allowed itself to be seduced into seasonal expansion until *folie de grandeur* took over and it has now done quite a Topsy.

To be fair, it has done it well. It has three excellent beaches, Lido, Reneceros and Casino; and its large and well-equipped port de plaisance is surrounded by inoffensive modern buildings given over to cafes, bars, restaurants and boutiques. It has been well converted and with its gardens, pines, palms and mimosa it is by no means soulless territory. Bandol vineyards produce some of the best-known Côtes de Provence wine. ∎

▬▬

BENDOR

43.07.07 N 05.45.01 E2   Tel. 94 29 44 34
Port B3   Town A3

Lights	E Jetty Head	OcR 4s	5m	7M	W/R Tower
	W Jetty Head	Fl(2)G 6s	3m	5M	G/W Base
Draught	2.5m **LOA**	13m **Berths**	610 (10 visitors)		

APPROACHES and ENTRY

From the east, pick up La Fourmigue and pass it at will, keeping watch for the fast ferries that ply in this vicinity. From the west, follow the rocky coastline of the island on the port hand, after which the port entrance will open.

Whether or not it will be open and accessible for you is another matter, since the traffic is heavy and visitors' berths are at a premium. The track is indicated by the exotic Afro architecture dead ahead. There is little room to manoeuvre in the confines of the harbour and you must keep well away from the ferries.

COMMENTARY

In spite of what must have seemed like an obvious appeal to many people, in 1950 the island was practically deserted. Henry IV offered it to Capitaine Henri de Boyer et Bendor, calling it a stone 'plus précieuse que le diamant de la couronne du Roi de France' – although not brilliant enough to attract royalty. However, the night fires lit by the 17th-century ruthless robber, le comte Robert, were unfortunately bright enough to cause many shipwrecks on its inhospitable coast.

A bright light of a different kind is the Universal Wines and Spirits Exhibition. It covers the production of wine, aperitifs and liqueurs in 45 countries, with 7000 bottles on view. ∎

ST CYR LES LECQUES
43.10.08 N 05.41.00 E
Tel. 94 26 21 98
Port B2   Town B2

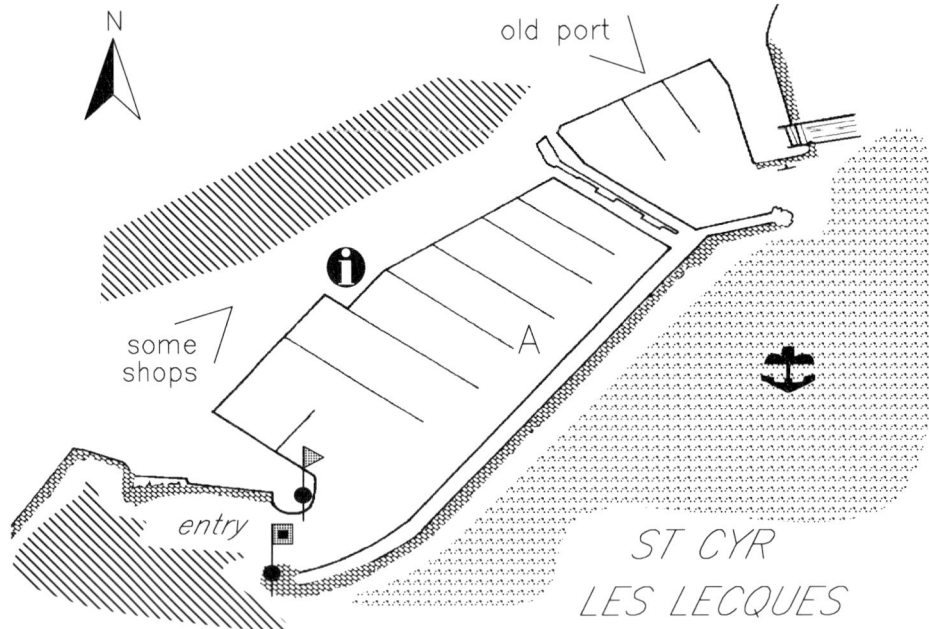

Charts	SHOM 5323, 6612 ECM 504 ADM 2164, 2165				
Lights	S Jetty NE Head	Fl(2)R 6s	8m	7M	W/R Tower
	S Jetty SW Head	Iso G 4s	10m	9M	G/W Base
	Inner Spur	Q R	3m	7M	R Structure

Marks Les Lecques is in the north east corner of the Baie de la Ciotat, and the main landmark is to the west. It is one of the most outstanding and eye-catchingly dramatic on the Mediterranean: the Cap de l'Aigle. Nearby is l'île Verte.

Reception Ends of the first three pontoons which are to port.

Moorings Lines: to laid chain.

Draught	2.5m	**LOA**	15m
Berths	431	**Visitors**	(Dependent upon vacancies.)

Fuel Immediately to port upon entry.

Weather Teletape: 94.46.90.11. Posted each morning to the storm signal mast.

Boatyard Services Reasonable.

Shops Reasonable.

APPROACHES

The approach across the Baie de la Ciotat, entered at leisure between Cap de l'Aigle or l'île Verte to the west and the Pointe Grenier to the east, is trouble free.

ENTRY

The main, south, jetty has a green topped white tower to the west marking the entrance to the recently built marina, and a red and white tower marking the entrance to the old port. Little purpose is served by trying the latter as there is little water at the best of times (hardly more than a metre); it is frequently silted up; and there is seldom a berth for visiting yachts even when they can get in. So the obvious choice is the equally obvious entry into the marina. The masts and vacation buildings behind them make the place difficult to miss.

COMMENTARY

The old harbour has had a marina three times its size added on to its south side. Shoresides, the feeling is the same: one of man made summer houses and facilities to service them. Otherwise, there is very little, although Les Lecques is popular in summer and winter alike. It has a fine extended beach that runs eastward to La Madrague where the coastline becomes at once rocky and rugged. At that point there is a small harbour suitable for only the smallest of craft.

Les Lecques is a pleasantly bland experience: unpretentious and middle of the road in every way. ∎

LA CIOTAT
43.10.05 N 05.36.06 E
Tel. 42 08 62 90
Port C1   Town A1

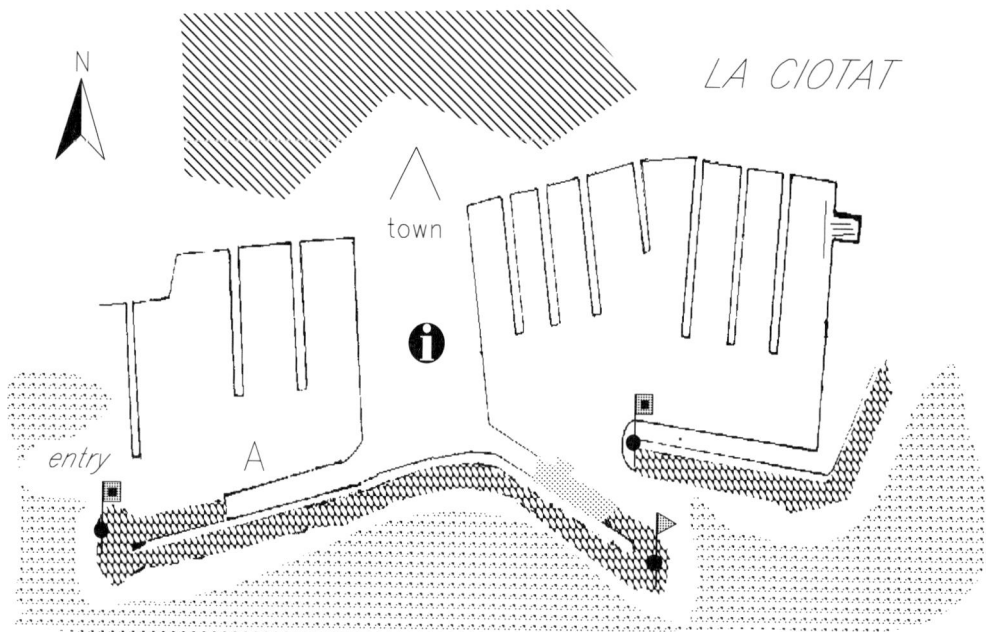

N

LA CIOTAT

town

ⓘ

entry

A

Charts	SHOM 5325, 6612, 6882, 6951 ECM 504 ADM 2164			
Lights	Breakwater	Oc(2)R 6s	21m	13M	R/W Tower
	Jetty Head	Fl R 4s	18m	9M	R/W Tower
	Bérouard	Iso G 4s	15m	12M	G/W Tower
	S Jetty Head	Oc(2)G 6s	8m	5M	G/W Tower
	E Capucins	Fl(2)R 6s	7m	9M	R/W Tower

Marks The unmistakable Cap de l'Aigle is all that is needed from east or west. The port itself is noticeable when cruising within the bay.

Reception To starboard immediately after entry into the Bassin Bérouard: the southerly basin.

Moorings Quay: to laid chain.

Draught 2.5m   **LOA** 15m

Berths 640   **Visitors** 25

Fuel Inner quayside immediately to starboard upon entering.

Weather Teletape: 94.46.90.91 and 91.90.30.00. Capitainerie daily; and Marseille R/T upon request.

Boatyard Services Comprehensive.

Shops A full range of excellence in the pedestrian (more or less) precincts.

APPROACHES

The approach is straightforward from all directions. The Île Verte may be rounded either side, but with provisos. To the west there are the two Cannoniers to be avoided. The Cannonier du Sud is marked by a blind green beacon, but the Cannonier du Nord is unmarked. In bad weather it is prudent to take the outside track.

From within the Baie de la Ciotat the sky pointing fingers of the shipyards and the steeply rising houses above the marina make it easy to spot.

ENTRY

The shipyards are to be completely avoided and a course set for the Bassin Bérouard, the more southerly of the two basins. Legend has it that you may berth in the attractively named Bassin des Capucins (not to be confused with the Port de Capucins which is a little farther to the north), but in fact that never seems possible and I have yet to meet a visitor who has stayed there. Once past the shipyards, the marina is dead ahead virtually northward. The entrance can be tricky with weather in the south east, giving rise not only to long swells and short surges but also sharp overfalls.

Visitors' berths are the first to starboard. It may be necessary to take a vacant place and report to the Capitainerie at the head of the basin, for the quayside is not always honoured by the presence of port de plaisance staff. It must be said, in fairness, that they can be equally reticent about the collection of fees.

COMMENTARY

Unfortunately, the berths in the Bassin Bérouard become extremely uncomfortable when there is southeasterly weather; and if it is really bad, you may well find that the berth becomes untenable if you are living on board. This is a pity, because southeasterly swells are uncommon here and the town of La Ciotat has much for cruising visitors.

There are two major attractions. First, the old fishing port which is tucked away in the north west corner of the old port. It is still more or less unaffected by the petroleum industry and the huge shipyard enterprises that overlook it. Ever since the Greeks first came, there has been a shipyard here, and the town of 25 000 owes much of its prosperity to the industry that builds shipping up to 60 000 tonnes.

The second attraction is the town. While it is tourist oriented, thanks to all the blessings of next door Ciotat Plage, it combines that side of its being with the sort of idiosyncratic character that is usually lacking in such resorts, and at night parts of it are almost classic fairyland. The shops seem to be owned by committed artisans who are assisted by loyal staff of ancient vintage or green but dedicated apprentices. Just to wander from shop to shop is a joy, and the food selection is magnificent. There are delis, butchers, fishmongers and greengrocers in sufficient numbers to make happy any devotee of Thatcherite competition. However, in the main, they are more than pleased to co-operate rather than compete with one another, and will send you on to their best contact if they are without your particular request. This is a pleasing phenomenon as infrequent in France as in England.

Historically, La Ciotat (the city) is not without interest. In ancient times it was a satellite port of Marseille known as Citharista, and up to the 16th century suffered first at Roman hands and then at those of various barbarians. After that time, it became one of the main merchant ports of the Mediterranean, an accomplishment that survives today.

It also has the honour of being the first place in the world where a motion picture was projected: the Lumière Bros, the famed cinematic wizards, showed their short film here, two months before it was seen in Paris.

For those interested in nature and with legs that can cope, there is the Parc du Mugel situated right at the top of Cap de l'Aigle (155m up and then down again). It is a protected area with mimosa, arbutus and cork trees growing in reddish soil of shingly sand. Below there is Île Verte and the Calanque de Muget. The other famous calanques (inlets) are also close by. Not surprisingly, and utterly rewardingly for those who achieve it, the view is stunning. ∎

CASSIS
43.13.00 N 05.32.00 E
Tel. 42 01 03 73
Port A3   Town A2

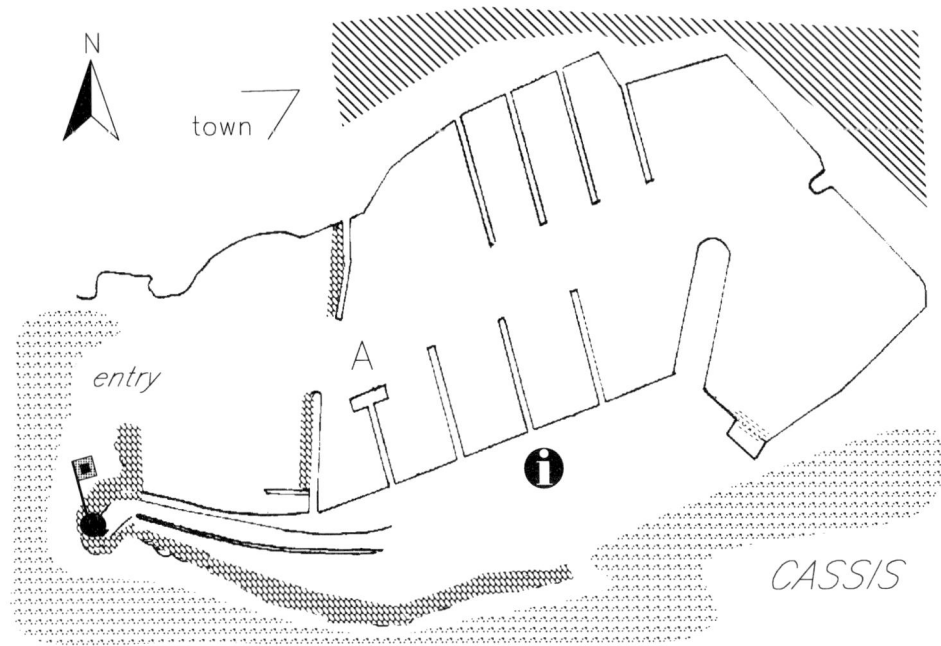

Charts	SHOM 5325, 6612, 6682, 6952 ECM 504 ADM 2164				
Lights	Les Empereurs	Q (96) + LFl WR 15s	18m	6/4M	Beacon
	La Cassidaigne	Fl(2) 6s	25m	8M	BRB Beacon
	Cassis Batterie	Fl R 4s	12m	7M	R Structure
	Cassis Mole Neuf	Oc(2)G 6s	17m	6M	W/G Tower

Marks La Cassidaigne is a rock almost immediately to the south of the port. It carries a BRB isolated danger mark. To the south east is the unmistakable headland of the Cap de l'Aigle, and to the west there are the detached rocks off l'île Riou known as Les Empereurs.

Reception On the fuel pontoon immediately to port upon entry.

Moorings Quay and floating pontoons: to laid chain.

For a visitors' berth, you can also contact the Association Nautique Cassidaigne on VHF 6 or Telephone 42 01 24 95. They have seventeen moorings with 5m draught for craft up to 15m. French only is the general rule.

Draught	6m	**LOA**	15m
Berths	450	**Visitors**	23

Fuel On the pontoon immediately to port upon entry.

Weather	Teletape: 91.90.30.00 and 94.46.90.91. Posted at the Capitainerie daily at 0900. The office will occasionally make the meteo call for you at no charge.
Boatyard Services	Only moderate.
Shops	Only moderate, but with a fair market.

APPROACH

There is no encumbrance in the outer seaward approaches to Cassis, and the port stands out clearly and attractively from some way out to sea. The Baie de Cassis between Pointe Cacau and Cap Canaille (names to conjure with indeed) is extremely pretty with its rocky fjords, creeks, inlets (or calanques, as they are called).

ENTRY

Up to the last few cables there is no difficulty. Close to though there is comparatively little water, say 5m or so. This in itself is no problem, but frequently there is swell that builds up in the close confines; and since there is no spending wall the surging and resurging can make for a very boisterous headway.

The entrance is also narrow and it is necessary to make quite a tight turn. To compound all this, the tourist traffic in fast ferry boats for the calanques is a non-stop ecstasy throughout the daylight hours during the season.

COMMENTARY

The small town of Cassis is situated at the mouth of a small gorge and is itself a major tourist attraction, with land-based sightseers flocking there. It was first made popular by Fredric Mistral, the poet who seems to have been everywhere and seen everything in Provence, when he featured it in his poem 'Calendal' in 1867. Later, it was pounced upon as a summer residence by a number of painters, among them Matisse and Dufy.

In times past it was renowned for the quality of its seafood and the strength of its musky wine. Indeed, at one time, the Muscat of Cassis was a contender with that of Frontignan or Rivesaltes. The seafood here is still worthy, but the wines are no longer quite what they used to be. Muscat is no longer made, and the local brews have lost something of their brilliance. Nevertheless, Cassis, a greenish white wine, somewhat akin to Portugal's vinho verde, is still one of the best wines to go with either the local *oursins* (sea urchins) or the big Cassis fish dish, *bouillabaisse*. The wine would not thank you for associating it, even remotely, with any glass or bottle connected with the blackcurrant.

Cassis does not live by tourism alone. The local work is the nearby quarry at Calanque de Port Miou, where a hard white stone is dug for use in quaysides and gateways. It was used in the 1920s Rove Tunnel under the Estaque Mountains, for the Suez Canal, and also at Campo Santo in Genoa.

In spite of their proximity to Cassis, the calanques are known as Les Calanques de Marseille. There are three, and two of them are confusingly called 'ports': la Calanque de Port Miou; la Calanque de Port Pin; and la Calanque d'En Vau. They are created by the valleys of the Marseilleveyre and Puget limestone ranges continuing under the sea.

What's in a name? An anchorage by any other name will moor you just as well. Port Miou may have pontoons along its flanks, but it still nowhere approaches what you really expect of a port. The essential attractions of the calanques are the breath-taking form and scenery provided by the vertigo-inducing rough white cliffs which rush to 150m, starkly perpendicular above the limpid deep blue to turquoise water.

Their secondary appeal is their 'away from it all' peace and quiet. The first endures, but the second is only to be guaranteed in the evenings out of the high season, so much have they to offer. Pleasant evenings can be spent sailing out of Cassis in the dinghy and by taking the walk, the Promenade des Lombards, along the beach and round the foot of the rocks of the castle of Les Baux. ∎

MARSEILLE

43.17.08 N 05.22.00 E
Tel. 91 33 63 72
Port B1   Town B1

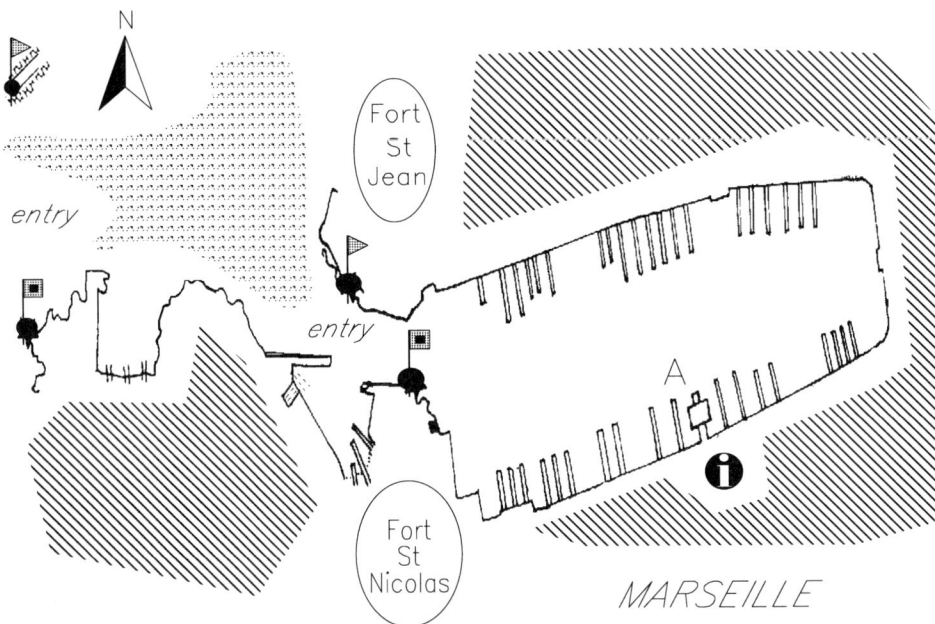

See also plan on page 61

Charts SHOM 6739, 6767 ECM 504, 505 ADM 2164, 150
Lights *Please note only those of major use to visiting yachts. The list is not comprehensive. Refer to ADM Chart 150.*

The major distant lights are:

Couronne	Fl R 3s	34m	21M	W/R	Tower
Arnette	Q(9) 15s			YBY	
Carro	VQ(9) 10s			YBY	
Planier	Fl 5s	68m	27M	W/R	Tower
Croisette	Oc(3)WG 12s	58m	11–9M	W/B	Tower
Riou	Q(6)+LFl WR 15s	18m	6–4M	W	Structure

The major close lights are:

Tiboulen	Fl(3)G 12s	34m	9M	W/G	Tower
Caveaux	Iso 4s	28m	10M	W/B	Tower
Île d'If	Fl(2) 6s	27m	13M	W/R	Tower
Sourdaras	Q(9) 15s	13m	8M	YBY	

Marseille:

Digue Catalans	Fl(3)G 12s	7m	5M	W/G	Structure
Digue Ste Marie	UQ(2)R 1s	20m	13M	W/R	Structure
Pte Desirade	Fl G 4s	13m	10M	W/G	Tower

Joliette	Oc(3)R 12s	7m	7M	W/R Structure
Joliette	Oc(3)G 12s	7m	6M	W/G Structure
Fort St Jean North	Q R	11m	7M	W/R Structure
Fort St Jean South	Iso G 4s	8m	7M	W/G Structure
West Tunnel	Fl G 4s	5m	5M	Dolphin
East Tunnel	Fl(3)G 12s	5m	5M	Dolphin

Marks *The major distant marks are:*

Northerly: Cap Couronne at the south east corner of the Golfe de Fos marks the beginning of the coast that runs almost directly eastward to Marseille. The headland also has two Cardinal marks, Arnette and Carro. Nearby is the main pilot station for the area.

Southerly: The main offshore light is on l'île de Planier, also marking the associated Le Souquet, la Pierre à la Bague and a cluster of wrecks. It lies off to the west of the other major landmarks, Cap Croisette and l'île Riou – both of which designate the end, in every way, of Mont de Marseilleveyre, to the south of Marseille. Cap Croisette is lit by l'îlot Tiboulen de Maire, which must not be confused with l'îlot Tiboulen 'plain' just off l'îles du Frioul to the north. L'île Riou is lit by l'îlot les Empereurs.

The major close marks are:

From the north, the Basilique de Notre Dame de la Garde is outstanding. The small îlot Tiboulen (not the 'de Maire' that lies just off Cap Croisette) marks the northwestern extremity of les îles du Frioul.

From the south, Cap Caveaux shows clearly as the southerly point of l'île Pomegues; and closer to the port are the large offshore beacons of lit Sourdaras and blind Canoubier, and l'île d'If.

Reception The public reception berth is opposite the Hotel de Ville on the north quay. The Société Nautique de Marseille, the well-known SNM, has a small pontoon for reception at the west side of its floating pavilion on the middle of the south side of the port, opposite the Capitainerie.

Moorings Quays and pontoons: to laid chain.

Draught 7m **LOA** 110

Berths 3200 **Visitors** 40

Fuel On the west side of the north quay.

Weather Teletape: 36.65.02.02, 36.65.08.08, 42.09.08.08, 94.46.90.11. At the Capitainerie and the SNM daily. The SNM printout is very good, but can be late in its posting.

Boatyard Services Comprehensive.

Shops Comprehensive.

APPROACHES

The approach to Marseille has no unmarked hazard, and all the landmarks are clear and plain to see. The run-in from the north is completely open. From the south, you need to negotiate a track between the YB Cardinal of the Basse Ste Estève off Frioul and the west side of l'île d'If, or between the east side of l'île d'If and the sandbank marked by Sourdaras and Canoubier.

ENTRY

The last few miles before coming into the harbour shows the city of Marseille at its architectural best, with a fantastic range of shapes, sizes and styles – stunning when seen in silhouette.

The long sea walls of Catalans to the south and Ste Marie to the north reach out to make the half-mile-wide entrance to the port. They are dominated by the Basilique de Notre Dame de la Garde, poised on its limestone spike some 150m and more above the port.

You tend northerly and use the main Entrée Sud between the Digue Ste Marie and the Pointe de la Désiderade. Round slowly to starboard, keeping a wary lookout for the many and varied craft that frequent the port, and most of which will be moving at a great rate of knots. Just after the Port de la Réserve to starboard, the walls close in as you approach the gap between the two forts of St Jean and St Nicolas. To port is the fuelling quay and to starboard the dolphins that mark the tunnel; the small inner harbour is entered under a bridge with headroom of 2.5m.

There are numerous possibilities of mooring – once you get to know the place, that is. I would advise the first-time visitor to use the facilities of the Société Nautique de Marseille. I found them most efficient and welcoming. Even after much looking and shopping around you will probably still decide that the discreet SNM is the better part of valorous experiment.

COMMENTARY

Large tomes have been written about Marseille, which, after twenty-six centuries of history, is the oldest of France's great cities and the greatest Mediterranean port. I can pass on a few tips.

For the founding Greeks and the ensuing Romans, as well as the ancient and modern citizens, the spirit of Marseille has always been vested in the Lacydon, now known as the Vieux Port. Predictably, prices are high and, not so predictably, quality amenities are few. Perhaps the area is to be most generously judged by its restaurants. Two are choice: the *choucroûte* experts on the south quayside and the Cloche de Fromage in the nearby square. There are plenty of options for that famous Marseille speciality, *bouillabaisse,* and edible fun is to be had in comparing and contrasting the various offerings. Ingredients and quality vary remarkably, but the price, never.

At the top of port, to the east on the Quai des Belges, are to be found the fishermen with their catches – some of which are sold straightaway on the quayside stalls. The displays vary from the substantial and first class to whole catches that are insignificant and meagre, and, in the best traditions of the sea, should never have been landed – the phrase 'small fry' being a euphemism here.

The long slog to the railway station is made worth while if you take the Afro back streets and raid them for their fabrics; some of these are rare and costly in the UK but go for a song here – that is, once you have dredged the gold thread from the dross and bartered in Pidgin Arab-AfrAnglais.

For those who cherish images of the old Marseille culled from the works of the likes of Maugham and Waugh, there are glimpses still to be found; that is, if you search patiently and persistently, but don't be put off by the first pseudo pimp who whispers in your ear. ■

Ports in the Rade de Marseille:
Pointe Rouge – L'Estaque – Frioul

POINTE ROUGE
43.14.00 N 05.21.02 E
Tel. 91 73 13 21
Port B2   Town B3

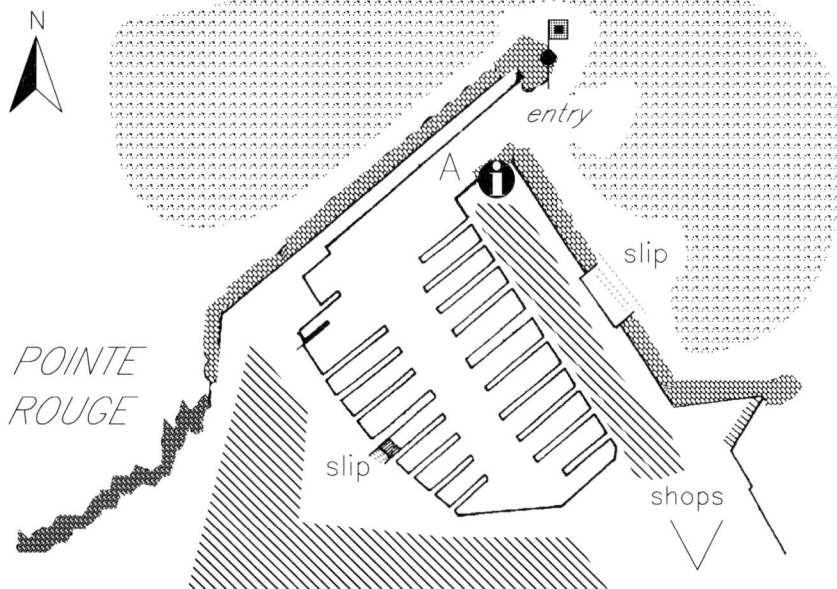

Charts	SHOM 6739, 6767 ECM 504, 505 ADM 2164, 150
Lights	Breakwater Oc(2)G 6s 10m 6M W/G Tower
Reception	Immediately to port upon entering.
Moorings	Quay: to laid chain.
Draught	3m
Berths	1200
Fuel	Reception quay in front of Capitainerie.

Draught	3m	**LOA**	25m
Berths	1200	**Visitors**	10

Fuel Reception quay in front of Capitainerie.
Teletape: 91.90.35.00, 42.09.09.09 and 94.31.38.38. Also posted at the
Weather Capitainerie daily.
Boatyard Services Reasonable.   **Shops**   Basics in the locality.

COMMENTARY

Because of its distance from all the facilities of Marseille, this modern bleak marina is not of great interest to visiting yachtsmen; but overlooking the bay is a pleasant restaurant that is extremely popular on Sundays. ∎

L'ESTAQUE
43.21.06 N 05.19.00 E
VHF 16, 12
Tel. 91 46 01 40
Port C3   Town C3

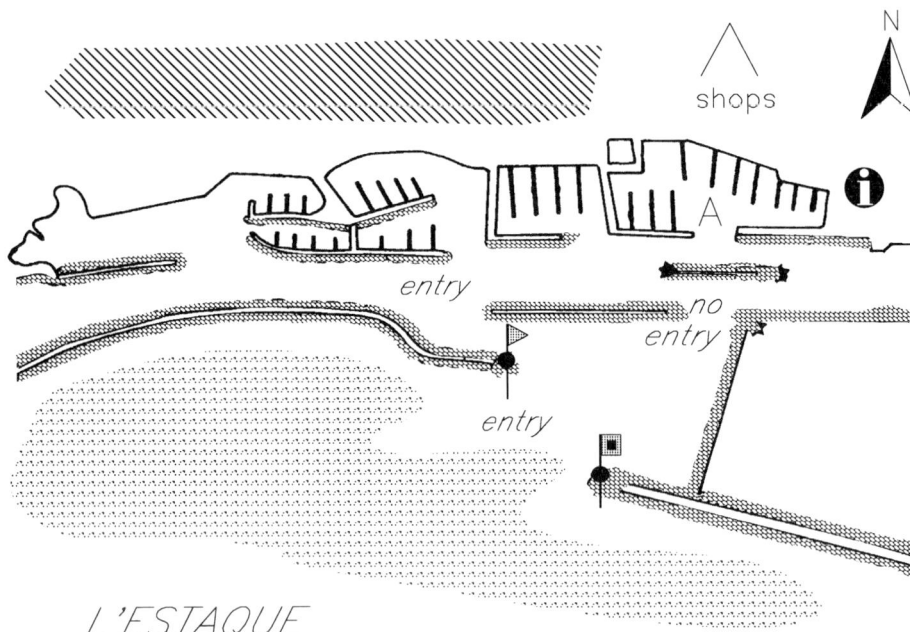

L'ESTAQUE

Charts	SHOM 6739, 6767 ECM 504, 505 ADM 2164, 150				
Lights	All major lights as for Marseille.				
	N Jetty Head	Fl G 5s	15m	15M	W/G Structure
	W Jetty Head	VQ	21m	16M	W/R Structure
	L'Estaque	Q R	11m	6M	W/R Structure
	Chalutiers	Fl G 4s	8m	6M	W/G Structure
	Chalutiers	Fl(3)R 12s	8m	6M	W/R Structure
	Chalutiers	Q(9) 15s			YBY

Marks	All major marks as for Marseille.
Reception	The Société Nautique d'Estaque-Mourepaine (SNEM) has a pontoon in Port Sud.
Moorings	Concrete and floating pontoons.

Draught	2.2m	**LOA**	20m
Berths	1450	**Visitors**	50

Fuel	Port Sud, Saturdays only.
Weather	No special facility.
Boatyard Services	Comprehensive in the vicinity, but not always available to visiting yachtsmen.
Shops	Rudimentary needs can be met locally.

ENTRY

Easy to identify and approach, with a large viaduct set well back from the port. Close in, you see the Blockhaus office set on a high footbridge with a mast.

Use the northerly entrance, nominated the 'passe plaisance', and not the passe des Chalutiers (trawlermen). After this, you turn smartly to starboard and follow the jetties until you reach the reception pontoon opposite the barrier jetty across the passe de Chalutiers.

COMMENTARY

Theoretically, there is room for visitors, and English is spoken. In spite of the presence of a number of yacht clubs in the port, there is no real sign of any welcome for visitors. Well, not for foreigners anyway, for this is real chauvinistic backwoods territory with a local accent that defies Parisians. And when it comes to English being spoken, you need to learn French. Unless you have a pressing reason for being here, you will be best advised to try elsewhere.

■

FRIOUL
43.16.07 N 05.18.05 E
Tel. 91 59 01 82
Port A2   Town B2

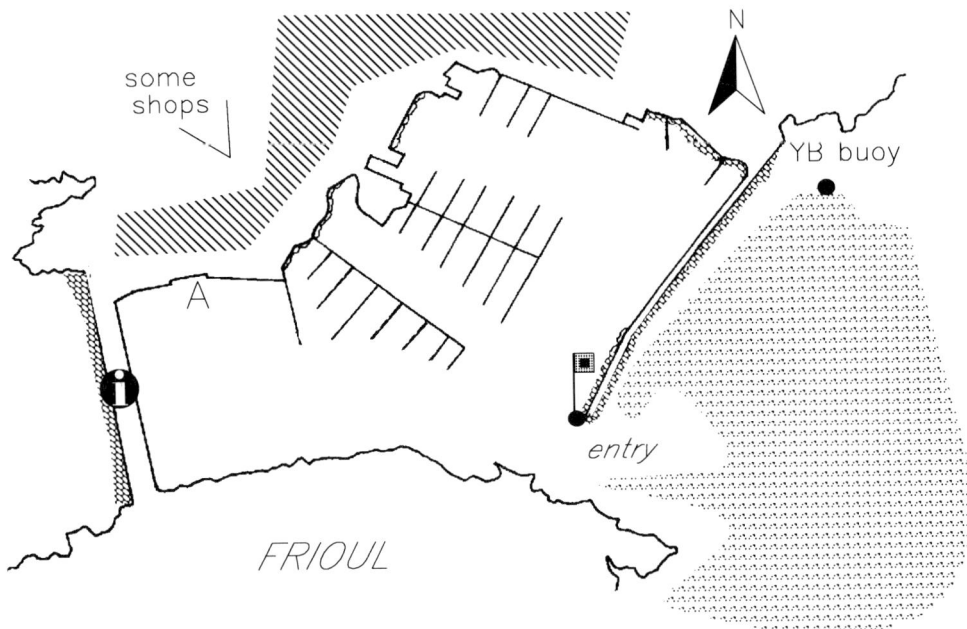

some shops

N

YB buoy

A

i

entry

FRIOUL

Charts	SHOM 6739, 6767 ECM 504, 505 ADM 2164, 150
Lights	All major marks as for Marseille.

L'Île d'If	Fl(2) 6s	27m	13M	W/R	Tower
Ste Estève	Q(6)+LFl 15s			YB	Cardinal
Port du Friou	Iso G 4s	7m	4M	W/G	Structure

Marks	All major marks as for Marseille.
Reception	No specific reception quay. Report to the office on the Quai Berry to the west in the inner harbour.
Moorings	Catwalks and buoys.
Draught	6m **LOA** 110m
Berths	750 (1500 proposed) **Visitors** 150
Fuel	On the north quay; that is, at the far side of the port from the Capitainerie.
Weather	Teletape: 91.90.35.00, 36.65.02.02, 94.41.38.38 and 91.73.11.14. Capitainerie daily.
Boatyard Services	Only limited.
Shops	Very sparse. Mainly for souvenirs and gifts.

ENTRY

Apart from the fact that the islands themselves are quite unmistakable, there is a 110m TV mast, fixed red light, to the north of l'île Pomègues. Entry is unencumbered and straight in between the jetty and the 'mainland'. There is frequent ferry traffic from Marseille and l'île d'If.

COMMENTARY

The port is popular for weekend visits from those who flee the delights of the Lacydon. It is usually jumping with tourists who have come across by ferry to escape the chaos of Marseille's Canebière. Others have been forced to retreat from If, having been irritated by the banality of much of the ambience in spite of the charm, intelligence and sheer brilliance of the guides.

Fictionally famous, the Château d'If is no splendour to behold, being in actuality quite small; however, it is a frightening wonder to explore. It does not do to let the mind dwell on fact or fiction, for the tales of the Huguenots, the Protestants, the Man in the Iron Mask, the young Mirabeau, the Count of Monte Cristo and the Abbé Faria are equally horrifying.

There is nothing as dramatic as If at Frioul, where the marina is sited between a jetty to the east and a breakwater sea wall to the west. This latter has joined the two previous islands of Ratonneau and Pomègues, so that the Îles du Frioul now consist of one Chief and a few outlying Indians. ∎

CARRY LE ROUET
43.19.07 N 05.09.03 E
Tel. 42 45 25 13
Port B2   Town B2

Charts	SHOM 6767, 5318 ECM 505 ADM 2164
Lights	Couronne Fl R 3s 34m 21M W/R Tower
	Carry le Rouet Fl R2.5s 7m 3M W/R Tower
	Carry le Rouet Fl G 4s 10m 3M G Structure
Marks	Cap Couronne to the west is the main landmark.
Reception	Immediately to starboard on entry by the Capitainerie. It is an alongside berth, and at night has orange lights.
Moorings	Floating pontoons: to laid chain.
Draught	3m
LOA	15m
Berths	500
Visitors	10
Fuel	By the Capitainerie.
Weather	Teletape: 42.09.09.09, 91.90.35.00. A local forecast is posted at the Capitainerie daily.
Boatyard Services	Reasonable.
Shops	Reasonable.

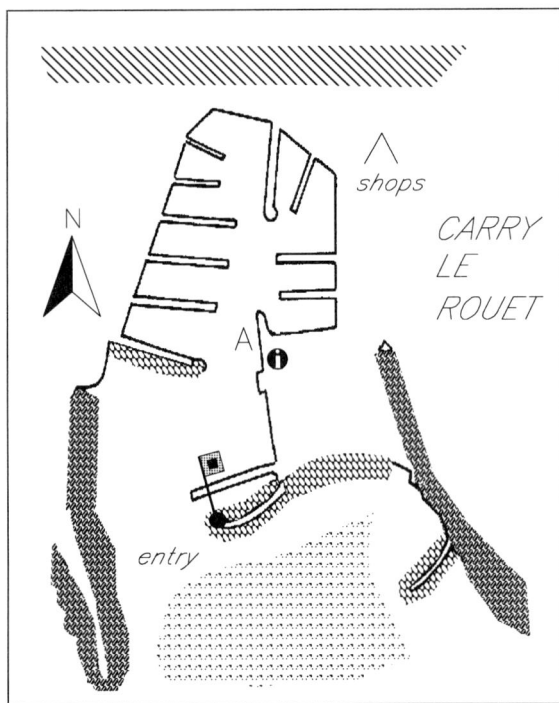

APPROACH
The outer approach is without problems, and the bright white and red lighthouse of Cap Couronne is conspicuous. As you close the harbour it is almost impossible to miss the seventeen-storey high rise block of flats immediately behind the port. On a good day, it is visible for 5 miles.

ENTRY
Watch out for the green buoy that marks the Estéo shoal bank. The rocky mini peninsula to the east of the actual entry known as the Pain de Sucre is marked by a white beacon. The ground shelves gently into the port.

COMMENTARY
Carry le Rouet is a place of which it is impossible to say anything derogatory. It is friendly, efficient and agreeable. ∎

SAUSSET LES PINS
43.20.00 N 05.06.05 E
Tel. 42 48 55 01
Port B2   Town B2

Charts	SHOM 6767, 5318 ECM 505 ADM 2164
Lights	Couronne Fl R 3s 34m 21M W/R Tower
	Sausset les Pins Oc(3)R 12s 10m 9M W/R Tower
	There is also a green starboard light on the east jetty.
Marks	Cap Couronne to the west is the main landmark, with the block of flats at Carry le Rouet running it a good second.
Reception	The Capitainerie immediately to port on entry.
Moorings	Quays: to laid chain.
Draught	2.5m **LOA** 12m
Berths	394 **Visitors** 10 (Improvements are in hand.)
Fuel	Capitainerie.
Weather	In theory it is posted at the Capitainerie daily.
Boatyard Services	Only modest.
Shops	Basic needs can be met; good bread and paper shops.

APPROACH

Outer approach: as for Carry. There is a small island, Aragnon, just off the Tamaris headland, which should be avoided to seaward. The onshore passage looks tempting, but is not safe. Closer to the port, Sausset castle and the large hotel are the only noticeable landmarks.

ENTRY

The Capitainerie advises a northwesterly course on to the head of the east jetty, after which you tend to starboard. This will bring you within hailing distance of the Capitainerie. The reception area has recently been improved.

COMMENTARY

Sausset les Pins is a friendly little port. Although in fact it is not all that small, it has an intimate ambience and everyone is friendly to a degree. This somewhat makes up for the very real discomfort to be suffered, not excluding physical damage to the boat, when there is weather from the east or west through south. The port is not large and shopping is restricted, but there are good restaurants and it is always possible to buy a fresh meal at the fishermen's quay. ∎

CARRO
43.20.00 N 05.02.06 E
Tel. 42 80 76 28
Port C2   Town C3

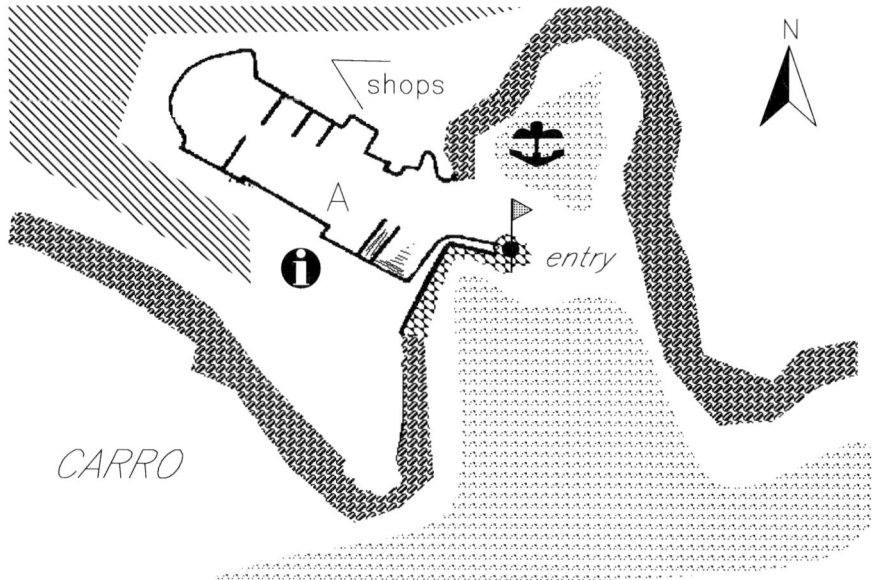

Charts	SHOM 6767, 6884 ECM 505 ADM 2164, 3498				
Lights	Couronne	Fl R 3s	34m	21M	W/R Tower
	Arnette Cardinal	Q(9) 15s			YBY Cardinal
	Carro Cardinal	VQ(9) 10s			YBY Cardinal
	Carro Jetty	Oc(2)WR 6s	8m	9/6M	W/R Tower

Marks Cap Couronne to the west, with its distinctive white and red lighthouse, is the main landmark. The Cardinal marks, Arnette and Carro, round the headland to the west, and the block of flats at Carry le Rouet will confirm.

Reception There is no official reception place or procedure. You take your chance with the small but busy fishing fleet to grab attention or a place as conditions indicate. Tact and prudence are called for.

Moorings Quay and pontoons with buoys. Mooring buoys possibly available.

Draught 2.5m   **LOA** 11m

Berths 200   **Visitors** 20 (It would be improper to call this official statement of numerical fact a fabrication. However, whether fact or fiction, there is not a lot of space for visitors.)

Fuel Tax-free for fishermen only. You must go to Carry le Rouet.

Weather Posted at the Capitainerie in season.

Boatyard Services   Restricted for visiting yachts.
Shops   The word 'modest' does them more than justice, but they are at least in characterful keeping with the spirit of the place.

APPROACH

The outer approach is without problems, and the bright white and red lighthouse of Cap Couronne is conspicuous. The Cardinals Arnette and Carro mark the shoal banks which in fact carry more than 2m. Although used by the locals, they are best avoided, except for careful exploration in calm settled weather. When approaching from the east, watch out for the small island rock Aragnon halfway between Carro and Sausset.

The final approach to Carro will bring you somewhere between Cap Couronne and the Pointe de Carro, a span that contains the large Anse du Verdon and the two smaller bays that make up Carro's protected position.

ENTRY

Verdon is left to starboard and Carro itself is entered between Pointe Riche to port which is marked with a small white beacon, and the rock-strewn Pointe Roquetaillade to starboard.

The final entry is open with plenty of water and you make a course for the head of the jetty marked by its red topped white tower. The anchorage is in the bay to starboard. Once the east jetty is rounded the port opens up. It is usually busy with fishing vessels. They are cautious and considerate navigators in their home port, not only when they move about what is a cramped harbour, but also as they steam in and out of the entrance: a pleasing experience rendered the more so by its infrequency.

COMMENTARY

There are some modern buildings in Carro, but on the whole the village is mainly old and appears to be well used. The anchorage in the bay is very pleasant and looks much older.

There are walks to be taken all round the headland and the sea can be approached by many routes, each with contrasting styles and textures. The various views are well worth the efforts of climbing, for you will get nowhere in Carro unless you are prepared to go uphill all the way.

Of all the small communities on the Provence coast, Carro is the one that will afford you the most questioning reception. There is no overt suspicion or boycott laid on visitors – just a misty veil between Carroites and strangers, be they foreigners or not, that categorically precludes the possibility of intimacy and tells anyone with an ear to hear or an eye to see that Carro is not the place to linger. Its attitudes are not all that much removed from those who cautiously, if not furtively, gain their livelihood by defeating the best efforts of the revenue men – all of which seems right and proper for an area that was largely uninhabited until the 1920s, when the oilman cameth.

Carro is the end of the road in all kinds of ways, including the literal sense. Its well-protected position lies right at the back of a veritably rock-strewn bay. Found as it is on the south west extremity of the Estaques peninsula, it is a halfway house in a no man's land. It is not sure of a wealthy place in the sun, or a position in the flickering shadows of the petroleum flares – not even after inhaling their noxious fumes whenever the north west breezes favour them. But Carro is a place not intending to suffer the poverty that has been the near perpetual lot of this isolated part of marginal Provence; it is not willing to tolerate the old order of fishing three days to make a living for one. It drifts from season to season, like Janus, looking both ways, with its feet in the past and its face towards the future.   ■

Ports in the Golfe de Fos:
Port de Bouc – Martigues – Fos sur Mer – Port St Louis du Rhone

PORT DE BOUC
43.24.02 N 04.59.00 E
Tel. 42 06 38 50
Port C1   Town C2

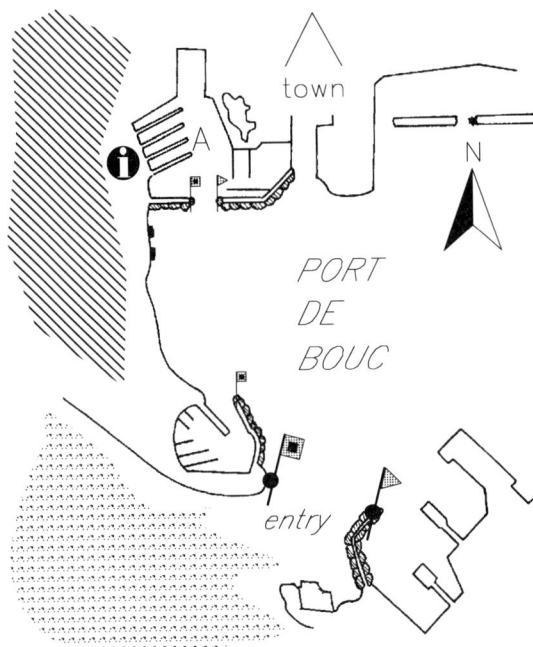

Charts	SHOM 6684, 6767 ECM 505, 507 ADM 2164, 3498					

Lights   *Please note only those of major use to visiting yachts. The list is not comprehensive. Refer to ADM Chart 3498.*

The major distant lights are:

Cap Couronne	Fl R 3s	34m	21M	W/R	Tower
Arnette Cardinal	Q(9) 15s			YBY	Cardinal
Carro Cardinal	VQ(9) 10s			YBY	Cardinal
Rouston	Q(6)+LFl 15s			YB	Cardinal

The major close lights are:

Port de Bouc	Fl Vi 5s	8m	9M	W/G	Structure
	Oc(2)WRG 6s	30m	12–9M	G/W	Base
	Fl(4)R 12s	15m	6M	W/R	Structure
Small Ship Basin	Oc(2)G 6s	5m	7M	W/G	Structure
Fishing Basin	Fl R 4s	3m	8M	W/R	Structure

Port de Plaisance	Iso G 4s	4m	6M	W/G Structure
Leading Lights	F R	17m	11M	
	F R	12m	11M	
Leading Lights	Q R	16m	14M	
	Q R	11m	14M	

Marks The Golfe de Fos is entered between the headland of Cap Couronne to the east and the Rhône to the west. Couronne can hardly be missed while the Rhône can hardly be perceived. The YB Roustan Cardinal marks the unnavigable entrance to the river.

Once in the Golfe, the approach to Port de Bouc on the east side towards the northern corner is marked by the multitude of tall chimneys, flares and tanks of the power station and many refineries.

Reception There is no special reception quay. Heads of pontoons tend to be used, especially towards the north. The Capitainerie is on the west quay.

Moorings Quay, floating pontoons and catwalks.

Draught	9m	**LOA**	16
Berths	448	**Visitors**	79

Fuel Immediately to port on entry.

Weather Posted at the Capitainerie twice daily.

Boatyard Services Satisfactory.

Shops Equally satisfactory, albeit boring. Extra large supermarket.

APPROACHES

The close approaches are without hindrance. The channels are well buoyed and all the marks are clear to see, although some of them are of no navigational significance. There is a lot of very mixed traffic in the area.

The chimneys of the power station on the east coast cannot be ignored; sometimes their 'safe emissions' soar and flare as if they are being stoked by Titans.

ENTRY

The entrance is widely open between the two huge sea walls. The leading marks (orange stripe on red) are not really needed by leisure craft. The port de plaisance is in the north west corner of the harbour where, once inside, leisure craft are to port and fishing vessels to starboard.

COMMENTARY

Port de Bouc is by no means an unwelcoming place in spite of its heavy commitment to big shipping and petroleum. But even the most pleasant welcome cannot make up for the surroundings.

There are beaches nearby and the locals play their own variety of bowls like crazy, but none of it is enough to distract the mind from the encircling gloom. If you want to be in this area, the Étang de Berre or Fos sur Mer are more attractive candidates. ▪

MARTIGUES

43.24.90 N 05.03.20 E
VHF 12 call sign: Fos Port Control
Tel. 42 42 13 35
Port B2   Town B2

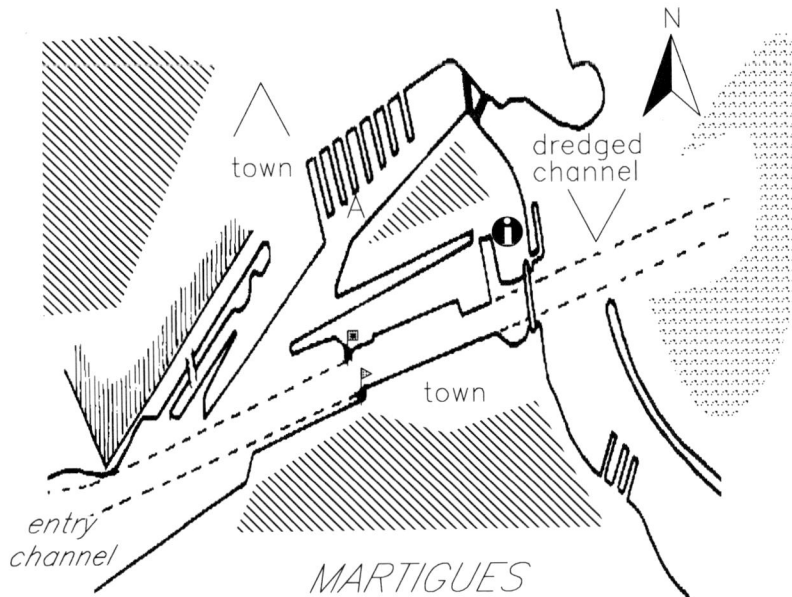

MARTIGUES

NOTE There are two leisure craft facilities in Martigues: the Floating Harbour in the Ferrières Basin and the Dry Port (Port à Sec) on the south bank of the Canal de Caronte between the railway viaduct (air draught 21m) and the motorway bridge (air draught 40m). All movement must be reported on VHF 12 to Fos Port Control at the Port de Bouc observation and control tower.

Charts SHOM 6684, 6907   ECM 505, 507   ADM 2164, 3498

Lights

Canal Caronte	Standard buoyage; some blind beacons.			
Caronte Shoal Corner	Fl G 4s			G Buoy
Traversee de Martigues	Q R	8m	8M	R Post
	Q G	9m	8M	G Post

Marks The entrance to the Canal de Caronte is marked to the south by a green buoy indicating the spit off the corner quay head and to the north by walls and jetties that are not in good order. The canal is buoyed. The two bridges are unmistakable and the entrance to Bassin de Ferrières is to port at the approach to the town and its small road bridge.

Reception	There is a reception quay at Dry Port, and enquiries should be made at the quayside in Ferrieres.		
Moorings	Quay and pontoons.		
Draught	2.5m	**LOA**	12m
Berths	320	**Visitors**	10
Fuel	South quay Ferrières Basin.		
Weather	Teletape: 42.09.09.09. Posted daily at Capitainerie of Dry Port.		
Boatyard Services	Extensive at the Dry Port.		
Shops	A thriving selection for this small community.		
Comment	Unless you have in mind to cruise the Étang de Berre, this is more a winter haven than a leisure port; when either wet or dry, all the accommodation is perfectly acceptable.		

FOS SUR MER/ST GERVAIS
43.25.06 N 04.56.05 E
Tel. 42 47 70 57
Port A2   Town A2

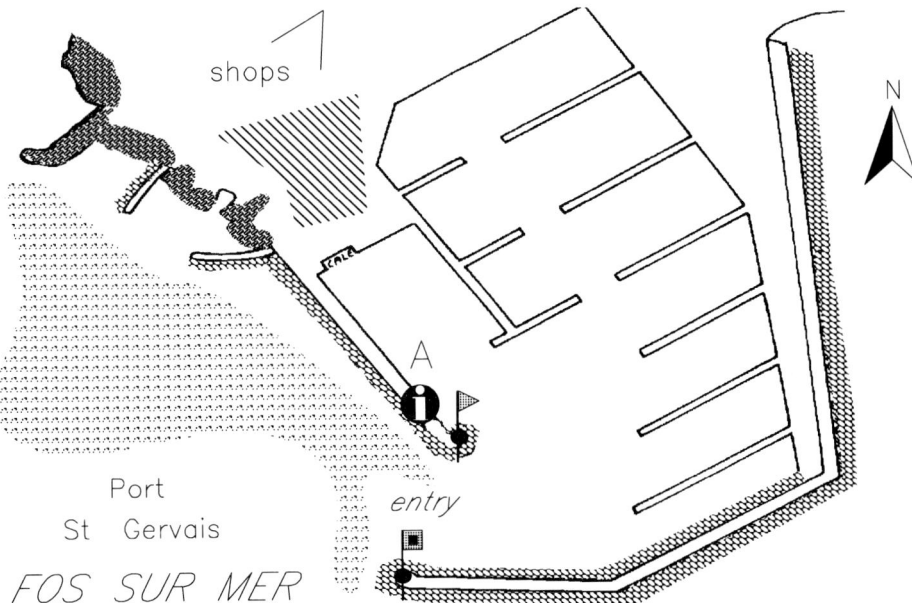

Charts	SHOM 6767, 6684, 6951, 6096 ECM 505, 507 ADM 2164, 3498
LightsMarks	St Gervais IQ(7)WRG 12s 45m 25-21M Tower
Reception	Breakwater Fl G 4s 7m 2M W/G Structure
Moorings	The tower of the St Gervais light.
Draught	Capitainerie: immediately to port on entry.

Moorings	Quays and floating pontoons: to laid chain.
Draught	3m **LOA** 17m
Berths	602 **Visitors** 35
Fuel	Self-service by the HM's Office: account registered inside.
Weather	Teletape: 42.09.09.09. Capitainerie daily; and there is a good weather station.
Boatyard Services	Modest.
Shops	There are shops close to the port for all everyday needs. The town has a good selection and is not far away.

APPROACH

Inside the Golfe de Fos, the chimneys of the power station and the plant of the petroleum refineries to the east are obvious. Of more eye-catching interest is the futuristic tower of the St Gervais light. It stands immediately above the port de plaisance and will lead you straight in.

ENTRY

The ground shelves gently and there is a hazard-free route in round the Digue Sud to where the Capitainerie is obvious to port.

COMMENTARY

This is a modern port de plaisance, artificially gained from the sea and with all reasonable facilities. It is a most amenable port for making adjustments to craft having come down or pre-paring to go up the Rhône – a much more pleasant proposition than Port St Louis.

However, to dismiss Fos sur Mer entirely as no more than a station for rites of passage is to do it an injustice, for the port, the environs and the village are among the friendliest along the coast. ∎

PORT ST LOUIS
43.23.04 N 04.51.01 E
VHF 16, 30
Tel. 42 86 09 63
Port C3   Town C1

Charts	SHOM 6767, 6684, 6951, 6096 ECM 505, 507 ADM 2164, 3498
Lights	St Gervais IQ(7)WRG 12s 45m 25-21M Futuristic tower
	Training Wall (4)WR 12s 14m 9-6M W/R Tower
	Channel Q G G Buoy
	The entrance channel is then marked with standard beacons.
	Tour St Louis Dir Q 16m 20M G/R Tower
	Basin Oc R 4s 8m 7M
Marks	The tower of the St Gervais light is the distant mark. Close in, look for the white and red tower at the head of the south jetty training wall.
Reception	You can try the lock office or the boatyard.
Moorings	Quayside.
Draught	Max 6m Min 1m
Fuel	Service tends to be capricious; it is certainly not reliable.
Weather	Teletape: 42.09.09.09, or go to Fos.
Boatyard Services	Erratic. The name used to be Bayle, and while the agency is still not utterly baleful, it is certainly neither cheerful nor lively.
Shops	Better than basic.

APPROACH

Once Port de Bouc or the St Gervais light has been identified, it will not be difficult to seek out the main entrance to the St Louis channel. It is important not to be misled into the Port de Carteau channel which is to the south. This latter is marked with lit buoys and has leading lights. The white and red tower at the head of the St Louis training wall is the key.

ENTRY

The Canal St Louis is dredged to 8m. Once inside, there is only traffic to look out for. A dead ahead course leads you to the basin where yachts can moor alongside, often rafted up. The mistral rushes right down the High Street and sweeps the quaysides clean – and clean on to all nearby craft.

COMMENTARY

If you do your masting or dismasting at Fos sur Mer, you will miss a face-to-face encounter with the uncultivated, unprocessed joys and fears that go to make up the rough and tumble of this town that developed round the St Louis Tower that was built in the 18th century to defend the mouth of the Grand Rhône. Not yet punch drunk, it is still defending.

There are shops and bars near the lock, and they are much better than any acquaintance with the boatyard would suggest and are particularly worth an early morning foray.

For visiting yachtsmen, the raison d'être of St Louis du Rhône must be vested in its right of passage: doorway to the Med. And like many of London's Soho doorways, it is what lies beyond the dismal, drab and dreary exterior that matters. ∎

Part Three

PORT GARDIAN (SAINTES MARIES DE LA MER) TO BANYULS SUR MER

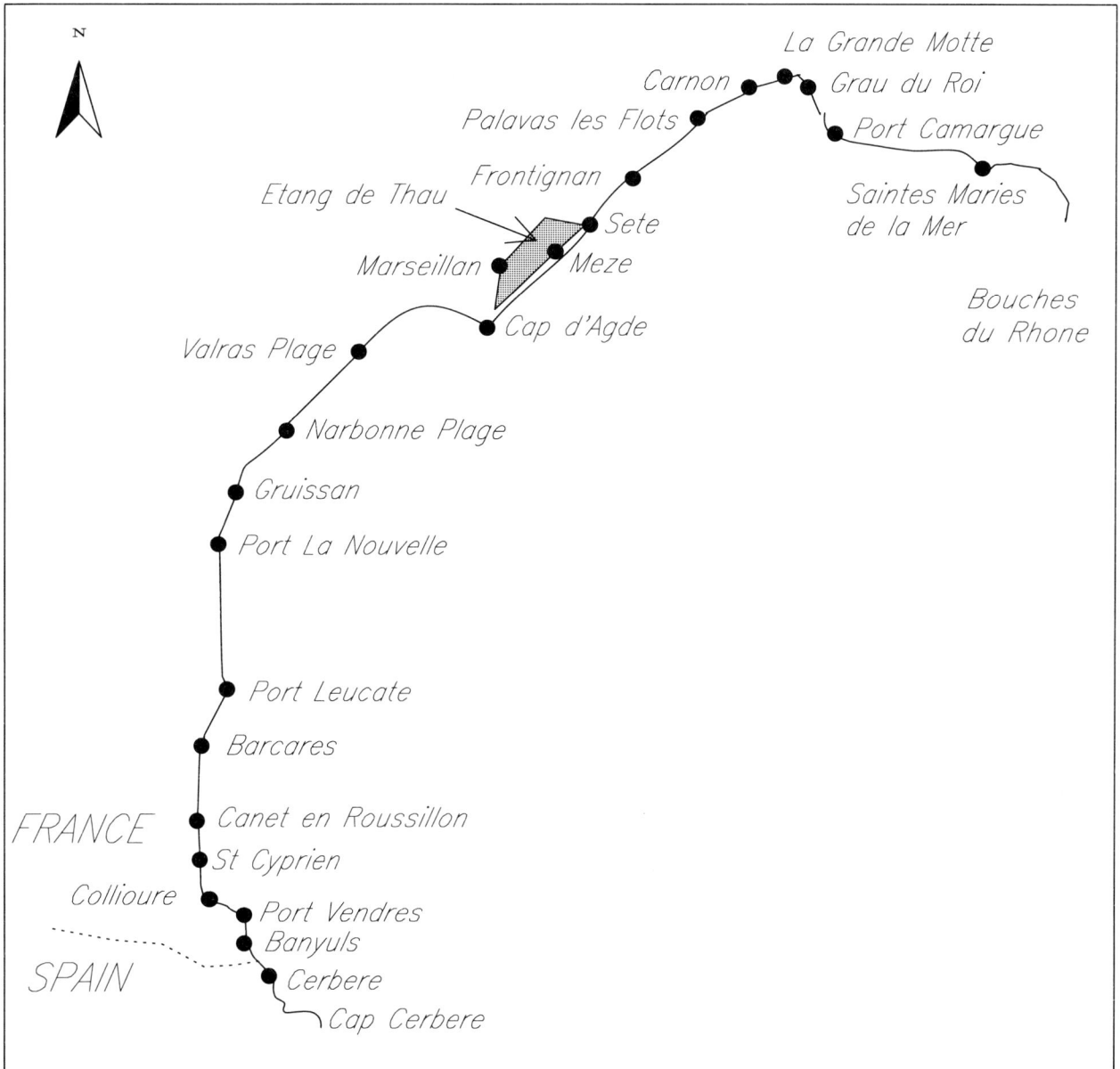

N

La Grande Motte
Carnon
Grau du Roi
Palavas les Flots
Port Camargue
Frontignan
Etang de Thau
Sete
Saintes Maries de la Mer
Marseillan
Meze
Bouches du Rhone
Cap d'Agde
Valras Plage
Narbonne Plage
Gruissan
Port La Nouvelle
Port Leucate
Barcares
Canet en Roussillon
FRANCE
St Cyprien
Collioure
Port Vendres
Banyuls
SPAIN
Cerbere
Cap Cerbere

PORT GARDIAN (SAINTES MARIES DE LA MER)
43.27.10 N 04.25.40 E
Tel. 90 47 85 87
Port A2   Town B2

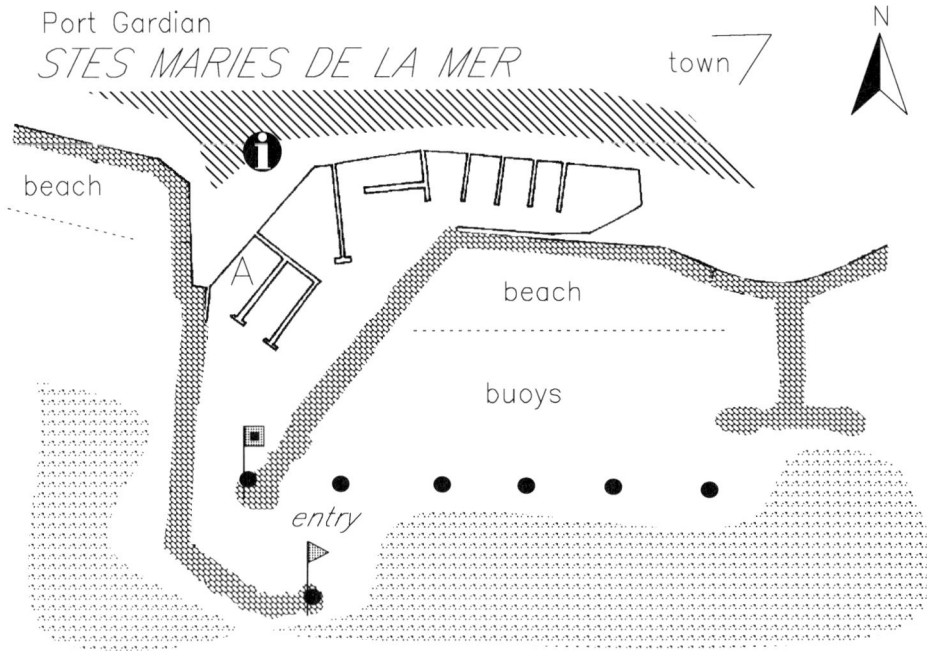

Port Gardian
STES MARIES DE LA MER
town
N
beach
A
beach
buoys
entry

Charts	SHOM 7004, 7053, 7008 ECM 507 ADM 1705
Lights	La Gacholle Fl WRG 4s 17m W13M R10M G10M W Square tower
	Petit Rhône
	Leading Lights: Q G 6m 14M
	Port Gardian Q G 13m 14M
	W Jetty Head Fl R 4s 7M W/R Tower
	E Jetty Head Fl G 2.5s 2.5M G/W Base
Marks	The 30m triple domed white church of Saintes Maries is unmistakable.
Reception	Special alongside quay to port on entry. It is usually attended.
Moorings	Quay, with piles: to laid chain, usually with piles.
Draught	2.8m **LOA** 14m
Berths	350 **Visitors** 60
Fuel	By reception and Capitainerie.
Weather	2–3 times daily in the season, otherwise once.
Boatyard Services	Modest.
Shops	A tourist-based service in the main, but not to be despised. Their afternoon hours relate more to Spanish late siestas than light local fiestas.

APPROACH

From the east, the low-lying Bouches du Rhône make for the hazardous aspects of this trip. It is best to wait for a good forecast before rounding, thus avoiding being caught between the devil of the shallows and the deeps – both of which can be fatal in a really bad blow. So, being able to stand off the appropriate distance, as guided by the excellent navigational aids all round, and keeping to the 20m contour, you will be led towards the red/white safe water mark of Saintes Maries.

At this stage, you will be able to distinguish the various beacons on the Pointe de Beauduc, notably the eponymous light with its white square tower and squat black top. Shortly after, you should pick up La Gacholle light, also with a white square tower and black top. After this, you pick up the Saintes Maries buoy and make for the port on a due northerly course.

From the west, similar care must be taken to keep well clear of the elongated shoal ground off the equally well buoyed Pointe de l'Espiguette, marked by another of the square white towers with black tops.

Once round the seemingly endless curving sweep of the headland, if you stand out to sea no less than half a mile you avoid all dangers. In the distance straight ahead, you will begin to see La Gacholle; and from the deep hinterland of the Golfe de Beauduc, the red sector of this light covers the dangers of the close inshore approach from the west. In particular, you should keep half a mile off until well past the 400m sandbar that builds up at the Grau d'Orgon, out from the mouth of the Petit Rhône. When the entrance is due north, you can turn and make your way into the port.

ENTRY

Along this flat, quite featureless coast, the church of Saintes Maries stands out like a good deed in a naughty world. Making an easterly entry into Port Gardian, you go straight in through the port and starboard light towers on the breakwaters; and from westerly, you round the port tower, giving its bottom stones a clear berth. There is also a submerged spur some 200m east of the leisure 'arena' by the entrance marked by a spar. It presents no threat, as visitors should not navigate near the area.

There is a line of yellow buoys marking the bathing area. Stretching from the starboard breakwater parallel to the beach, it does nothing to help with the traffic problem that can build up in the entrance due to a narrow passage with its blind right hand turn. The reception jetty is then to port. Conditions that make for difficulty in the entry are brought about exclusively by strong easterlies.

COMMENTARY

Port Gardian describes itself as, first of all, the port of a welcoming village: The Saintes Maries de la Mer; and, to sum up, the 'plus joli port de la Mediterranée'. It certainly does all it can to make visitors especially welcome, including a long list of rules and regulations (some unusual) designed for quiet comfort. For example, yachtsmen are requested not to gather in groups on the quays, and not to light fires on the quays or the port platforms. Also, transactions of any kind are prohibited within the port area.

The church is special: built as a fortress with mere holes for windows, it was a place of refuge against the marauding Saracens. The sculptured lions devouring their prey are symbolic.

There is legend in profusion surrounding Les Saintes, as it is known locally (or Li Santo in Provençal). The most dramatic is that which tells of a vessel without oars or sails being set adrift from the Holy Land with a full complement of men and women all of whom were destined for sainthood – including at least three called Mary, Lazarus and Sidonius. Miraculously and safely they landed here to go their separate proselytising ways. Mary Jacobé and Mary Salomé stayed at the landfall, together with a black servant, Sara. This last soul appealed to the gypsies. Because she was the only member of that motley crew who was dark skinned and not a saint, she became their patroness. Nearly twenty centuries later, tremendous pilgrimages are made in May for two of the Saintes Maries and in October for the other two. This latter is the famous gypsy celebration, when they take over the whole area.

But even at other times, both in and out of season, you will find that there are market touts of assorted types, garrulous gypsies, geriatric *gardians* and pseudo farandolers who all trade on the holy reputation of the village. These, and all other vagrants who possess the knack of discerning every possible soft touch, should be studiously avoided. Avert your gaze, for it takes only acknowledgement of their presence, even if that is a firm 'Non', for them to be attached to you inordinately. ∎

PORT CAMARGUE
43.31.20 N 04.07.50 E
Tel. 66 51 43 09
Port and 'Town' Both B1

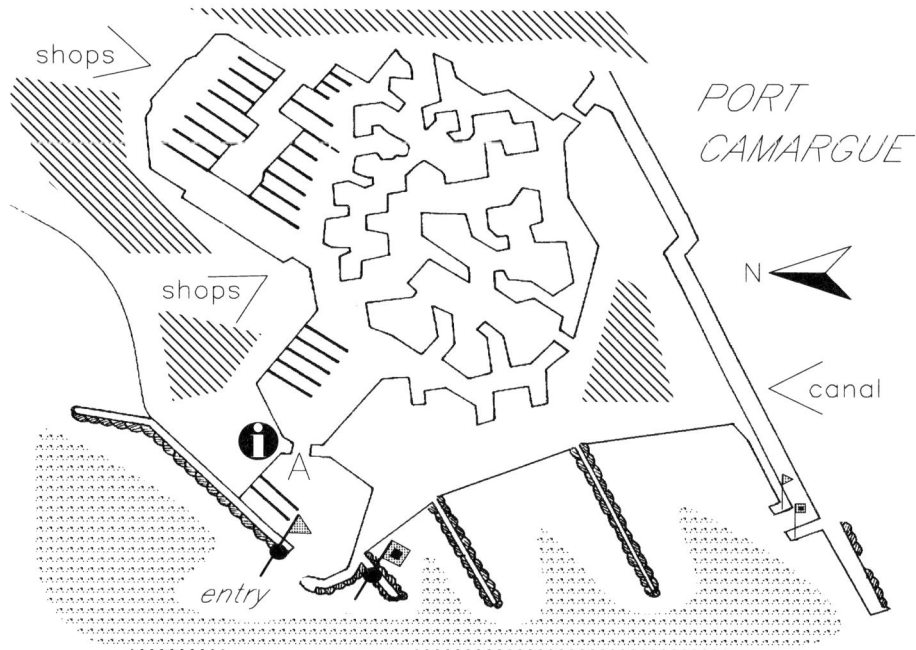

Charts	SHOM 7004, 7053, 7008 ECM 507, 508 ADM 1705			
Lights	L'Espiguette	Fl(3) 15s	27m 24M	
	Canal Entrance	Oc G 4s	4M	W/R Tower
		Oc R 4s	4M	W/R Tower
	Canal Breakwater	Q(9) 15s	8M	YBY Cardinal
	Port Entrance	Fl R 4s	6M	W/R Tower
		Fl G 4s	9M	G/W Base
	Port Breakwater	VQ(9) 10s	6M	YBY Cardinal

Marks From the east, L'Espiguette lighthouse and the two Cardinal buoys should be identified. From the west, the unique architecture of the pyramid at La Grande Motte and the old light at the more recent water tower at Le Grau du Roi stand out well.

Reception At the unmistakably architectured 25m tall, white and stylish Capitainerie. You will see it to port when you have crossed the outer harbour.

Moorings Concrete jetties and floating pontoons: some with catwalks, some with piles, and some with buoys.

Draught 5m–3m   **LOA** 40m

Berths 1995 + 2140   **Visitors** 200

Fuel At the junction of the Boucainville and Lapérouse Quays. Upon leaving the Capitainerie, proceed past the five rows of visitors' floating pontoons to port and then take the first major turn to port, where the fuel station will be visible straight ahead. There is a large jetty with ample pumps.

Weather Twice daily at the Capitainerie and at various points around the harbour. Antiope in season. Also, Telephone: 66 51 80 81.

Boatyard Services Comprehensive.

Shops These are good. They are in the Centre Commercial, behind the Capitainerie and lead to gardens that overlook the bay. There are various supermarkets, boutiques and artisans galore. Bearing in mind the size and ambience of Port Camargue, prices are not unreasonable.

APPROACH

From the west, the whole approach through the Golfe d'Aigues Mortes is hazard free, and it is impossible to miss the famous pyramid of La Grande Motte, the old tower of the Grau du Roi, and the conglomerate that is Port Camargue.

From the east, care must be taken to get clear of the shoal ground off the well buoyed Pointe de l'Espiguette, with its two Cardinal buoys and square white tower and black top. Once round the long haul of the headland, if you stand out to sea no less than half a mile you avoid all dangers.

ENTRY

From whichever direction you approach Port Camargue, you will find it difficult to pinpoint the entrance until quite close, such is the confusion of buildings and backgrounds. From the west the Grau du Roi is unmistakable, but from the east there is a canal entrance that looks misleadingly like the real thing.

In any case, you will know for sure when you are close, because of the presence of the mini-multitudes of fishing craft of all shapes and sizes that foregather here in a density that I have not encountered in any other area off the Mediterranean coast of France.

However, once you are close to, there is a strangely dark and dismally half-threatening sculpture on the sea wall. Beyond it, well inside the port, the singular white building of the Capitainerie is eye-catchingly contrasted.

Keep well away (some 250m at least) when approaching from the SW because of the sandspit that builds up outside. Entrance is usually problem free except in the extremes of bad weather, since Port Camargue is blessed by a uniquely protected position.

You may well come across boats at anchor in the outer harbour, some even in the fairway, and also unlit – in spite of the obvious dangers and harbour regulations strictly prohibiting it. At night, extra care should be taken when crossing. The Capitainerie is always plain to make out.

COMMENTARY

The Port Camargue project, which was begun in 1969, is the most eastern of the Languedoc–Roussillon coastal developments. It is made up of nearly 400 acres, of which half are of water. There is no high-rise growth here: the buildings are never more than two storeys and are laid out with gardens in near-symmetry throughout the port.

The shops are accessible and inexpensive, so it is a good idea to eat on board, since the restaurants do not, on the whole, offer very much in the way of the best of Provençal or even French cuisine, and they have become much attracted to London prices.

The essence of the surrounding countryside is contained within the romantic name of the port: The Camargue, famous for its pink flamingoes, white horses and black bulls; and its gypsies and *gardians* and their (now modern and attractive) cabins. Thanks to a local planning edict, all buildings in that area must be designed and built within the local tradition. It is a discipline that has worked well.

All the services, domestic, boat and leisure, are within striking distance and everything within Port Camargue is up to date and smoothly organised. Not too far away are the splendidly extensive beaches of the Pointe de l'Espiguette, where the lighthouse stands in the middle of a sparse Camargue landscape, and where, among the dunes, constantly wind-blown, you can find tamarisk, sea rockets, cakiles and thistles.

However, for anything seriously more historical, beyond the last two decades that is, you must turn to next door Grau du Roi or inland to Aigues Mortes. ∎

GRAU DU ROI
43.32.00 N 04.08.00 E
VHF 11
Tel. 66 51 66 08
Port A2   Town A2

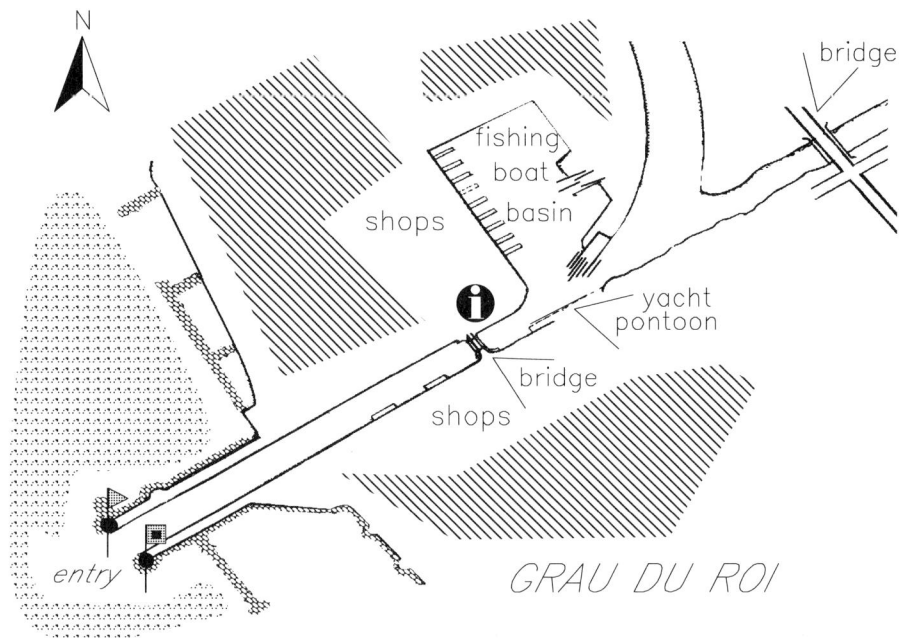

Charts	SHOM 7004, 7053, 7008 ECM 507, 508 ADM 1705
Lights	Oc(2)R 6s 9m 9M W/R Tower
	VQ(3)G 2s 10m 10M G/W Base
Marks	From the east, L'Espiguette lighthouse and the two Cardinal buoys should be identified. Virtually halfway between La Grande Motte and Port Camargue, there are two unusual light towers at the entrance. Together with the water tower, the old lighthouse makes a clear landmark.
Reception	In the fish dock, but it is necessary to find a berth in the approach channel to wait for the opening of the bridge.
Moorings	Floating pontoons.
Draught	2.3m–4m **LOA** 15m
Berths	162 **Visitors** 15
Fuel	From the quay at the north-west corner of the harbour.
Weather	Twice daily at the town hall and fire station.
Boatyard Services	Good.
Shops	This is an old town and shopping here is excellent in the traditional local manner.

112

APPROACH

If you are coming from Port Gardian at Saintes Maries, you need to stand half a mile off the headland of l'Espiguette, as for Port Camargue.

Coming from elsewhere, east or west, there is no hazard. However, the coast shelves and shoals, and there is no point in trying to see how close in you can navigate; a sober half mile is prudent. The pyramid of La Grande Motte to the west and the buildings of Port Camargue bracket the port which is itself marked by its classic old lighthouse. The light towers at the entrance are singular and obvious.

ENTRY

Weather from the south and west can cause problems: first a heavy swell; second, a residual sandbar to the south of the breakwaters. However, the entry is generally straight in and hazard free; the only problem is the narrow (40m) entrance with the possibility of heavy fishing traffic, in and out at all times. There can also be quite a strong current flowing out of the canal, which is no wider.

Fishing and pleasure ferry boats are moored along both sides, two and three deep. There is nowhere to berth here, except when waiting for the bridge to open. It is then deemed acceptable to ask a fishing boat if you can go alongside.

COMMENTARY

Situated at the entrance of the Grande Roubine, Grau du Roi is one on its own. The word Grau is Provençal for estuary or river mouth (the equivalent of the Catalan of Grao) and all round there is an ambience of this non-contemporary world. It is a small, self-contained fishing port that has withstood the ravages of time and weather as well as the assaults of invading brigands and, more recently, the onslaughts of tourism. It is not without modern services and facilities, but the essence of the place is rooted in its past.

Two of its food specialities are *bourride,* a combination of boiled fish and potatoes coated with hot garlic mayonnaise, and *rouille,* a mixture of boiled octopus and potatoes with garlic mayonnaise. This either sounds tempting or sickening depending on your taste, but there are always the classic local wines of the Listel cellars, where tasting is freely available.

The surrounding area has been created by alluvial deposits from the vast Rhône Delta. In 1580 a flood caused a breakthrough in the then offshore bar, which is where the present town is sited. It was then known as Consac de Gagne Petit. Henry IV planned the exploitation of the breach, and it was then, for the first time, called Grau du Roi. Since then, and through the revolutionary troubles, it has been known variously as Grau le Pelletier and Grau Napoléon.

In 1806 only a few fishermen's cabins existed, but in 1822 the lighthouse that still stands on the west breakwater was built; and in 1830 the present community was born. By the end of the century there were still fewer than a thousand souls living here, but today there is a 100-strong fishing fleet and a busy tourist industry based on the (somewhat optimistic) boast of 300 days of sunshine a year.

Not far up the canal is the old walled town with its name permeated in melancholy: Aigues Mortes, the City of Dead Waters. The place has been the scene of so many wars that they are not all commemorated. It was taken, lost and taken again by the king's troops and his opponents during the old adversarial wars between the Armagnacs and the Burgundians, the Hundred Years War, and all the religious wars. It was the point of departure for the Crusades of Louis IX in 1248 and 1270, from which latter he never returned, having succumbed to the plague in Tunis. It was also the meeting place, in 1538, of those powerful rulers, François I and Charles V.

The first view of Aigues Mortes that you get coming from Grau du Roi is probably the best there is, and it affords a splendid introduction to a tour of the ramparts that date back to 1272. The famous Constance Tower was built in 1740–49 by Louis to protect those of his subjects he had managed to lure to the bleak spot by promises of tax exemption.

There are many eye-catching facets to Aigues, but two others in particular are the Gothic Church of Notre Dame des Sablons; and, for those who want to take their history whiling away the hours outside, there is, right in the heart of the town, the pleasant old square called, predictably, the Place St Louis. ■

LA GRANDE MOTTE

43.33.30 N 04.04.55 E
Tel. 67 56 50 06
Port B1   Town B2

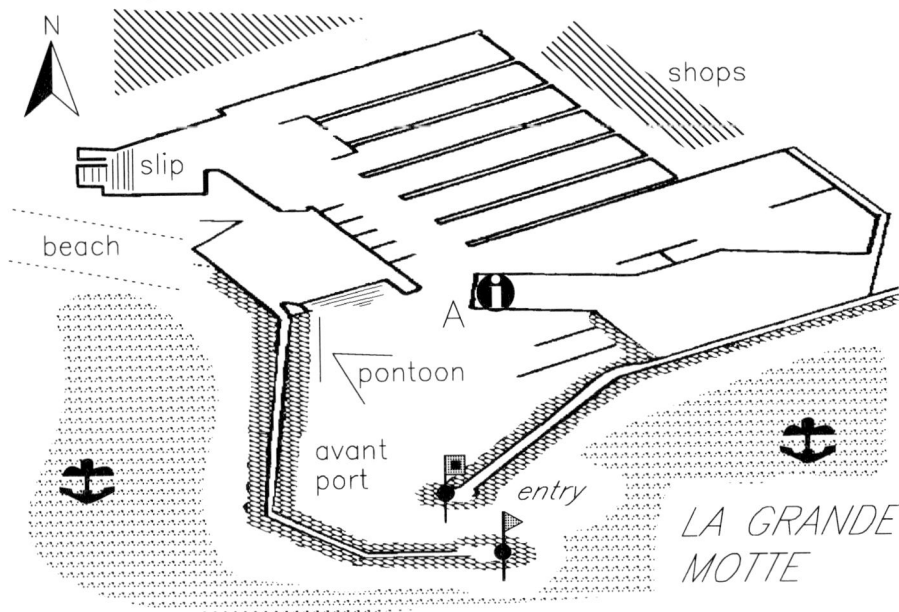

Charts	SHOM 7004, 7053, 7008 ECM 507, 508 ADM 1705
Lights	W Jetty Head Fl(2)R 6s 12m 9M W/R Tower
	E Jetty Head Fl G 4s 9m 3M G/W Base
Marks	From the east, L'Espiguette lighthouse and the two Cardinal buoys should be identified. From all directions, the great pyramid stands out, and there is an almost equally splendid eye-catching white edifice at the end of the west jetty.
Reception	There is a quay at the Capitainerie, immediately ahead, once you have passed through the outer harbour.
Moorings	Quay and fixed/floating pontoons.
Draught	3m **LOA** 30m
Berths	1364 **Visitors** 15
Fuel	Towards the Zone Technique: past pontoon O and opposite pontoon C. NB: maximum draught at the fuel quay is 2.5m.
Weather	Posted four times daily at the Capitainerie. Telephone: 36 65 08 08/09; also 67 56 52 78.
Boatyard Services	Comprehensive.
Shops	No more than is sufficient and necessary.

APPROACH

There is no offshore problem of any kind here in the well-protected Golfe d'Aigues Mortes. The renowned architecture of the pyramid of La Grande Motte means, in literal translation, Great Clod or Lump (of earth), but whatever it means, it is the biggest and best landmark for miles.

ENTRY

The sea wall sculpture that welcomes you on the end of the southern jetty, which must be left to port, carries the legend of a large M; and if that is not enough, it flames in brilliant red at night.

The entrance is 95m wide and is dredged to 3.5m. However, craft with more than 2.5m draught are advised to keep to the centre of the channel and not get too close to the green light. The only difficult conditions for entry are when there is wind, weather and/or swell from the south east which can also cause a heavy surf.

COMMENTARY

It is impossible to visit La Grande Motte without viewing and then forming a view of the outstanding pyramid architecture, which the inhabitants claim is unique on the Mediterranean coast. The project was conceived, designed and constructed all of a piece, starting in 1967, by a team led by Jean Balladur. The main buildings, decisively if not aggressively modern in their ziggurat-like traps, were created in the pyramid style so that maximum exposure to the sun could be obtained. The smaller apartments were, perhaps as a sop to the conventional and the many objectors, built at lower levels and in accordance with traditional Provençal profiles. Critics condemn it as tawdry and heartless in human terms, and cheap and 'contemporary brutish' in its architecture – such opponents call it La Grande Grotte.

Whatever its opponents may have had to say, it has proved a success and has an attendant population of something in excess of 80 000, and is still expanding. It is a leisure centre without equal, if not par excellence. Certainly it is one in which the government takes much pride, being the first of the six major unités planned in 1963 to transform the little-known and less explored coast of Languedoc–Roussillon into a holiday-maker's paradise.

Before it could be thought of as a plausible proposition though, it was necessary to drain the stagnant lagoons that had been mosquito hotbeds for centuries. After this, and much conservationist controversy about spraying, the area was rendered less troubled by the little pests.

Surprisingly then, after all this effort, the marina is not well served by the easily available shops; and this is a project where yachtsmen were served first. One would expect better things of this modern miracle of the Big M. The shops do, of course, suffice, since many folk live here full time, but they do not excite. Except, that is, for one minor diversion: there is an expensive discovery for those devoted to the arts and crafts of interior decoration, as well as choice fabrics. It is a branch of the international Souleiado.

Lawrence Durrell lived in Languedoc at one time, and here is his impression of the area:

'The horizon like some keystone between soil and air

Halves out all earth in quiet satisfaction,

In tones of dust or biscuit, particularly kind to

Loaves of the sunburnt soil the plough turned back ...' ∎

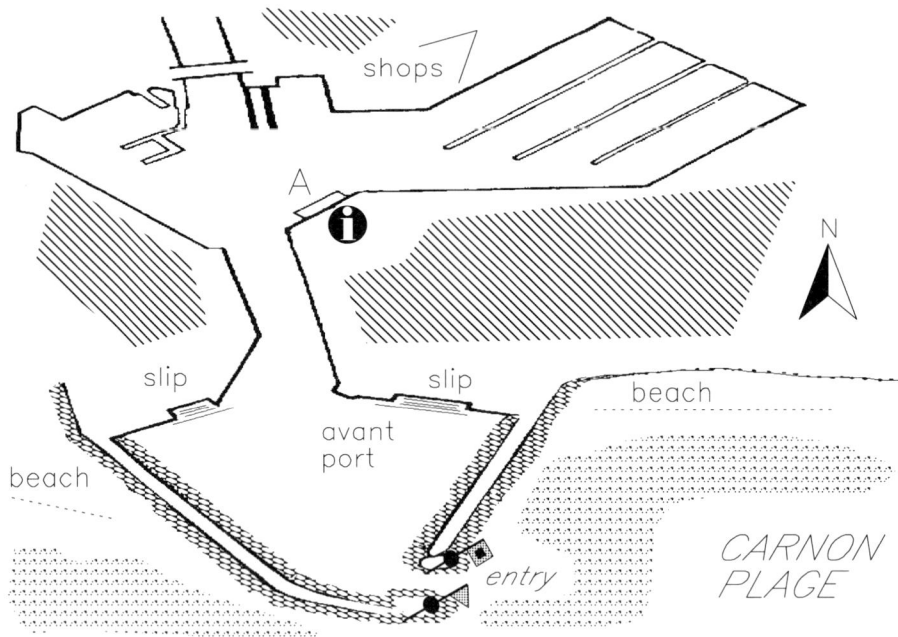

CARNON PLAGE
43.32.30 N 03.58.30 E
Tel. 67 68 10 78
Port B2   Town B2

Charts	SHOM 7053, 7008 ECM 507, 508 ADM 1705
Lights	SW Jetty Head Fl(4)R 12s 8m 10M W/R Tower
	E Jetty Head Fl G 4s 8m 3M G/W Base
Marks	The Carnon water tower and the two light towers on the jetties are conspicuous.
Reception	Can be clearly seen at the far end of the approach canal on the starboard hand.
Moorings	Floating pontoons and quays to piles.
Draught	3m **LOA** 15m
Berths	700 **Visitors** 50
Fuel	The quay is to starboard, just before the Capitainerie, as you reach the end of the canal.
Weather	Posted twice daily at the Capitainerie. Telephone: 36 65 08 08/09.
Boatyard Services	Moderate.
Shops	Adequate but uninspiring.

APPROACH

The approach is straightforward whether from Palavas les Flots, La Grande Motte, or from seaward. However, there is little in the way of substantial landmarks to identify the place. Palavas is fairly distinctive with its high-rise flats, and the pyramid of La Grande Motte is unmistakable. Carnon has a water tower.

ENTRY

The entry should be made by tending slightly to the red port light tower on the west jetty. The final entry is secure under all conditions except strong weather from the south east.

COMMENTARY

There is little to say about Carnon, other than it is a popular lido for many folk from nearby Montpellier. It is one of those beach and marina resorts that exist for no other purpose than tempting crowds down to the sea in ships, and down to the beach in (or out of) bikinis. This is where La Jeunesse Dorée pursue La Dolce Vita, and it has been perhaps unflatteringly dubbed the French Florida.

It is purposeful and it works, but this particular venue has little to offer other than convenience for the sea, the sun, and the miles of sand, sand, and more sand. ◼

PALAVAS LES FLOTS
43.31.35 N 03.55.60 E
Tel. 67 68 00 90
Port C2   Town B2

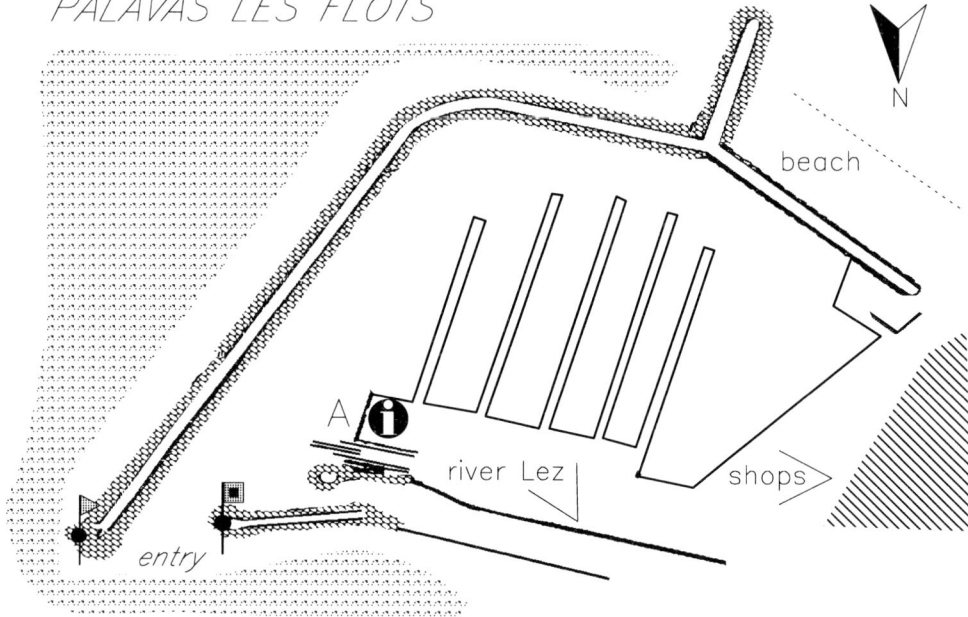

Charts	SHOM 7053, 7054, 7008 ECM 508 ADM 1705
Lights	W Jetty Head Fl R 4s 8m 8M W/R Tower
	E Jetty Head Oc G 4s 8m 8M G/W Base
Marks	The especially massive water tower in the town to the east and the vast blocks of flats are easy to identify.
Reception	Once through the breakwater entrance, leave the river to starboard, and the fuel quay with crane will appear ahead immediately to starboard. The Capitainerie is on the corner by the first reception pontoon, designated E.
Moorings	To pontoons, fingers and quays.
Draught	2m **LOA** 14m
Berths	Port 620; Bassin 200; **Visitors** 40
	Canal 200
Fuel	At the reception quay by the Capitainerie.
Weather	Posted once daily. Telephone: 36 65 08 08/09.
Boatyard Services	Modest.
Shops	Full range in the town.

APPROACH

Roughly halfway between La Grande Motte and Sète, there is little to distinguish it other than its dominant water tower and high-rise flats, both of which are conspicuous.

ENTRY

A straightforward standard entry. Visitors are advised to tend towards the red port light tower on the end of the SW jetty. The entry is difficult only in winds from the south or east.

COMMENTARY

Different from its neighbours – Carnon Plage to the north and the port de plaisance of Frontignan to the south – Palavas les Flots was already something before it became a holiday resort, and it has retained a goodly taste of it. Basically, Palavas was a small fishing port and, like many of the fishing communities in this area, it was particularly devoted to the tuna sport.

It is situated at the mouth of now dredged River/Canal Lez, with the marina to the west and the main drag of the beach to the east. It came to the forefront as the main seaside resort for the people of Montpellier in 1872 when a minor miracle for the area was established: a celebrated little train service that shuttled to and from the coast. It was for a long time the only stretch of beach along the Languedoc–Roussillon coast that had been 'civilised' for holiday-makers, and it continued in its unique position until the government development scheme of the 1960s.

Upon entry, the most eye-catching feature is the cable car that carries people across the river at its seaward end, saving them the hike up the main street to the road bridge. On both sides of this river lie the characterful halves of the old town, which the Lez successfully divides. One side of the water is supposed to provide the superior neighbourhood in which to live, but I have never been able to determine which that may be. There is the usual conglomeration of tourist restaurants and giftshops, but they do not drown the less superficial side of the town. All the worthwhile shops are in the back streets, many of them behind closed dark doors – but which open to disclose choice goods, bits and pieces.

Palavas is one of the centres of the regions that is quite fanatical about its Joutes Nautiques. These water jousts are famous in Languedoc–Roussillon, because they were born of the embarkation of St Louis for the Crusades, and they represent one of the oldest pieces of local folklore. Special Catalan-type craft, one in classic blue and the other in classic red, are fitted with a kind of elongated bowsprit, a for'ard outstation on which stands a 'knight' with shield and lance. The boats are rowed ferociously towards one another by a crew of eight, and each forward lance/spear-holder attempts to lance the other into the water. Much of the time both fall into the water, and no one ever seems the worse for the butting or the dousing. Eventually, of course, blues or reds prevail, and there are many loud and proud salutes to the noise of the bands that accompany the cheering and jeering of the crowds at the quayside. Les Joutes Nautiques symbolise the spirit of this ancient fishing port in a unique and unforgettable manner.

If a quieter life is more your style, just down the coast among the étangs and sandbars is Maguelone, the port for Montpellier in the Middle Ages. It is supposed to have a history going back to the 2nd century, and it is the site of a list of religious wars as long as your arm. Its fortunes rose and fell with Catholics and Protestants alike, until Louis XIII lost patience entirely with the Protestant inhabitants of that time and in 1633 destroyed the defences and houses in one fell swoop.

Maguelone used to be an islet, but is now permanently joined to the mainland. Today there is only the Romanesque Cathedral, restored in the 19th century by the Fabrège family who owned the estate in which it stood. More a fortress than a church (like that at Saintes Maries), its thick walls with only narrow openings for windows, its vast single-arched nave, and housings for nearly a hundred cannon are all there is left to speak of the glory that once was paramount here. ■

FRONTIGNAN
43.26.00 N 03.46.30 E
Tel. 67 48 75 21
Port C2   Town B2

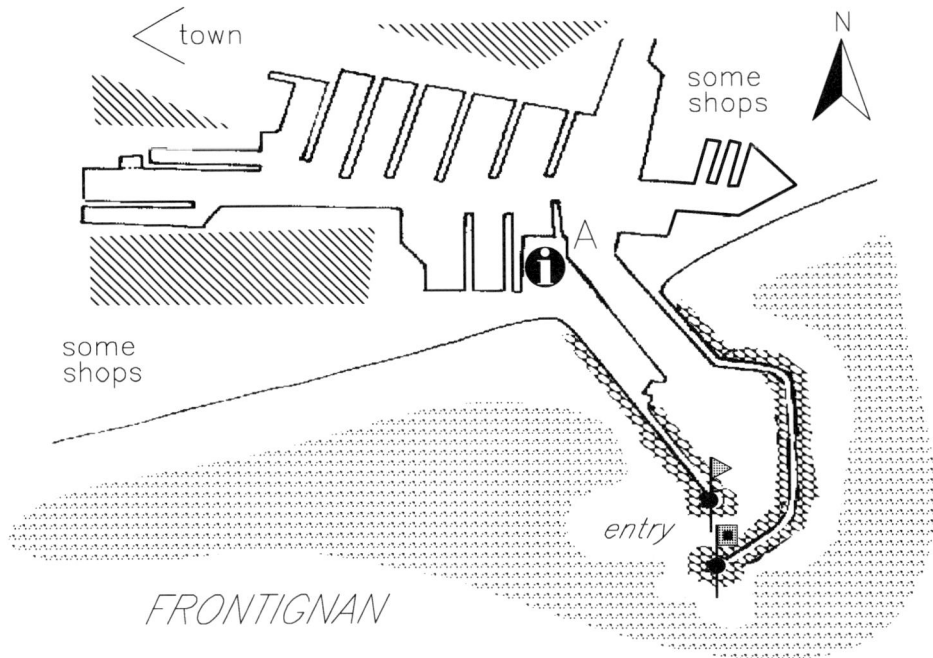

Charts	SHOM 7053, 7054, 7008 ECM 508 ADM 1705, 2606
Lights	N Breakwater Fl(2)R 6s 9m 7M W/R Tower
	S Breakwater Fl G 4s 9m 7M G/W Base
Marks	To the west, the light at the peak of Mont St Clair at Sète is dominant; just above sea level the seemingly endless low line of oil refinery works almost reaches it, punctuated by the occasional high-flying chimneys and cooling towers.
Reception	Once through the small outer port, the present low-key portacabin office and fuel berth are obvious on the port hand.
Moorings	Mainly to floating pontoons with fingers. Some berths are to piles.
Draught	2.5m **LOA** Pontoons 11m; Piles 18m
Berths	600 **Visitors** 60
Fuel	At the reception quay by the Capitainerie.
Weather	Posted twice daily at the Capitainerie. Montpellier-Fréjorgues Airport Telephone: 67 65 81 81.
Boatyard Services	Adequate to comprehensive.
Shops	Minimal on site; only the bare essentials are available. The nearest good centre is in the town of Frontignan (2.5km distant, and no public transport).

APPROACH
With the exception of the end of the long line of refinery apparatus, there is nothing to help you distinguish this small port from its background. However, the refinery works stretch all the way from Sète, where Mont St Clair is unmistakable.

Approaching from the west, it is the first sign of marina life on the shore. From this direction, it is necessary to watch out for the large unlit buoys that stand out to the east of Sète.

ENTRY
The final approach should be from the south west, and is on the 3m contour line. Keep as far out as this until you move in as the bottom shelves quite rapidly in places. Entry is not advised in strong winds and weather from the south east, when rolling, sometimes breaking, waves make the entrance dangerous. There is an immediate turn to port after you pass the light towers, and the channel to the canal then opens straight up.

COMMENTARY
A marina is a marina is a ... and so on. Here, a few kilometres distant from the town from which it takes its name, there is an absolutely standard marina with all standard services and facilities. The staff, somewhat unexpectedly bearing in mind their office and general conditions of work, are among the most helpful and efficient along this stretch of coast. These are important attributes when choosing a marina.

If all you want is a base for cruising the area, it could not be better, but if you have in mind something more characterful, or even entertaining, then Frontignan will not be for you. However, it will certainly give you a good night's rest at a calm berth, which, it is worth noting, is more than can be said for the next port of call going south – namely, Sète. There is a night club, the Cythere, close to the berths most often used for visitors.

If you are near the crossroads of the canal and the marina, you will be able to observe with interest and some amusement the coming and going of the unusual local fishing craft, each one usually powered by a massive outboard – or two or three.

Clearly, they are more at home in the étangs than in the open sea, but there is little in the way of Mediterranean weather that keeps these hardy souls and their small craft from venturing seaward. They leave the amateurs to go after the tuna – their own catch being almost exclusively shellfish. When they go out in the small hours in their peculiar craft and strange clothes, it is difficult to know whether they are Musselmen or Musulmen.

The darker side of Frontignan for many is the presence of the massive refinery project of Mobil Oil Française. When the wind is wrong, you get a mild-to-powerful taste of the sweet-to-sickly odours from the chimneys. No perfumery this.

On the bright side is Frontignan town itself. It is an old town, on the Étang d'Ingril and the Canal du Rhône à Sète. There is very good shopping in this traditional centre; but nothing will lift the spirits as much as a visit to the Coopérative du Muscat for a taste of the golden/amber liquid known as the Muscat de Frontignan. It is a delicious wine, deliciously strong, and to be taken as an aperitif or with/or after dessert. There is more however: you must not leave without marking (as in mark, learn and inwardly digest) the local variety of their Marc.

After savouring the Muscat, you may feel up to scrutinising yet another church fortified against the world, with a cannon platform masquerading as a clock tower. ■

SETE

43.24.00 N 03.42.00 E
Tel. (Société Nautique) 67 74 98 97
Port C1   Town A2

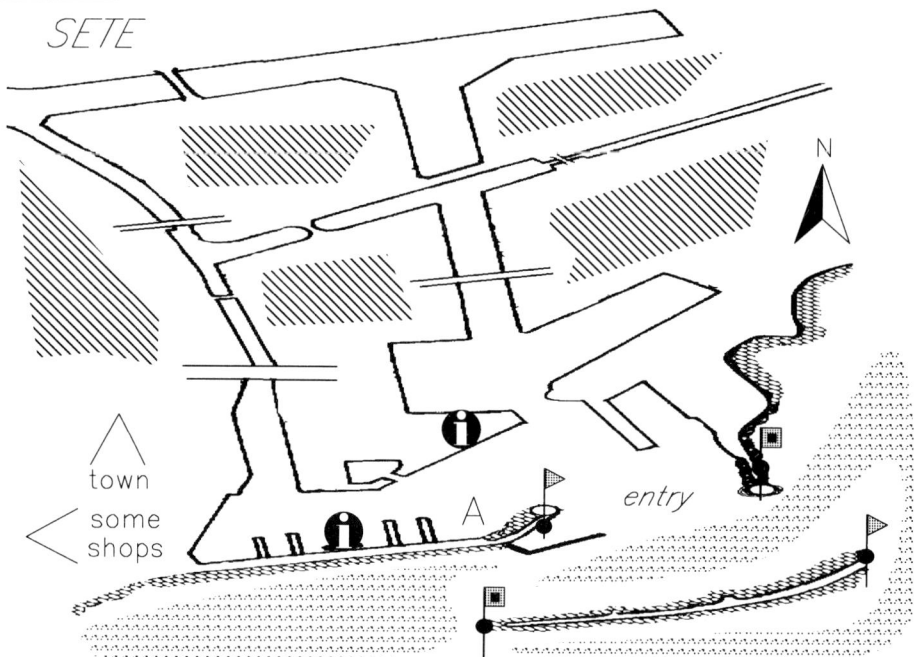

Charts	SHOM 6839,7053,7054,7008	ECM 508,509		ADM 1705,2606		
Lights	Mont St Clair	Fl 5s	93m	29M		
	East Breakwater	Q R	12m	9M	W/R	Tower
		Fl(2)G 6s	10m		G/W	Base
	Centre Breakwater	Oc R 4s	21m	10M	W/R	Tower
	West Breakwater	Iso G 4s	10m	6M	G	Structure
		Fl(2) 6s	10m	7M	R	Structure
	Môle St Louis	Fl(4)WR 12s	34m	15/11M	W	Tower R Top

Marks   Mont St Clair and its light are prominent, as are the light towers on the harbour's sea wall and jetties.

Reception   The pontoons of the Société Nautique de Sète are to port in the 'inner' outer harbour, by the Môle St Louis. There is no reception quay as such, but visitors' moorings are immediately to port. There is also a small quay by the crane. The able and helpful staff are very often in attendance in the area and you may find yourself summoned, if not by bells, then by a whistle. Jilling around usually brings forth signs of life. Reception is in the upper office by the floating restaurant.

Moorings   Floating pontoons to buoys.

Draught	4m	**LOA**	30m
Berths	280	**Visitors**	30

Fuel	On the quay near the reception office.
Weather	Posted daily at the Société Nautique.
Boatyard Services	Comprehensive.
Shops	Excellent.

APPROACH

From west and east, Mont St Clair dominates the approach. From Frontignan, you need to be aware of the large unlit mooring buoys just to the east of Sète. From the other direction, there is a prohibited area just off Marseillan Plage. Otherwise, the way is clear and plain; it is frequently marked by the passage or anchoring of the big commercial ships that use the port.

ENTRY

There are two entries – east and west – and both are made very noticeable by their large light towers. Yachtsmen are asked to use the west passage, as the east is reserved for commercial traffic; and, if you do use it, you are asked to call the Capitainerie on VHF 12 for traffic movements. Many local leisure craft ignore all the foregoing.

Yachtsmen are also advised by the Capitainerie that the entry is safe under all conditions except when there are winds from south/south east/east – blowing at Beaufort Force 10!

Moorings for leisure craft are in the old port, which is on the inner side of the Môle St Louis. Turn to port round the end of the vast sea wall with its conspicuous light tower, and they are on your port hand.

COMMENTARY

The guide book to Sète (or, as of old, Cette, Bains de Mer, Reine des Plages de la Mediterranée) gets off to a flourishing start: 'Between the blue shades of the sky and the sea, Sète embroiders its lace with the streets and canals, coiling up round the Mont Saint Clair.' Sète is also one of the major outlets from the Canal du Rhône à Sète, by the famous Étang du Thau, and the town is a splendid place. However, the same cannot be said of its harbour – one of the biggest in France.

There are five mobile bridges to be negotiated, and their operators suffer neither fools nor yachtsmen gladly. If you are to get through safely, you must be prompt to the minute and very fast. Other than the Société Nautique in the old port, there are few berths of any kind, and even fewer that have services or are secure. Most are alongside the noisiest parts of the port. Some may be gratis, but you pay a high price for that gratuity. The fishing boats demand right of way at all times. Indeed, it was put to me this way: 'The Captain of the Port is not the Captain of the Port: the fishing mafia is king.' They make life intolerable at the Société Nautique moorings from three until six morning and evening, storming in and out at full speed and creating near havoc. That they then have to wait in line 100m ahead makes it all the more lunatic.

However, the Société Nautique does what it can. Masts can be easily craned and they will help arrange your bridge exits and entrances.

In the town itself there are excellent markets. The central covered market is open daily for meat, fish and veg. On Wednesday mornings there is a grand open air market, and on Friday mornings there is a street market near the railway station. Here local traders sell their personally tended small crops, home-made breads and cheeses, hand-raised eggs and poultry, and strange-looking biscuits, cakes and buns.

Some of their stalls carry so little that one wonders how it can be worth their while to make the early morning journey and spend the hours behind a miniature display of (say) carrots. For it is a fact that they specialise; not only, for example, in root crops, but also in just one kind of root. However, French men and women have developed a sophisticated knack of choosing between this man's leeks and that woman's onions, that girl's ducks' eggs and that bearded youth's smelly goat's cheese. In fact, it seems obligatory to handle the goods to show your appreciation of their virtue. To reject the tomatoes without having inspected them fully is taken as a slur on the integrity of the trader.

When it comes to eating out, there is an even greater choice. There are hundreds of restaurants, with many specialising in the regional dishes of Languedoc. Red wines abound and can be drunk abundantly at less than 10F a litre.

Sète was the birthplace of Paul Valéry, and one of his most famous poems was written about the Cimetière Marin (in fact, 'St Charles'). A special visit should be made to the Musée Paul Valéry, which is at the top of a hill. The climb up to this, hopefully, won't quite put you in the nearby Cimetière Marin, where rest Valéry and Jean Vilar. ■

Étang du Thau

MARSEILLAN
43.19.00 N 03.33.00 E
Tel. 67 77 34 93
Port B2   Town A2

Lights					
Les Onglous	Oc(2)WR 6s	10m	14/10M	W Tower R Top
N Head Breakwater	Q	5m	10M	YB Cardinal
S Head Breakwater	F W			
NE Jetty	Iso G 4s	7m	5M	G Structure
N Head New Jetty	Oc R 4s	1m		Strip light
Spur Head	F R			
SW Jetty Head	Iso W 4s	2m		Strip light

Marks The lighthouse of Les Onglous is conspicuous; and at the entrance, both the light tower with its clear town legend, and the Château du Port, are obvious.

Reception Once within the main body of the port, visitors' moorings will be seen to starboard on the NE Quai Autouin-Gros opposite the Capitainerie.

Moorings Quay and pontoons.

Draught 1.2m–2m   **LOA** 15m

Berths 200   **Visitors** 15

Fuel Quayside near the Capitainerie.

Weather Posted daily at the Capitainerie. Telephone: 67 26 00 21.

Boatyard Services Modest.

Shops This is an excellent venue for shops of all kinds. Sound and traditional.

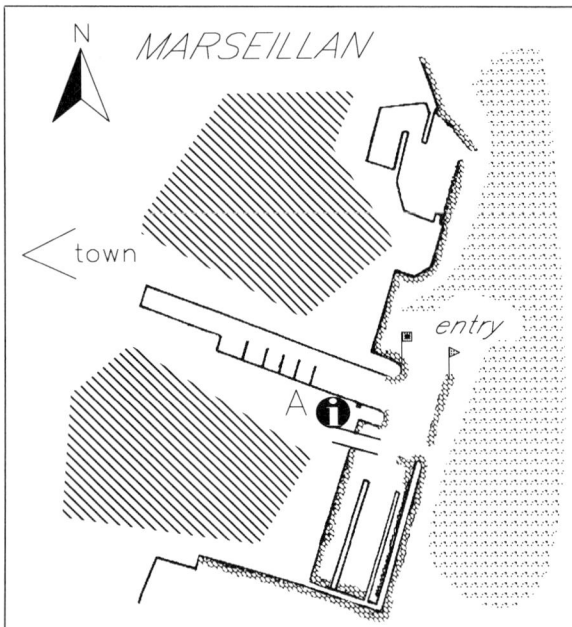

APPROACH
Basically the approach is a simple one: you head due west after the southern end of the oyster beds. Although the port is open to the mistral and the tramontane as well as the classic sea breeze from the south or south east, usually there is no problem.

ENTRY
Enter from the north round the breakwater and then take the immediate turn to starboard. The Capitainerie is on the SW Quai Toulon, with visitors' berths opposite.

COMMENTARY
The town is much more charming than one would expect from its unprepossessing façade, and makes a good base for a few days' relaxation from the rigours of life at sea. Marseillan probably goes back to the 6th century BC, and throughout its history it has been a fishing port.

MEZE
43.26.00 N 03.40.00 E
Tel. 67 43 85 25 (Seasonal)
Port B3   Town A2

Lights	Rocher de Roquerols	Fl(2)WR 6s	6m	11/8M	BRB Tower
	West Jetty	Fl R 4s			
	East Jetty	Fl G 4s	8m	7M	

Marks The old clock tower in the town and light tower at the entrance stand out.

Reception At the Quai Baptiste Guitard, close to the fuel jetty.

Moorings Quayside to buoys.

Draught	2.5m	**LOA**	11m
Berths	122	**Visitors**	11

Fuel At the Quai Baptiste Guitard.

Weather Telephone: 67 65 81 81.

Boatyard Services Very modest.

Shops A reasonable selection in the town.

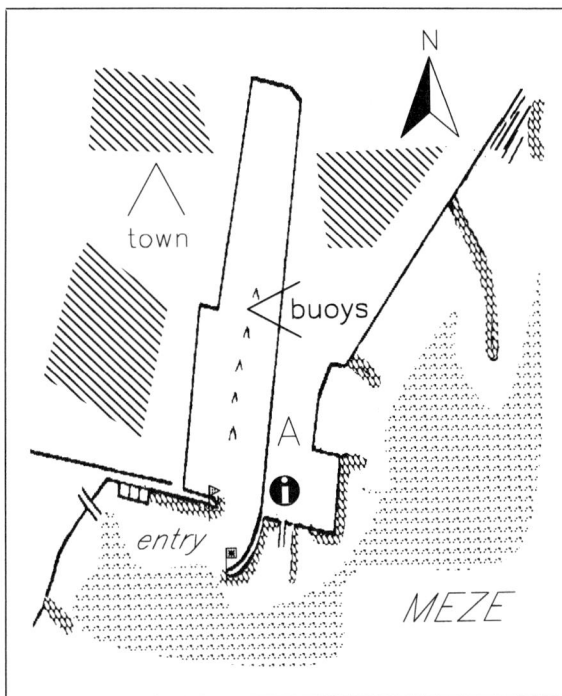

MEZE

APPROACH
Keep a watch out for the unlit shellfish layings and farms, and follow the buoyed approach channel.

ENTRY
The port is well protected from all winds and the actual entry is problem free.

COMMENTARY
Another great shellfish centre, based on the Étang du Thau. Like Marseillan, it is also a tourist centre. The port and its restaurants are the big pull, but its narrow streets are well preserved and a real attraction. There is an intriguing tropical fish aquarium and an exhibition known as the Station de Lagunage. ■

CAP D'AGDE
43.16.10 N 03.30.20 E
Tel. 67 26 00 20
Port B1   Town B1

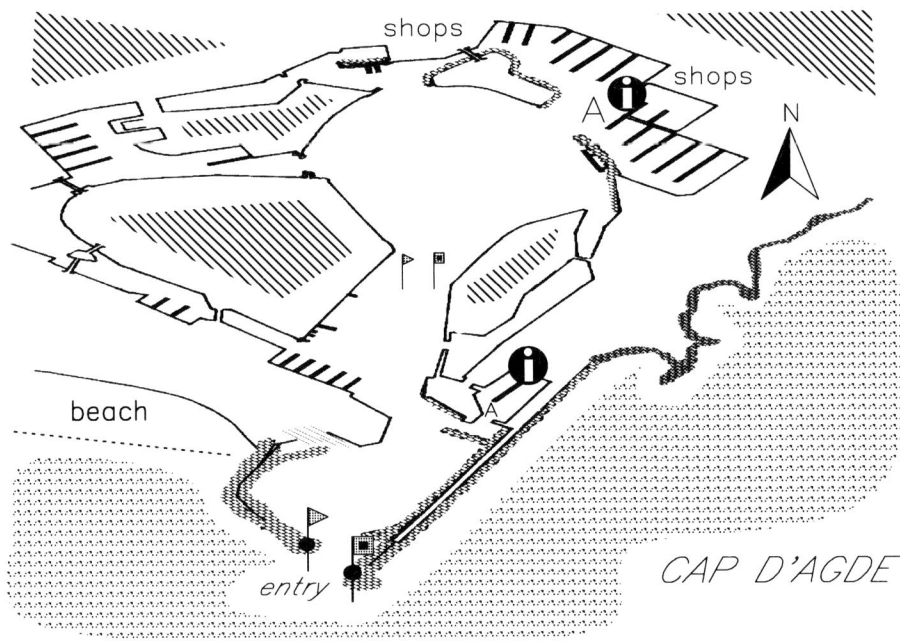

CAP D'AGDE

Charts	SHOM 7054, 7008 ECM 509 ADM 1705, 2606			
Lights	***Marseillan Plage:***			
	W Jetty Head	Fl R 4s	7m	9M	W/R Tower
	E Jetty Head	Fl G 4s	8m	5M	G/W Base

Lights   *Marseillan Plage:*

W Jetty Head	Fl R 4s	7m	9M	W/R Tower
E Jetty Head	Fl G 4s	8m	5M	G/W Base

Port Ambonne:

SW Jetty Head	Fl(2)R 6s	9m	7M	W/R Tower
NE Jetty Head	Oc W 4s			
Île de Brescou	Fl(2)WR 6s	22m	13–10M	W Tower R Top
Buoy	Q(6)+LFl 15s			BYB Cardinal
La Lauze	Fl G 4s	10m	6M	G/W Tower

River l'Hérault:

W Jetty Head	Oc(2)R 6s	14m	7M	W/R Tower
E Jetty Head	Oc G 4s	14m	7M	G/W Base

Cap d'Agde:

W Jetty Head	Fl R 4s	8m	5M	W/R Tower
E Jetty Head	Iso G 4s	8m	9M	G/W Base

NB: Standard navigation lights operate within the port.

Marks   The modest hills of St Martin and St Loup stand out well behind the port. The latter is the more dominant and is surmounted with communications pylons and the old signal station.

	Île de Brescou is a helpful mark, but will probably be slow to detach itself from the mainland.
Reception	There are two. The first is within the starboard enclave, but is only open in season and on an irregular/informal basis (Telephone: 67 26 000 08). The second, the main office, is right within the body of the port to the north east in what is known as the Port de la Clape. There is a modest waiting quay.
Moorings	Quayside and pontoons with buoys and posts.

Draught	3m	**LOA**	20m
Berths	2450	**Visitors**	30

Fuel	Near the Capitainerie in Port de la Clape and also by the secondary Capitainerie near the outer harbour.
Weather	Posted twice daily at the Capitainerie. Telephone: 67.26.00.21/2.
Boatyard Services	Comprehensive.
Shops	Plentiful in the marina and the nearby town of Agde.

APPROACH

Coming from the north east, after Sète it is a straight drag down to the small but noticeable island, the Île de Brescou off Cap d'Agde. Similarly, from the south west, there is little to take the eye.

On a close approach, there is the isolated danger of the rock La Lauze. Some locals take an inner passage between this easily discernible tower and the east jetty, the Digue Richelieu, but I am persuaded that it is wiser for visitors to use the recommended route which takes you to seaward of this rock, keeping it at least 50m distant. You then turn gradually to the north until the actual Mont d'Agde is lined up centrally between the two jetty heads at almost due north. This leaves the Île de Brescou and its Cardinal marker to port.

While there is also an apparently completely safe passage inshore of the Île de Brescou, I have always thought it prudent to round it to seaward, and then proceed as above. However, many local 'youthful' motor cruisers move through that small passage like a dose of salts, but I have not seen your old sea salts taking this route.

ENTRY

Once between the jetty walls, the entry is straight ahead along the buoyed channel. It can become difficult in winds from the east/south east when there is a build-up of swell and high rising surf.

COMMENTARY

The marina at Cap d'Agde is of the large variety (one of the largest in fact), but somehow it manages to keep itself within decent physical and social bounds. It never gets above itself nor stifles you with overkill. It has the services and facilities that you would expect of a well-run, modern marina, with an excellent variety of shops and restaurants. Choice is no problem. Extras are the Musée d'archéologie sous-marine for those wanting a quiet introspective break, and the merry acres of Aqualand for those with excess energy and a penchant for water sports.

The nearby town of Agde was founded by the Greeks as far back as 2500 BC. It was among the first of their colonies and is one of the oldest towns in France. Its name was originally Agathé, meaning the Good Place, although such was an unlikely concept since it is dominated by Mont St Loup. This mountain used to be volcanic, and its black, basilic lava came to be used for many of the town's buildings – the most noteworthy being the cathedral, raised on a commanding site overlooking the River Hérault.

Back from the river, near the Rue de la République, based in a Renaissance hotel in the old quarter, is the Musée Agathois. Founded privately, it houses a vast collection devoted to local archaeology, history, culture and Agde's life at large.

And that is what contemporary life is in this town now almost entirely based on the seasonal tourist industry. Not only does it attract by regular and regularly packed bus services crowds of folk from Cap d'Agde, but even more crowds from the nearby naturist resort of Port Ambonne. The town is extremely pleasant by the river, and there are some intriguing back streets. While some of the market stalls and shops still sell ordinary goods, you will find it difficult to avoid the all-pervading displays of tourist trappery. ∎

VALRAS PLAGE
43.14.50 N 03.17.50 E
Tel. 67 32 33 64
Port C3   Town B2

Charts	SHOM 6844, 7054, 7008	ECM 509, 510	ADM 1705		
Lights	West Jetty	Fl(4) 12s	9m	9M	W/R Tower
	East Jetty	Fl G 4s	8m	7M	G/W Base
	NE Port Entrance No 1	Iso G 4s	2m		G Structure
	SE Port Entrance No 2	Iso R 4s	2m		R Structure

Marks There are two: the fifteen-storey residential tower block just over a mile to the west of the entrance, and the water tower to the east.

Reception There is a floating pontoon in the river on the west bank with easy land access to the Capitainerie on the fuel quay, but I have always found it occupied. The alternative is to try for reception at the fuel quay which is immediately ahead after entry from the river. Space is usually at a premium here also.

Moorings Floating pontoons to concrete quays with buoys.

Draught 2m   **LOA** 12m

Berths 270   **Visitors** 36

Fuel At reception quay.

Weather Posted daily at the Capitainerie.

Boatyard Services Limited.

Shops Only modest in the immediate environs.

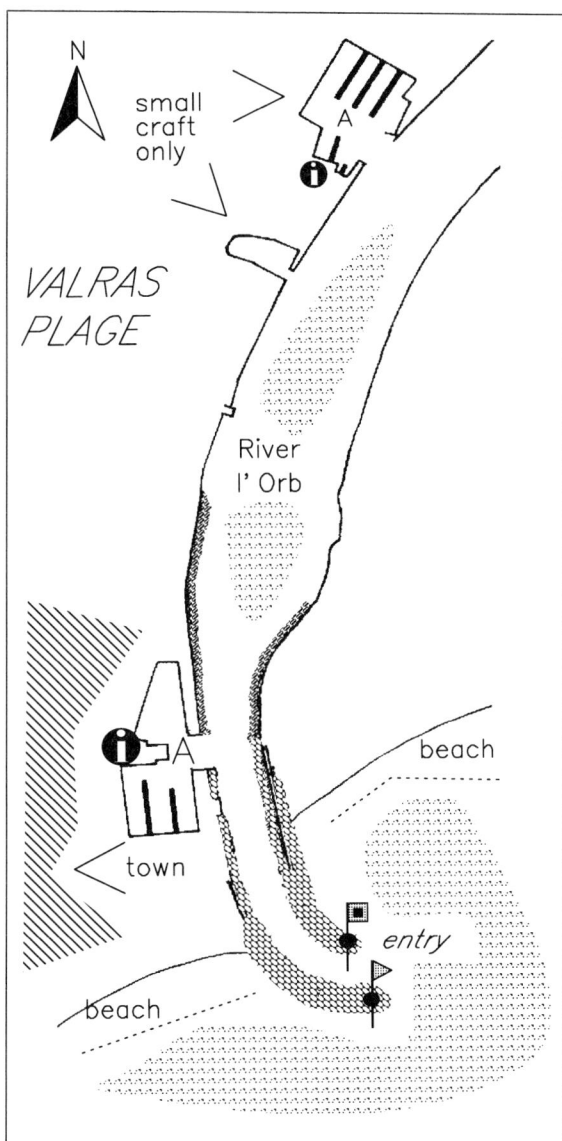

APPROACH

There is little in the way of landmarks between Cap d'Agde and Narbonne Plage. However, near to Valras there are two signs: to the west a large high-rise block of flats, and in the town itself a large water tower. Closer in, the light towers on the sea walls are easy to spot.

ENTRY

It is wise to take a slow central route into the River l'Orb. It is used by all kinds of craft with all kinds of skippers, and not all are navigated according to the best rules of roadsteads or fairways. In addition, sight lines are not good and there are the additional hazards of the rock-bestrewn jetties. But there is nothing that straight-forward seamanship will not overcome.

Once inside the river, the way ahead is clear and plain, past the optimistically described 'waiting pontoon' and up to the harbour entrance on the port hand.

COMMENTARY

Valras is a fairly well-sheltered port at the mouth of the River l'Orb. In every way it is a small experience: depth of water; size of boat; services and facilities, both afloat and shoresides. The river is a popular base for local cruising, fishing and water sports in general. There is not a great deal for a visiting yacht and there seems little point in using the port unless emergency dictates.

Farther up the river, there are two more small ports, each smaller in their own way than Valras. Both are to port on the north west bank of the river. The first, Port Jean Gau, is just past the crane and boatyard, and the second, the Port de l'Orb/Sérignan, is a mile upstream from the entrance. Both can, depending on how many locals have left space, accommodate some visiting craft. They should be approached, if at all, with circumspection; craft that are much in excess of 10m and/or 1.25m draught should not venture there.

Their attraction is their near-complete removal from the sun'n'sand oriented ethos of the rest of the coast. ∎

NARBONNE PLAGE
43.10.00 N 03.11.00 E
Tel. 68 49 91 43
Port B3   Town B3

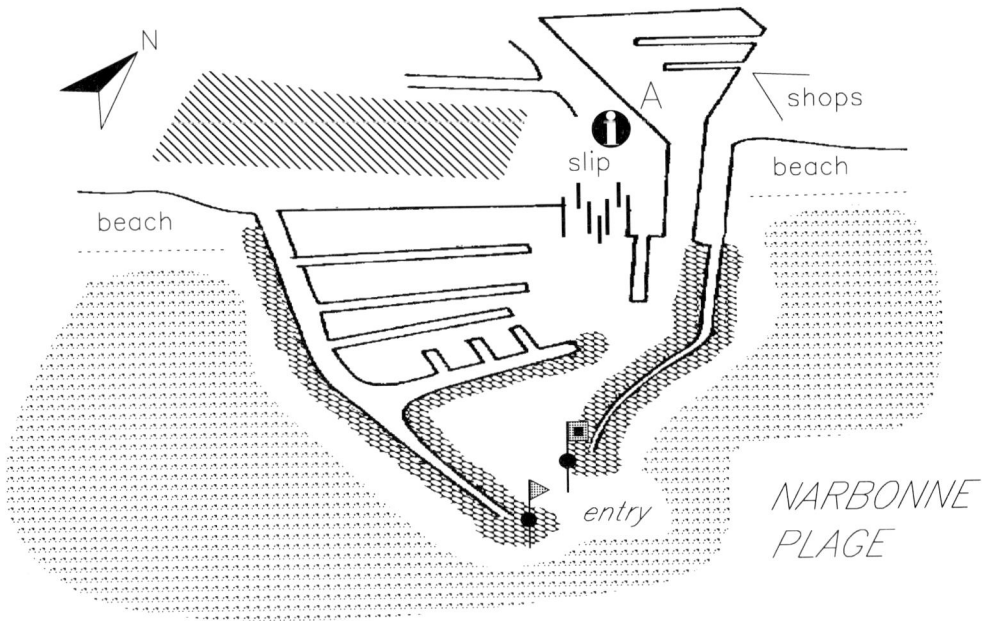

Charts	SHOM 6844, 7008 ECM 510 ADM 1705

Lights	North Sea Wall	Fl G 4s			G Structure
	South Sea Wall	Fl R 4s	7m	4M	R Structure
	East Sea Wall	Oc R 4s			Strip light

Marks The two radar domes (one light, one dark) at the summit of La Clape mountain are conspicuous, as is the old water tower. Closer to sea level, standing just above and inside the entrance, there is an unusual, slender monument.

Reception You take a vacant berth on the No 1 quay which is the first after the outer harbour, or on the Quai d'Honneur, the western quay No 5. You may be met by a member of staff; if not, report to the Capitainerie.

Moorings Quays and floating pontoons, some with fingers.

Draught	2.5m	**LOA**	10m
Berths	400	**Visitors**	Available, but indeterminate.

Fuel In the dredged canal to the Bassin Brossolette.

Weather Posted daily at the Capitainerie. Telephone: 36 65 08 08.

Boatyard Services Modest.

Shops Sufficient and necessary, but this is not a place where you set out to enjoy yourself.

APPROACH

Situated halfway between Gruissan and Valras Plage, there is little to distinguish Narbonne Plage. Behind, on the mountains, there are the radar domes, otherwise there is nothing; and that means also no problem in the approach. Closer in, the 'little houses on the hills' and the unusual, slender column monument help somewhat in identification.

ENTRY

From the northerly direction of Valras, the entry is straight in due south west. From Gruissan and the south, it is necessary to round the south breakwater, keeping a good distance from its rocky surrounds. According to the Capitainerie, access is not good in strong winds from the south east to north east; and by that they specify Beaufort 7–8. My experience was that it required considerably less than that to make the final entry extremely lumpy. It is also uncomfortable when there is any swell from the same direction.

Once through the 60m entrance between the jetties there is a small outer harbour giving on to the east jetty that is marked with a light tower.

COMMENTARY

Narbonne Plage is not the same thing as Narbonne. Here is a small yacht harbour given over in the main to small local yachts. Maximum size is dictated not only by the length of the berths, but also by the tight turns you must negotiate in order to gain entry. There is little here to detain a visiting yachtsman other than a trip inland to the mother, Narbonne itself.

There is an additional small attraction: sometimes, you are permitted a free berth for a 24-hour visit; however, this is not guaranteed, and it would be indelicate to press for it – especially at the height of the season. The Bassin Brossolette provides shelter for small craft with less than a metre draught.

Not far distant along the road between the marina and the next one at Gruissan is a Cimitière Marin; like the one at Sète, it is dedicated to local sailors lost at sea.

So it is to Narbonne that interest and attention are to be directed. As old cities go, it must be said that this one has the lot: ancient capital of Gaule Narbonnaise; host to the kings of the Visigoths; old bishopric city; and, in addition, it is today the thriving centre of its excellent wine industry and a major intersection for road and rail traffic.

The original old port of Narbonne, Colonia Narbo Martius, was founded by a decree of the Roman Senate in 118 BC. It was to remain the Romans' favourite for decades. In 410, after the sacking of Rome, it became the Visigoth capital, and later it fell into the hands of the Saracens. Like other towns in the region, its fortunes came and went with various rival religious factions.

Up to the 14th century, Narbonne had continued in its role as a major trading port; but the silting up of the area brought about its decline, and at the time of the Revolution there were less than 1000 inhabitants. Happily today it blossoms, blooms and flourishes as a wine centre.

The tourist information centre is a very good one, although their command of any language other than French is surprisingly slender. There is so much to see in Narbonne that a decent guide is essential, and fortunately they are well stocked. Above all, however, the inescapable 4th-century church, which is now the Cathédrale St Just, dominates the place and must be a priority: vast, steeped in history, and above all macabre and awesome if not terrible even, it can occupy you for days – and haunt you for ever. ■

GRUISSAN
43.06.20 N 03.07.10 E
Tel. 68 49 08 20
Port A1   Town A3

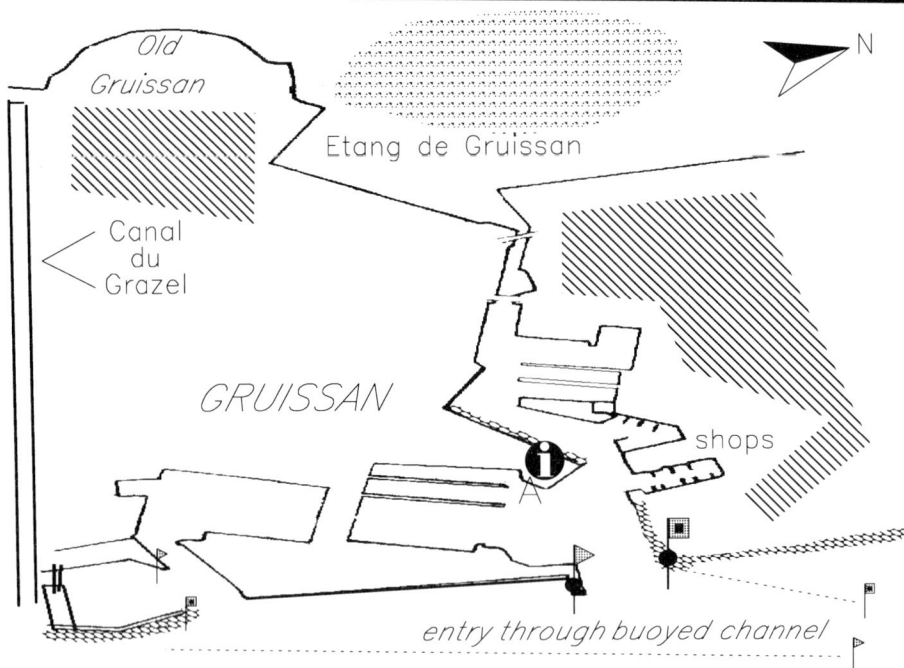

Charts	SHOM 6844, 7008 ECM 510 ADM 1705
Lights	North Jetty Fl G 4s 11m 7M G/W Base
	South Jetty Fl R 4s (Temporary Light)
	(NB This a buoy marking the collapsed end of the jetty.)
	Designated South Jetty Light:
	Fl(2)R 6s 11m 7M R/W Tower
	The approach channel (dredged to 3m) is marked by buoys and beacons, after which standard navigation lights operate within the port.
Marks	The two radar domes (one light, one dark) at the summit of La Clape mountain are conspicuous from a distance. Closer in, the Barberousse Tower in the old village stands out.
Reception	Follow the buoyed channel from the outer port and the spacious quay by the Capitainerie is straight ahead. The offices are unusually attractive – in no way 'businesslike'.
Moorings	To pontoons and fingers, quays and buoys.

Draught	2.5m	**LOA**	30
Berths	750	**Visitors**	150
Fuel	By the Capitainerie.		

Weather	Posted twice daily at the Capitainerie. Telephone: 36 65 08 08, also 68 61 03 92. Antiope in season.
Boatyard Services	Very reasonable.
Shops	Comprehensive.

APPROACH

At 20 miles to the south west of Cap d'Agde and 10 miles to the north of Cap Leucate, the massive marina at Gruissan is overlooked by the radar domes on La Clape 2 miles behind it. Closer in, it is easy to spot the unusual light towers (especially the one that is damage inclined and never seems to get repaired), and also the tower of the old Barberousse Tower on the hill of old Gruissan just to the rear of the port.

Nearby to the south, there are the entrances to the Canal du Grazel and the Grau du Pêche Rouge. They are not likely to lead to confusion since they are isolated from all the signs of civilisation that surround the maritime community of Gruissan.

Half a mile to the south east of the channel entrance, there is a 'field of buoys' marking what is called Aquaculture. I noted them as being indeed multitudinous.

ENTRY

The entrance into the channel suffers from a bar when there have been strong winds from the east to south and a big swell from the south east.

There is a vast area of open water that was once associated with the Étangs of Gruissan and Grazel. The channel is dredged to 3m and well buoyed. It leads to an intersection, marked and lit, when you tend to starboard for the Capitainerie.

COMMENTARY

It makes a pleasant change to be able to anchor inside an outer harbour without causing offence or offending against some local law. It is a well-protected spot and, although (predictably) popular, it is never crowded enough to be uncomfortable except at weekends in the high season.

As you progress along the dredged channel, to port on the south bank, you can see some of the best examples of houses built on stilts that are to be found in Languedoc–Roussillon. Although not ancient monuments, they are nevertheless the real thing, being no mere modern decorative substitute. As such they have an air of battered and forsaken havens. They are built that way to afford maximum security and protection against the floods and inundations that frequently occur at the equinoxes.

Within the new port, the tone for the modern/traditional architecture is set by the Capitainerie itself. It seems more Afro than Franco, but is a delight to gaze on as the sun sets its slanting rays across it, thus slightly drawing out the nightfall.

Shopping is neither a particular delight nor a special challenge in the new port. The goods are there for the searching, and careful selection will bring to light the artisans who really care about what they sell. The alternative is the pleasant short walk to the old town of Gruissan, where under the shadow of the castle you will find a small collection of old-fashioned shops who go in for old-fashioned service – and, of course, endless local gossip. There is an interesting market on Mondays. It is best to get there early, since it is never overstocked with the best.

The old town is intriguing. In concentric circles, the houses built for the fishermen and salt marsh workers all fall under the spell, shadow and command of the Barberousse Tower, sited on the top of the small but outstanding hill.

In days gone by, it used to be a hard-working centre for those fishermen who took their boats to the open sea off the coasts of Spain and Algeria. Today the old town has turned its back irrevocably on the sea, although there is always a grand fishermen's celebration for the June Fête of Saint Pierre. ∎

PORT LA NOUVELLE

43.01.00 N 03.04.00 E
Tel. 68 48 17 64
Port C2   Town C2

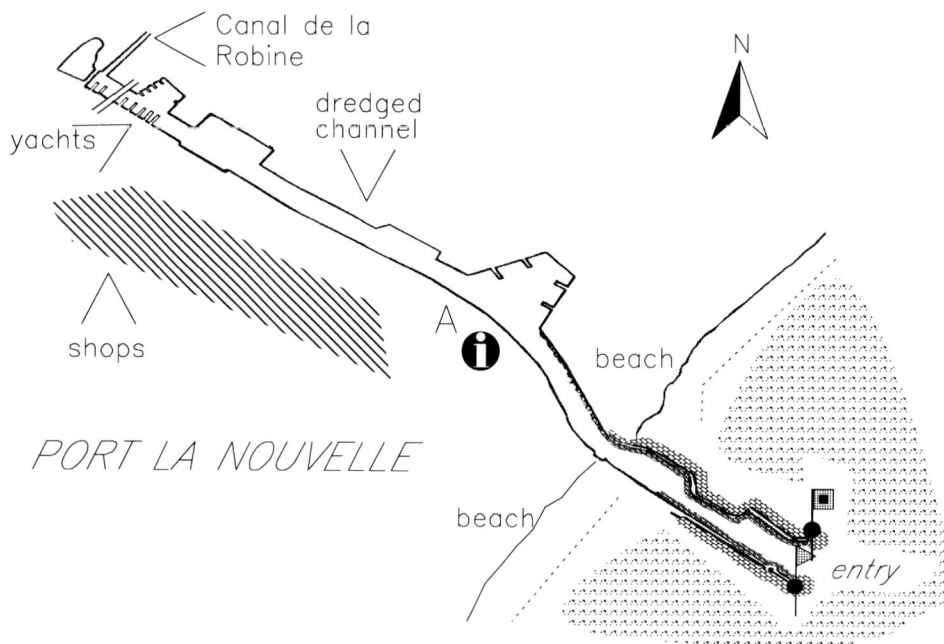

Charts	SHOM 6844, 7008	ECM 510	ADM 1705		
Lights	Pipe Line	Q(3) 10s			BYB Cardinal
	Front Leading	Q	23m	14M	W/R Tower
	Rear Leading	Q	48m	17M	Tower
	North Jetty Head	Iso G 4s	15m	5M	W/G Tower
	South Jetty Head	Oc(2)R 6s			W/R Tower

Marks The chimney of the Lafargue cement plant and the imposing light tower at the entrance are noticeable, and the 60m high silo is visible for up to 10 miles in clear weather.

Reception There is no reception quay as such. The Capitainerie is to port shortly after entering between the breakwaters. There may be space to moor and report. Otherwise, make for the head of the port, where there are basic visitors' pontoons on the port hand just before the main fish dock. Beware: depths decrease to less than a metre towards the sides.

Moorings There are pontoons just below the bridge on the port hand. At present, they are without services, and a stay of five days maximum is allowed. There are also three berths suitable for visitors in the boatyard.

Draught	4m	**LOA**	
Berths	130	**Visitors**	See above
Fuel	Near the small yacht pontoons.		

Weather Posted daily at the Capitainerie. Telephone: 67 65 81 81.
Boatyard Services This is a commercial port, so all services and facilities are available, but they are not necessarily very easy to come by if you are a yachtsman.
Shops A reasonable selection of everyday basic goods, but tending to the depressed.

APPROACH

From north and south, there is no hazard in the general approach, but you should look out for the large, well-marked, fishery protection areas that are laid out on both sides of the port. Closer in, the entrance towers and the cement factory chimney become obvious.

There can be a sandbar formed at the entrance in strong winds from the north east/south east. In anything above Force 6, entry is not advised.

ENTRY

Align the red and white banded chimney of the Lafargue plant with the 20m tall cereal silo and proceed in a northwesterly direction. The final run in between the outer jetties is clear and plain. Inside, the channel soon narrows as you near the Capitainerie.

COMMENTARY

Port la Nouvelle describes itself as a Port of Refuge, and that just about says it all. It is not disposed to accommodate leisure craft, although it does, predictably, offer a modest service for its own amateur fishing fraternity. Visitors are just not a part of its organised life. It is worth while noting that, thanks to its commercial trade,

it is the only harbour between Sète and Port Vendres where there is not a fall-off from the standard services out of season. But since they are not massive in the first instance, this is not so much of a consolation.

However, it does afford access to the Canal du Midi via the Canal de la Robine. Since this is the most westerly point where you can join the inland waterways, this is important. Sadly, the Canal de la Robine's tiny channel is narrow, tending to silt up and become weed covered and encumbered.

Port la Nouvelle is mainly devoted to industrial shipping and commerce, being the largest redistribution port and centre for fuel supplies in the south west. It is also a base for fishing. Yachtsmen are not refused entry; indeed, the harbour staff are friendly, willing and helpful as far as they can be, but they have few services and facilities with which to work. Basic repairs and mast craning can be dealt with without problem.

Because of restricted berthing and the problems of silting in the canal, it is wise to check with Port la Nouvelle Capitainerie before planning on using the port. You can contact the office on VHF 12 or Telephone: 68 48 17 64. ∎

PORT LEUCATE
42.52.25 N 03.03.15 E
Tel. 68 40 91 24
Port B2   Town B2

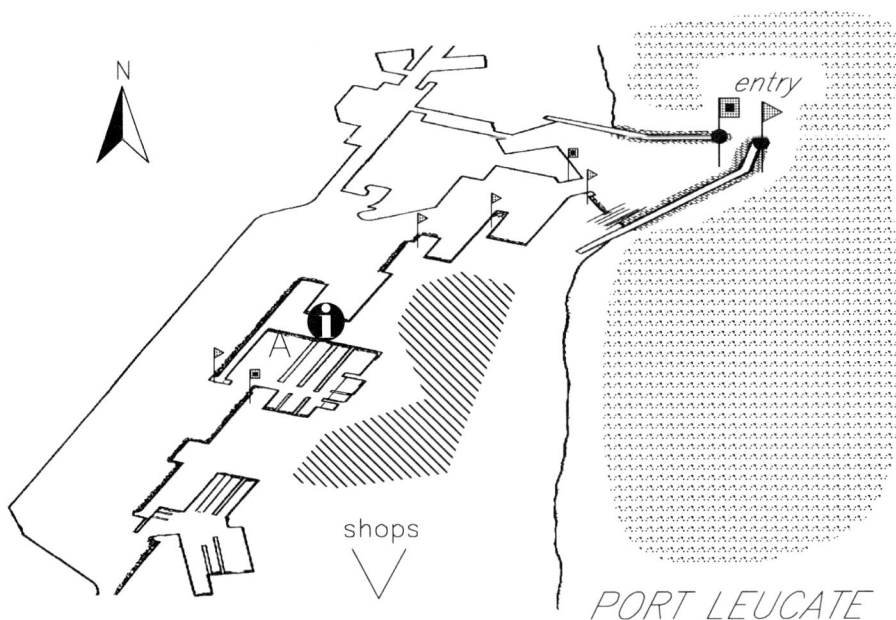

shops

PORT LEUCATE

Charts	SHOM 6843, 6844, 7008 ECM 510, 511 ADM 1705				
Lights	West Jetty	Fl G 4s	8m	6M	G/W Base
	East Jetty	Fl R 4s	8m	8M	W/R Tower
	S Entrance	Oc R 4s	3m	6M	R Tower
	N Entrance	Oc G 4s	3m	6M	G Tower
	Standard navigation lights operate within the port.				

Marks   Three miles to the south, on the beach, there is the unexpected sea/landmark of the passenger liner *Lydia*; it is unmistakable. Two miles to the north, Cap Leucate is conspicuous with the white tower of its light, its television pylon and its old signal station.

Reception   In the centre of the port. The Capitainerie is tucked away in the Bassin Central and not obvious on entry. Visitors are received on the Quai d'Honneur (pontoon No 9) where there is a noticeable legend: 'Visiteurs'.

Moorings   Pontoons and quays to buoys.

Draught	3m	**LOA**	20m
Berths	1000	**Visitors**	100

Fuel   At the reception quay.

Weather   Posted daily at the Capitainerie.

Boatyard Services   Good.

Shops   There is a selection in and around the marina.

APPROACH

The coastal and seaward approaches are all unencumbered. The white pyramid of the Cap Leucate lighthouse, with its red top and grey corners, and the TV relay centre are to be noted to the north; while to the south, the unmistakable ex-cruise liner *Lydia* perches on the beach like a stranded whale. Close in, the jetty walls can be identified with difficulty from the background.

ENTRY

Once inside the jetty walls, it still feels fairly unprotected – not like the seaway, true, but there is plenty of open space and a long haul to the large marina itself. There is still much work to take place on this massive development site, and this part of the entry, to both sides, is pretty bleak: to starboard are desolate natural flats, while to port are the foundations for what may well become desolate man made flats.

With a tramontane from the north west blowing up round here very quickly to Force 8, this route can be unpleasant; and with a sea breeze (or marine wind) from the south east, at anything from as little as Force 3 upwards, the swell in the entrance can be most unpleasant.

The inner entrance to the marina facility is well marked to port. You can frequently tie up alongside near the Capitainerie to report.

COMMENTARY

The official handbook for Leucate goes out of its way to point out that, among the many glories and riches of the surrounding region, there is one that is outstanding, and brings visitors in hordes from the four corners of Europe. It is the wind; and in very truth it is never in short supply.

The massive development that embraces Leucate and Barcarès is not yet finished, in spite of it already being the largest combined yachting and leisure base on the Mediterranean coast of France. It must be said that while the marina staff are charming and efficient, the same cannot be claimed for the scheme at large, nor for those who provide the facilities – domestic or social. Basically, all shopping tends to be done on site, so there is a captive clientele; the nearest large town is Perpignan, miles away.

The wines of the area are worth investigating, and there are plenty of them. At the last count, Leucate had 265 vine growers. Their wines, in particular the notable AOC Fitou, are characterised by a rich and lively dark red colour. It is best kept for a while, since even the locals suggest it is somewhat rough and tough when young. Not to be overlooked are the other two great joys for the bibulous: the famous 'vin doux' of the area, the AOC Muscat de Rivesaltes; and the equally well-known AOC Corbières.

The history of Leucate is essentially one of warding off the Spaniards from as far back as the 16th century. It would seem that long lessons have been well learned. It was in this area that I was continually approached by the customs. Their first question was always the same: 'Have you come from/been to Spain?' I am afraid that what I called research, they insisted on referring to as eccentric cruising. ■

BARCARES

42.47.55 N 03.02.35 E
Tel. 68 86 07 35
Port B3   Town B2

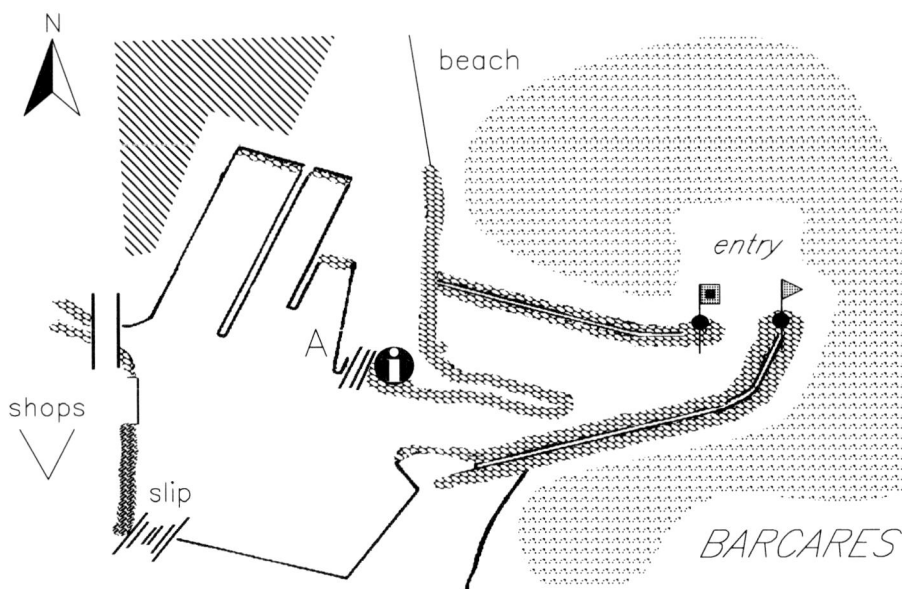

Charts	SHOM 6843, 6844, 7008 ECM 511 ADM 1705
Lights	E Breakwater Fl(2)R 10m 10M W/R Tower
	N Breakwater F W
Marks	Two miles to the north, on the beach, there is the sea/landmark of the unmistakable passenger liner *Lydia*, and there is a conspicuous water tower to the south.
Reception	There is no reception quay as such, although the quay by the fuel quay at the Capitainerie is pressed into service. In general, a member of staff appears and signals you to a berth. If not, try for a vacant place on the pontoons to the north, near the bridge.
Moorings	Floating pontoons to buoys.
Draught	2m **LOA** 13m
Berths	293 **Visitors** 10
Fuel	By the Capitainerie.
Weather	Posted three times daily at the Capitainerie. Antiope. Telephone: 36 08 08 08.
Boatyard Services	Not really.
Shops	Some nearby, others in the village.

APPROACH

The general approach is hazard free. The old cruise ship *Lydia* lies about 2 miles to the north. Closer in, the apartments, the port light towers and the unusually small but very decorative tower of the Capitainerie are all clear to see.

ENTRY

The way in is straightforward: a clear run in from the north, while from the south, the southern jetty must be rounded. The Capitainerie is obvious on the starboard hand immediately after entering.

COMMENTARY

This is one of the few ports that categorically offers a free berth for a 24-hour stay, outside the high season. In fact, if you arrive well out of season and you make a good impression, you will be permitted to stay free of charge for much longer.

Although Barcarès is frequently described as a modern yacht harbour, it is basically a small fishing port. Any largish craft are best advised to go to next door Port Leucate, but that will mean missing the novelty of the miniature experience that is to be found here. There is a body of locals who use the port and its surrounding facilities, and the atmosphere is redolent of a large, extended family. They take a great personal interest in visitors, and you will frequently find yourself boarded by folk who have just dropped in with a small gift (a local sausage; wild asparagus from the hinterland; a bottle of wine), to say a fond hello in passing, or just to be plain inquisitive. The local shopkeepers are the same. I consider it a gem of a place.

There is no shop on site, but there are basics available close by, and the village itself is only walking distance away. Once again on this coast, the necessary practice of having to search out the best shops obtains, for they are not all on the main drag, which is a classic village ribbon stretch.

The curiosity of the ex-cruise liner *Lydia* is nearby. She was beached in 1967 to end her days as a leisure and pleasure house and casino. Investigation is best left to the brave. He who dares wins. ∎

CANET EN ROUSSILLON
42.42.10 N 03.02.20 E
Tel. 68 80 20 66
Port B2   Town B2

Charts	SHOM 6843, 7008 ECM 511 ADM 1705
Lights	Ground Light (local lighthouse):

	Fl(4) 12s	27m	16M	W	Tower
North Jetty	Fl(2)G 6s	5m	5M	G/W	Base
South Jetty	Oc R 4s	9m	9M	W/R	Tower

Marks	Just to the north of the port, the Canet Plage light structure is unusual and eye-catching. Nearer the port is the white water tower, much higher at 34m.
Reception	There is a small pontoon immediately after the fuel station, which is the first quay to port once through the dredged outer harbour.
Moorings	Floating pontoons with buoys or posts, and some with fingers for craft over 15m.
Draught	3.5m **LOA** 24m
Berths	977 **Visitors** 117
Fuel	Near the Capitainerie.
Weather	Posted three times daily at the Capitainerie. Telephone: 36 65 08 08. Also, 48-mile radius radar.
Boatyard Services	Comprehensive.
Shops	Good choice.

APPROACH

From north, south and seaward, the approach is without hazard. The only landmarks are the unusual pylon light structure and the high white tower. Wind and weather from the north east/south east bring up bad swell and surf in the entrance, and entry is not advised when gusts are more than Force 7.

ENTRY

The light towers on the jetties can be identified well in advance from the north and seaward. From the north, the way in is dead ahead, while from the south, the southern jetty must be rounded.

COMMENTARY

Canet en Roussillon, also known as Canet Plage and Port Père Noël, doesn't really live up to more than one appellation, and that must be Canet Plage; for the community is utterly given over to the marina, water sports and related leisure and tourist activities. It is not entirely soulless, but you need to dig beneath the surface/service if you are to contact style and warmth in buildings or people.

The marina is well served by a very good choice of shops in the nearby town, and Perpignan is not too far away. Indeed, just as Palavas les Flots was the seaside resort for the residents of Montpellier, so was this the beach and leisure centre for those of Perpignan.

It is to Perpignan that the student of history must go. It was the old capital of the counts of Roussillon and the kings of Majorca. In the 13th century it benefited vastly from the trade that was engendered by the Crusades. It was shortly to become the second city of Catalonia, apparently acknowledging only Barcelona as a contender.

Like other communities in the region, Perpignan suffered from continuing assaults from the Spanish, coming and going consistently; and it was not until the Treaty of the Pyrénées in 1659 that Roussillon and, as they say, its jewel Perpignan, was fully reunited with the French monarchy. While Catalan is still undoubtedly around, it is very much the local variety and Perpignan sees itself as thoroughly French.

There is much to see in Perpignan, and time and a good guide book should be made and found. Priorities must be the unusual Palais des Rois de Majorque and the Musée Hyacinthe-Rigaud, equally unusually named after the 17th-century portrait painter. It contains not only the obligatory historical styles and studies, but also a section devoted to the Primitive Catalan School and another to contemporary works by Maillol, Dufy, Picasso and Calder.

Other less predictable enticements are the charming gardens behind the St Jacques church known as La Miranda. Also to be found in beautiful gardens is Saint Vicens, the local ceramics workshop and centre. ∎

ST CYPRIEN

42.37.20 N 03.02.30 E

Tel. 68 21 07 98

Port B1   Town B1

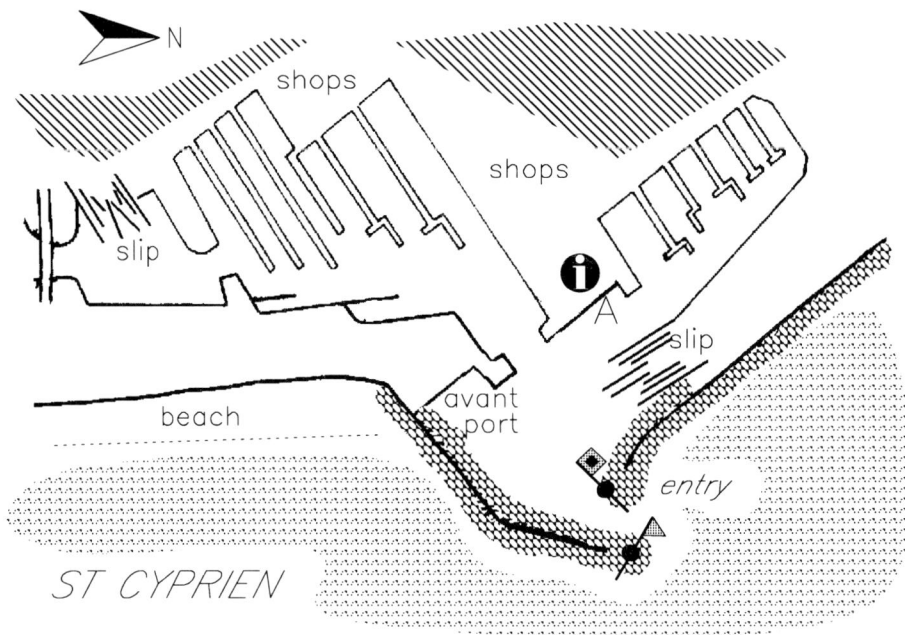

Charts	SHOM 6843, 7008 ECM 511 ADM 1705			
Lights	St Cyprien Rock Buoy	Fl(3)Y 6s		
	North Jetty	F W	3m	Strip light
	South Jetty	VQ(4)R 2s	10m 12M	W/R Tower
Marks	Cap Béar lighthouse is 7 miles to the west. Closer in, there is a water tower and the usual apartment blocks, but nothing that can qualify as an actual landmark.			
Reception	The obvious Capitainerie marks the spacious reception quay, which lies immediately ahead after entry.			
Moorings	Floating pontoons to buoys.			
Draught	3.5m	**LOA**	20m	
Berths	2200	**Visitors**	440	
Fuel	At the head of the reception quay by the Capitainerie.			
Weather	Posted three times daily at the Capitainerie.			
Boatyard Services	Good.			
Shops	Very good choice.			

APPROACH

This is the last harbour going south down the French coast where the approaches can all be said to be completely clear, plain and uncluttered. Cap Béar and its lighthouse are prominent at 7 miles to the south, while the massive apartment developments and water tower all become visible at about 3 miles off. East to south east winds make the approach, as they say, 'delicate'.

ENTRY

Once inside the vast outer harbour, where anchoring is permitted, the reception quay and Capitainerie become obvious. Unfortunately, there is no alongside mooring at the reception quay, and it can be quite boisterous with wind as it is an open spot; it can also be extremely busy with boats, as it is a popular place, being for many a point of departure for Spain. So, it is particularly worth while to be completely ready before making your bid. However, there is plenty of space in the outer harbour approach to jill around if necessary.

COMMENTARY

Going south, St Cyprien is the last of the big spenders as it were. This is the end of the huge Languedoc–Roussillon development, although the development itself is not yet finished. Indeed, it seems as if, like Spanish hotels, it never will be. It is used a lot by the French and Germans on their way to the Costa Brava and the Balearics, since it is such a useful and well-equipped staging post. It is not an intimate, cosy experience, but you can get plenty of exercise walking round the shops, the restaurants and all the other comprehensive facilities.

It is possible to buy local wines here from the *recolteurs* at their small stands, and it is really good to talk to them: they are interesting about their wines; interested in their wines; and more than ready to be interested in you. They are particularly chagrined that their wines are neither better known nor sell better, except at hugely marked up prices in the UK. I found these earnest yet witty folk one of the best parts of the working life and soul of St Cyprien. ∎

COLLIOURE
42.31.50 N 03.05.50 E
Tel. 68 82 05 66
Port A3   Town A2

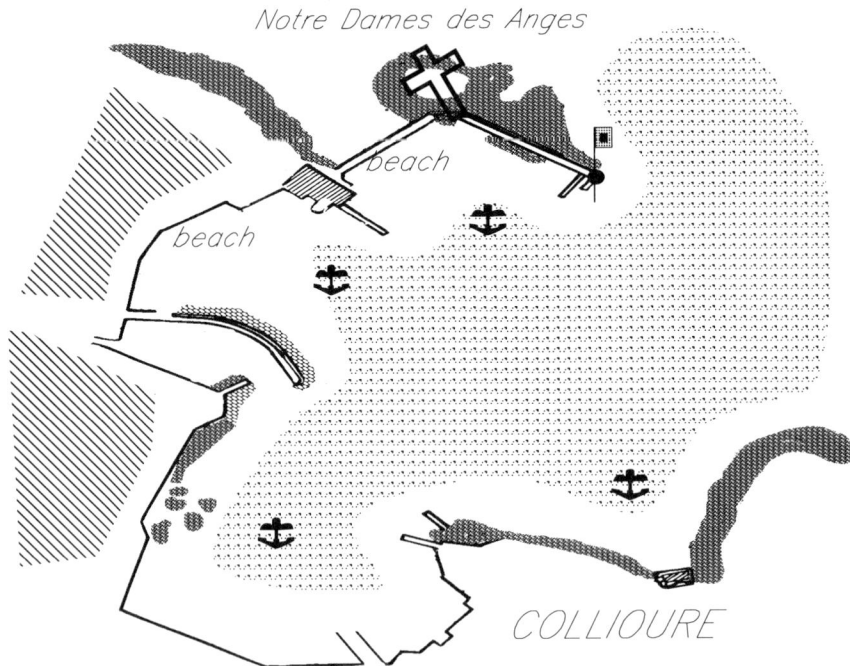

Charts	SHOM 6843, 7008 ECM 511 ADM 1705
Lights	N Breakwater Head Iso G 4s 14m 8M G/W Base
Marks	Cap Béar is to the west, and Fort St Elme stands up well above the port. The Tour Madeloc is conspicuous just over 2 miles distant. Nearer to sea level, the clock, the castle, and the remarkable ancient tower are all eye-catching.
Reception	There is no reception quay.
Moorings	Mooring facilities are all but non-existent except for the smallest of craft, which moor to the quay with buoys. The usual practice is to anchor in the small bay, where there is a restricted zone (see below).

Draught	2m	**LOA**	6.5m
Berths	90	**Visitors**	None

Fuel	Not here. The nearest is at Quai de la Presqu'île, Port Vendres.
Weather	Telephone: 36 65 08 08; Perpignan 68 61 17 18; and VHF 9.
Boatyard Services	Not really.
Shops	Charming: see opposite.

APPROACH

Collioure lies under the dominance of the local Madeloc Tower in particular, Cap Béar in general, and the Pyrénées at large. Any approach from the sea will find all three useful in identifying this tiny port that is hidden and not at all easy to discern.

There is no hazard in the approach, only the difficulty of finding the place. Fort St Elme dominates the entrance from the south east, while, closer in, the Château des Templiers, the church clock and the old pillar tower at the foot of the rocks and jetties are obvious.

ENTRY

Entry is made round the head of the jetty that stands to the north, and has a green light tower. The anchorage and small port lie immediately ahead.

COMMENTARY

It is well worth going to the bother of finding a safe (and approved) spot to anchor off in this quiet-time, very pretty village on the Côte Vermeille. It has a charm all of its own, having somehow managed to sell itself completely to the tourist trade but without ever having seemed to have done so. This is no mean feat for a community that is inordinately invaded each year by throngs of visitors.

There may be too many art galleries and artistic boutiques for the taste of some, but most of them contain a high proportion of unexpectedly unusual pieces. And nobody seems to mind how long you stand and stare without buying, so long as you are actually looking and appear to be interested.

If you don't fancy buying a piece of art as a keepsake of the place, the next best buy must be the anchovies – for which Collioure is noted. Unless you are an experienced hand with these delicacies, it is a wise precaution to declare your innocence and take advice – since they come in many shapes and sizes, and with weird and wonderful treatments. There is much use of salt and oil, among other pickling features, and you need to know just how much you can take.

There is a small, central car park by the small channel of Douay river; and it is from here (perhaps best reached by bus from Port Vendres) that you can explore the delights of the place.

The two main buildings are the Église Notre Dame des Anges and the Château Royal. The church, internally an extremely dark affair, was built towards the end of the 17th century to replace the previous edition that was destroyed by the orders of Vauban. The singular clock tower was the major light of the old port. The triptych is something very special indeed.

In spite of the fact that Collioure is the training HQ for some of the French Marine forces (who appear all over the place, ashore and afloat, in all kinds of guises), there are nevertheless quite calm and peaceful walks to be enjoyed all round the village and its back-to-back beaches. All in all, it is a joyful place that never actually goes over the top. ∎

PORT VENDRES
42.31.20 N 03.06.50 E
Tel. 68 82 08 84
VHF 12
Port C1   Town A1

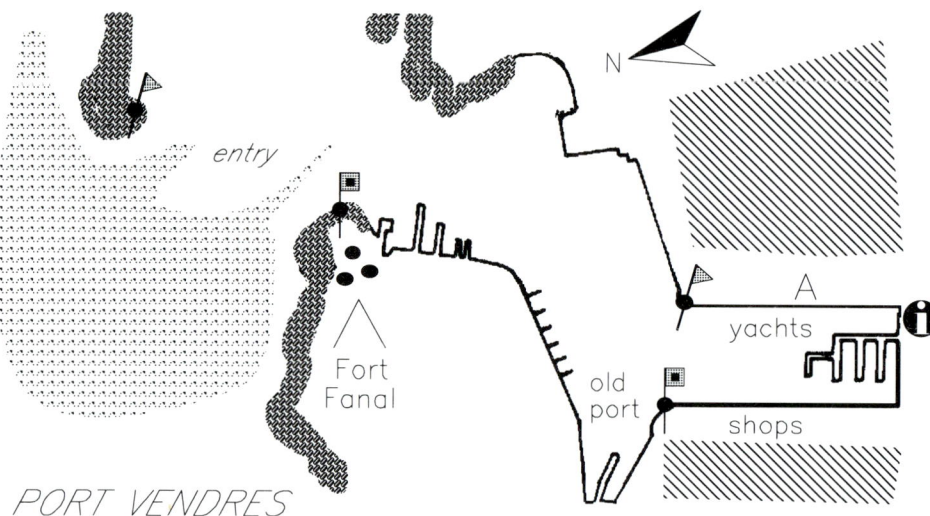

PORT VENDRES

Charts	SHOM 6843, 7008 ECM 511 ADM 1705			
Lights	Cap Béar	Fl(3) 15s	80m	30M
	Fort Béar Leading Lights:			
	Front	Q	12m	10M
	Rear	Q	23m	18M
	Breakwater	Oc(3)R 12s	20m	11M	W/R Tower
	Fort du Fanal	Oc G 4s	29m	8M	G/W Base
	Fanal Point	Q G	9m	7M	W/G Tower

Marks The lighthouse and old signal station on Cap Béar at no more than a mile from the port are noticeable. Fort St Elme on the mountains behind is outstanding. The light tower of Fort Fanal and the stilted outer light are plain to see.

Reception There is no quay labelled 'reception'. You tie up at the inner easterly jetty known as the Quai de la Republique, which is on the port hand just by the Customs Office (Quai de la Douane). Report to the Capitainerie of the port de plaisance at the head of the port in the Quai Joly.

Moorings Floating pontoons to buoys.

Draught	7m	**LOA**	40m	
Berths	243	**Visitors**	30	

Fuel	At the Quai de la Presqu'île, round the south west corner before the customs quay, near the commercial shipping berths.
Weather	Posted daily at the Capitainerie. Telephone: 36 65 08 08.
Boatyard Services	Good.
Shops	Good.

APPROACH

There is no offshore hazard lurking in the approaches to Port Vendres. From every direction, the way to Port Vendres is indicated by the looming presence of Cap Béar to the south. Its square towered light and old signal station are unmistakable. In addition, Fort St Elme, on the high ground immediately behind, is an obvious indication.

Closer in, the many-columned light tower, with its strange red top, on the east outer sea wall is unusual and eye-catching. To the west of the entrance, the large square white light tower at Fort du Fanal is noticeable.

ENTRY

Once the marks have been identified, the wide entrance is plain sailing. That is, except in strong weather from the east and north east; this is, after all, the territory of the infamous winds that haunt Cap Béar. When these occur, there are very troubled waters before the outer sea wall.

Once inside the outer port, progress southwesterly, past the Fort to starboard and commerce to port. A large dog leg to the right and then left eventually leads to the inner harbour, where the marina is at its head, with the Customs Quay to port.

COMMENTARY

It appears that Port Vendres means the Port of Venus, but its ambience is much more one of a sales port. In any case, its origins more closely appertain to the god Mars, for it was established towards the end of the 17th century as a port for military and naval vessels and was accordingly fortified in its own right.

At one time, Port Vendres had very strong trading links with Algeria, but with the end of the French connection that traffic died away. It is still a commercial port and there are passenger ferries, but it relies more and more on leisure craft and the fleet that fishes off the coast of Roussillon.

The floating pontoons in the yacht harbour have seen better days and the power points can be doubtful, but the staff are always helpful. When you can find them that is, for sometimes you need to lurk invisibly near the office in order to entrap one of them.

The good news is that improvements have been in hand for some time on the marina facilities. Even now, there may be new services at the head of the westerly jetty known as the Quai Pierre Forgas. The part of this quay to seaward and near the old port is reserved for the substantial fishing fleet.

At first sight, the shops of Port Vendres are not inspiring, but a full expeditionary research brings its rewards. The two tiny struggling artisan-bakeries overlooking the fishing port are worth discovering and worthy of support. They sport the classic corner shop 'Use It or Lose It' legends.

In keeping with its proximity to the Spanish border, the cash tills of the major banks ask you if you want your money in francs or pesetas when you insert your plastic. ▪

BANYULS SUR MER
42.29.00 N 03.08.00 E
Tel. 68 88 30 32
Port B3   Town A2

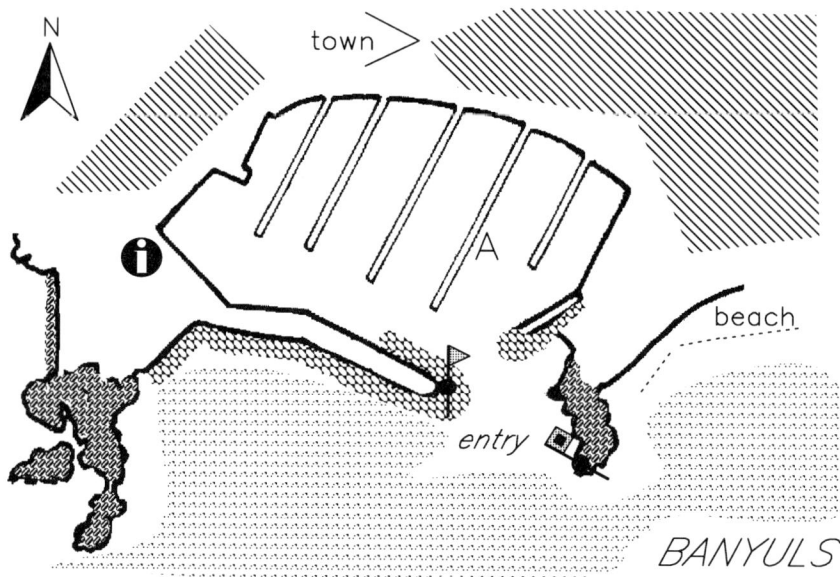

Charts	SHOM 6843, 7008 ECM 511, ECM E.03 ADM 1705			
Lights	Cap Béar	Fl(3) 15s	80m	30M
	Île Petite	Fl WG 4s	10m	10–7M W/G Tower
	NE Jetty	Oc(2)R 6s	9m	W/R Tower
	NW Jetty	Iso W 4s		

Marks The approach is dominated by Cap Béar and the signal edifices and accessories. Within the port are the outstanding buildings of the Oceanographic research centre. There are two islands just outside the port: Île Grosse to the east, and Île Petite to the west.

Reception The official reception quay is at Quay C. This is immediately to starboard after entry.

Moorings Concrete pontoons to buoys, but see below.

Draught 2m–3m   **LOA** 12m

Berths 400   **Visitors** 120

Fuel Only in the town.

Weather Posted daily at the Capitainerie, telephone: 36 65 08 08; also Perpignan, telephone: 68 61 17 18.

Boatyard Services Only modest.

Shops Plentiful in the town.

APPROACH

From the north, it is necessary to round the conspicuous Cap Béar, with all its noticeable lights and buildings. Following the coastline at a prudent distance brings Banyuls into view as you proceed into the second bay; that is, after Cap Oullestreil. From the south, the tiny port cannot be seen until you have rounded Cap l'Abeille.

ENTRY

Île Grosse should be studiously avoided (at least 50m) and also its yellow buoys marking the bathing areas. So should the rocky conglomerate that is known as Île Petite. (Neither of these 'islands' is in fact detached from the mainland. They form the outer protection of the harbour.) Entrance is made straight to the jetty heads, leaving the marked rocks of Île Petite well to starboard: their hazard is clear to see.

Visitors' berths are almost straight ahead and the office of the Capitainerie is to port at the end of the quay on the sea wall.

COMMENTARY

At the reception quay, C (the first to be seen on entry) berths 30 to 61 are reserved for visitors. There is seldom a member of staff in sight, and even when there is he may well be either a student on a vacation job and not be very skilled in his rope work – or he may be a member of the permanent staff and think that such endeavours are beneath him.

All this becomes of some import when it is appreciated that all these berths are open to the worst ravages of any inclemency in the weather. It is worth remembering that this is the famous Cap Béar territory where the elements tend to be at their worst in France. So it is a good idea to try to find a place near the Capitainerie at the eastern head of the small harbour on the north quayside – if only to report. If you are lucky, you may be able to stay in the inner sanctum for 48 hours.

Banyuls sur Mer is the last French harbour before the border with Spain. Except, that is, for what is known as the Port de Cerbère, but it is no more than a protected anchorage in a small *calanque* (creek) and usable only in calm, settled weather. Banyuls reeks neither of Spanish nor of Catalan influence; strangely enough, that is to be found farther to the east. But neither is it aggressively French, apparently combining the best of all those worlds and so achieving a unique blend.

Two Spanish elements do however feature as quite separate entities: the French tapas bar, that was as good as any I have used in Spain; and the nomad musicians who visit the town every year. Their street performances are vigorous-to-robust, with powerful breathy flute playing.

The seawater around Banyuls is so clear and well stocked with fish that the town is the home of the Arago laboratory of the University of Paris, which in fact dominates the port and its modest Capitainerie. Respecting these qualities, there is a vast protected area offshore clearly marked by yellow buoys.

Wine flows freely hereabouts, and special attention should be paid to the power of the local brew known just as Banyuls. It is similar to the Muscat de Rivesaltes, drunk in a similar way as an aperitif or with dessert, and goes down just as smoothly, but, if anything, packs more of a punch. It is possible to visit the Cave Templiers for a tour of inspection and the (obligatory) tasting.

The Île Petite marks the end of the easterly town bathing beach and the Île Grosse marks the end of the harbour, being connected to the mainland by a sea wall. Atop this, overlooking the whole scene, is the massive monument to the dead by the famous sculptor Aristide Maillot, the child of Banyuls whose monument is a couple of miles to the south west. There is a bracing walk up the rocks to inspect the monument to the fallen.

If you first approach the Mediterranean coast of France from Spain, you could not find a better community in which to spend a few days acclimatising. It is not as cosmopolitan as Menton on the borders of Italy, but neither is it so much under the influence of its foreign neighbour. A splendid place. ■

Part Four

CORSICA

━━━━━━

Charts SHOM 7025, 6969, 6970, 6822, 7050, 6823, 6942, 6855, 7162, 6929,
7024   ECM 1006, 1007, 1008, R3   ADM 1999, 1985, 1992, 1213, 1424, 1425

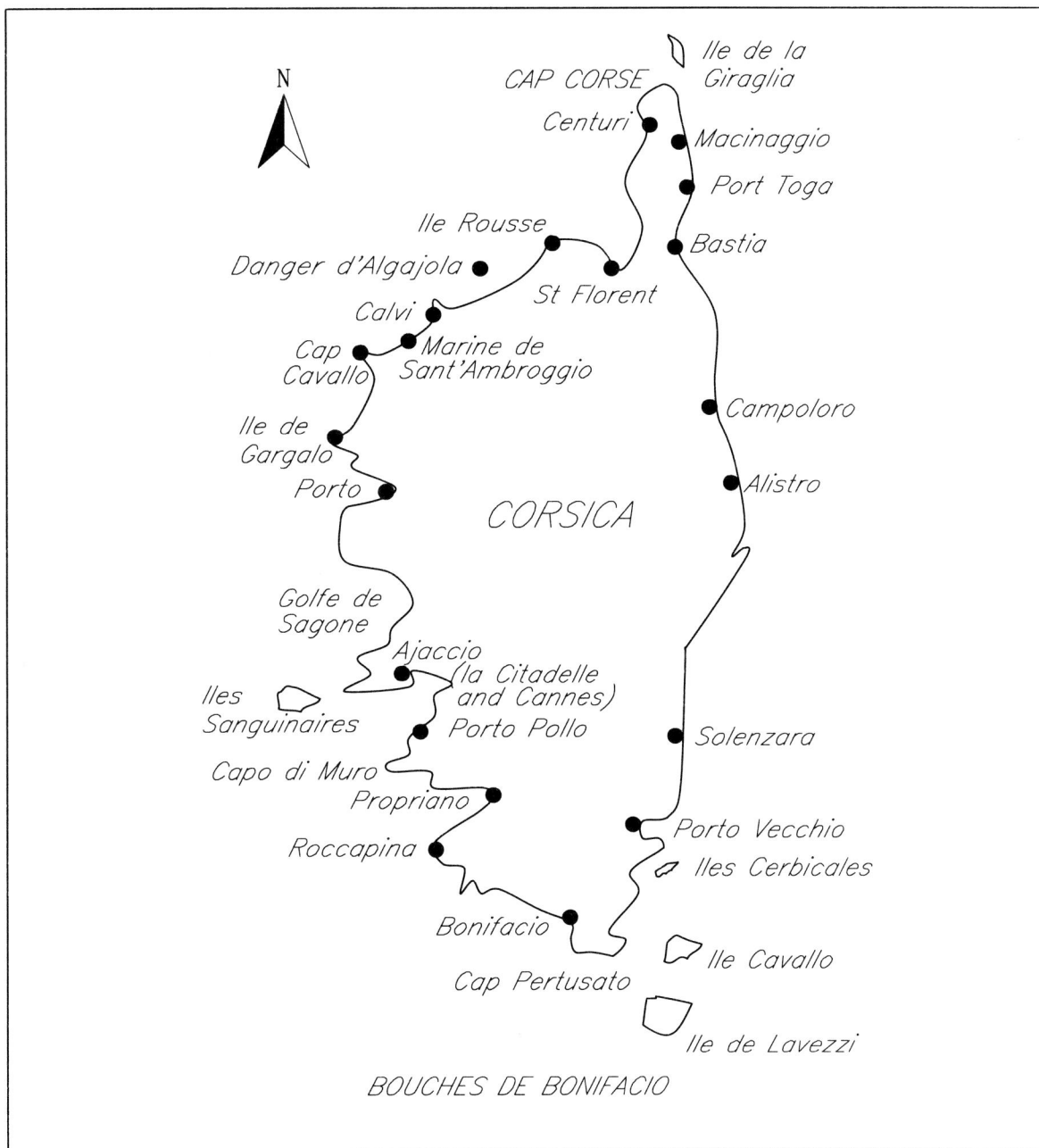

N

*Ile de la
Giraglia*

CAP CORSE

Centuri

Macinaggio

Port Toga

Ile Rousse

Bastia

Danger d'Algajola

St Florent

Calvi

*Marine de
Sant'Ambroggio*

*Cap
Cavallo*

Campoloro

*Ile de
Gargalo*

Alistro

Porto

CORSICA

*Golfe de
Sagone*

*Ajaccio
(la Citadelle
and Cannes)*

*Iles
Sanguinaires*

Porto Pollo

Solenzara

Capo di Muro

Propriano

Porto Vecchio

Roccapina

Iles Cerbicales

Bonifacio

Ile Cavallo

Cap Pertusato

Ile de Lavezzi

BOUCHES DE BONIFACIO

Cap Corse to Calvi

Lights Cap Corse
Île de la Giraglia   Fl 5s   85m   29M   W Tower B Top

Marine de Barcaggio
43.01 N 09.25 E
Just to the south of the dramatic, rocky island of Giraglia is a tiny inlet between two rocky headlands, exposed to the north. There is a large sandy beach, and it has a small inner quay, where craft of less than 1.5m can creep in. The anchorage is 120–150m from the easterly beach in 3–5m. There are shallow rocks in the middle of the bay extending out some 300m.

Marine de Tollare
43.01 N 09.24 E
A shallow, rocky anchorage in front of a small beach on which is sited an old tower. It is not much frequented, and is tenable only in calm settled weather. The anchorage is to the east of the tower, in 3–5m.

Port de Centuri
42.58 N 09.19 E
A small picturesque fishing village, with something of a tortuous entry only suitable for craft up to 10m; and it is usually full of resident working boats. However, thanks to the presence of Île de Centuri there is a partly protected anchorage just outside in the bay. The bay and the entrance can be dangerous in winds from the west to the north. Since this is one of the prettiest spots on the island, it is predictably popular.

Anse d'Aliso
42.55 N 09.22 E
Just over 2 miles to the south of Centuri, this is an attractive anchorage that penetrates deep into an inlet between high-rising hills. The little village of Pino is close by to the south. Since it is exposed to severe weather from the east, it is only suitable in calm, settled conditions. The approach is free of hazards and the anchorage is in front of the beach in 3–5m.

Marine de Giottani
42.52 N 09.20 E
Like Aliso, this small bay with a diminutive haven is open to weather from the east and is only suitable in calm, settled conditions. The tiny port, 11 miles north of Saint Florent, accessible only to the smallest of local fishing craft, is found in the northerly corner of the bay. The anchorage is 120m from the shore in 6–7m.

Marines d'Albo et de Nonza
42.48 N 09.20 E
Due to the sand encroachment along this stretch, there are pleasant anchorages at both Albo and Nonza. The former is easily recognised by its vast asbestos factory and is not of great interest or beauty, and care must be taken not to approach the rocks that reach up to 100m offshore by the tower. The latter can be distinguished by the more splendid ruins of its own tower. The anchorage is just to the north of the village, where there is a dramatic vista of the miniature headland. The approaches shallow quickly from 50 to 10m. Protection is limited because of the direct, uninterrupted line of the shore, so settled conditions are desirable.

De la Farinole a Punta Vecchiaia
About 3 miles to the north of Saint Florent, there are numerous anchorages suitable for calm weather or wind from the land. The beaches are separated by small headlands with a Genoese tower; and the pyramid formation of Farinole is unmistakable. By taking the usual precautions you can find sandy anchorages in 100–150m from the shore in 4–6m. ∎

SAINT FLORENT
42.41 N 09.18 E

Lights	North Jetty	Oc(2)R 6s	6m	W9/R6M	W/R Tower
	South Jetty	Fl G 2s	4m	2M	G/W Base
	Ecueil de Tignosu	Fl R 2s	6m	2M	R Tower

ACCESS AND ENTRY

Approach is indicated by the major lights of Punta Vecchiaia and Punta Mortella, while closer in are those of the square, baroque-style Fornali and the light on the Tower of Tignosu (Tegnoso); a course should be made midway between these two latter. Care should be taken not to risk the rocks of Tignosu, and a 50m clearance is recommended. In addition, it should be noted that the bottom shelves steeply in the south of the bay, towards the area known as La Roya.

Access across the bay is straightforward, and the actual entry into the harbour is through the 35m entrance: a soft bottom at nearly 3m. Reception is at the butt of the first jetty and the Capitainerie is straight ahead in the body of the port. In general, the harbour is well protected from weather, but part of the reception quay is susceptible to winds from the west.

In settled weather, it is possible to anchor in the west of the bay and to the south of Tignosu in 5–6m.

COMMENT

There are good services and facilities in this magnificently situated little port. Craft can be left in perfect safety if you want to explore inland. In season, you may well want to do that for it is a popular spot, frequently crowded with revellers and carousing crews whose antics can seem endless. ∎

Anse de Fornali
42.41.N 09.17 E

This tiny bay lies about a mile to the north west of Saint Florent. It is a fine-weather anchorage. There is an isolated rock in the middle of the bay just to seaward of a line joining the two mini headlands. It draws not much more than a metre.

The safe approach is therefore from either side at between 250m and 500m. A prudent entry will take you to a secure anchorage about 50–100m off in 3–4m.

Baie de la Mortella
42.42 N 09.16 E

This is a largish bay with good opportunities for anchoring. There is no hazard in the approach if you keep a good 300m offshore, and make sure to keep well clear of the Pointe de Cepo, which has a shallow patch off its rocks just to the east of north.

There are good grounds above and below the Anse de Fiume Santo, which itself is a tiny bay. To the south is the Plage de Vaghio, encumbered by rocks close in, and to the north, near the ruin of a Genoese Tower, a series of tiny beaches separated by rocks. In each case, 200m off will find you in 3–5m.

Plage de Loto
42.43 N 09.14 E

A little to the west of Pointe Mortella, this is a tiny place, where you can anchor 100m off in 4–5m. Prudent navigation and a careful lookout can take you much farther in.

Plage de Saleccia
42.44 N 09.12 E

This is the neighbouring mirror twin to Loto, on the other side of the Curza headland, which should be given a clearance of 500m. There is an extremely long beach here, and it has the air of the Caribbean. Sadly, it is only possible in calm, settled weather because of the severity of the open sea swell. At about 150m from the beach, you will find 4–6m.

Anse de Malfaco
42.44 N 09.07 E

Here, in this deep creek, is a beautiful miniature experience, where you can anchor in the centre in 4–6m in all safety. This is a place to unship the dinghy and proceed to the head, where, past the rocky section, there is a small sandy area in 2–3m. ∎

L'ILE ROUSSE
42.38 N 08.56 E

Lights	La Pietra	Fl(3)W G 12s	64m	W15/G11M	W	Square Tower
	Port Jetty	Iso G 4s	12m	7M	G/W	Tower

About 20 miles from Saint Florent and 10 from Calvi, this is an intriguing spot with a fascinating self-contained community. Sadly, its approaches are by no means without hazard.

Coming from Calvi, you must watch out for the isolated rock off Algajola, known as the Danger of Algajola, marked with a BRB beacon in a failing state. The Pietra tower and the bulk of the Grande Île Rousse can be seen from afar. Closer in, a hotel and Genoese tower become visible. From Saint Florent, the rocky outfalls of La Pietra are to be avoided by standing well off. When the headland has been rounded, the end of the jetty will come into view.

In the absence of ferries and commercial shipping, you can take a berth at the jetty on the west quay before reporting to the Capitainerie. ∎

Algajola
42.37 N 08.52 E

Beware! About a mile off the main headland of San Diamiano to the north west lies the notorious Danger of Algajola: a small, proud and isolated rock that lives up to its name. The rock itself is never easy to spot, even on the calmest of days. It is 'marked' with a vestigial BRB beacon.

It stands, a sea guardian to the sentinel of the land fort, as part of the 17th-century defence constructions of the Genoese. The citadel and clock are immediately recognisable. There is an anchorage some 150m offshore east north east of the clock tower in 3–4m. It is also possible to take the dinghy into the small haven in the bay of the village, where there is a sandy beach (scattered rocks). Small craft can rest in 2–4m. ∎

MARINE DE SANT'AMBROGGIO
42.36 N 08.50 E

Lights   North East Jetty   Fl G 2s   7m   2M   G/W Base
              South West Jetty   Fl R 2s   7m   2M   R   Tower

ACCESS AND ENTRY

Avoid the Danger of Algajola (see above), and make your final approach from the south. The entrance channel is marked with red buoys, but so is the waterski channel a little to the north. They should not be confused.

There should be a minimum of 2m in the approach channel at all times, but there is a problem of sand silting or even building up. In addition, the marina quays are fringed with rocks, so extreme caution should always be exercised. About 3m off seems to be the standard precaution. Take extra care at the small jetty to the north.

COMMENT

This is a vast leisure development just a mile to the west of Algajola, built on the Sant'Ambroggio headland. The marina is on the east face. Once inside it is well protected, but the approach is secure only in calm, settled weather because of the swell that can make the shallows treacherous. There are good services and facilities in season, when it is extremely busy – and virtually none otherwise. ∎

Calvi to Porto

CALVI
42.34 N 08.46 E

Lights	La Revellata	Fl(2) 15s	97m	24M	W	Square tower, B Top
	Citadel	Oc(2)G 6s	30m	10M	G/W	Base
	Breakwater	Fl R 4s	6m	7M	W/R	Tower
	Pier Head	Q G	10m	9M	G/W	Base

Berths From 1.5m to 5.5m in the outer port. There are 350 berths, including some 150 for visitors. Maximum LOA is 60m.

ACCESS AND ENTRY

The Golfe de Calvi is entered between the two headlands of La Revellata and Spano. The close approach is imposing, and the ancient fortifications on this dramatically rocky peninsula stand out well from afar. The harbour is tucked under the south of the citadel on the east face of the headland. From it, to the east, there stretches a long sandy beach.

Entry to the port is problem free. Care should be taken to note the presence of large unlit mooring buoys. They should be left to port. Also, attention should be paid to the (swinging) movements of the car ferries.

Reception is at the second quay after the entrance. If the harbour is full (or too full for your liking) it is possible to anchor 200m off the long beach in more than 3m. The strong wind that causes trouble is from the north east, but that is rare in the summer; otherwise there may be good gusts from the north west and south west, and because of this, and the possibility of long swells, it is wise to lay an especially long scope of chain in the not-best-holding sand. The yellow beach marker buoys are to be respected.

COMMENT

Calvi is an immensely good-looking place, attractive and popular. It is usually a very busy spot, being the standard port of entry for yachtsmen from mainland France. There are full services and facilities, all social and domestic needs can be met, and comestibles abound. ∎

Baie de la Revellata
42.34 N 08.44 E

On the other side from Calvi, on the west face of the headland and just to the south of Pointe Bianca, are three fine weather anchorages. The surroundings are dramatic and severe, and there is usually plenty of room. They are, in order from the north, **Porto Vecchio**, where you can anchor 150m off 5–9m. There are isolated, but noticeable, rocks to be avoided. Close by is **La Grotte des Veaux Marins**, where there is 12–15m in front, but it is perhaps best visited by dinghy. Next is **Recisa**. There are isolated rocks to the north of this small bay. Anchor 110m off in some 10m. Last of the trio is the deep gully of **Port Agro**. Take a central course in and anchor 100m off the clearly visible rocks in 8–10m.

Baie de Nichiaretto
42.32 N 08.43 E

This a large bay, surrounded by the heights, and well protected from weather from the south west. It has a pleasant beach. A central entry to the south east avoids rocks. Anchor 100–200m off in 5–10m. There is also a small anchorage with 4–5m towards the south of the bay in front of a small hut.

Golfe de Galeria
42.25 N 08.39 E

There is secure tenure here in winds from the south west, although the swell may be bad; but when the weather is from the north west it becomes quite untenable. There is a shallow rock to the north of the hotel with little more than 1.5m. Anchor 100m off the beach from in front of the houses to the tower in 5–8m.

Marine d'Elbo
42.23 N 08.34 E

The bay comprises the shoreline between the headlands of Nera to the east and Palazzo to the west. The anchorage is exposed to weather from the north west but well protected from the south west. Entry is best advised by approaching the noticeable tower tending to a course on a north west/south east axis. This avoids the double rocks (Rocher Rougeatre) that head the smaller ones that extend from the mini peninsula below the tower. It also avoids the isolated rocks, closer in, to the west of the entrance to the creek.

Under the shadow of the tower and the surrounding hills you can hide away in one of the most appealing locations round the island: isolated, savage, steep and splendid. Anchor centrally off in anything from 20m at the entrance itself to 5m at the head. There are rocks off the south shore. ■

ÎLE DE GARGALO
42.22 N 08.32 E

Lights   Île de Gargalo   Fl W R 4s   37m   W8M/R6M   W Pillar R Top

This is a small island of steeply rising rock topped by a conspicuous tower, and with a slender light pillar at its north west headland. It is a place best explored in calm settled weather in the dinghy. There is a narrow (25m) pass between the island and the mainland with no better than 3m. To the north, just off Palazzo Point, is another small island, Ilot Palazza.

Anse de Girolata
42.21 N 08.37 E

A small inlet fronting a small haven of pontoons (fishing and trip boats, 1.5m only) with a sandy beach and some habitation below the vast mountain range. It is best to anchor centrally 250m from the beach, for to the west there are rocks under the Genoese tower; to the east the shore is thoroughly encumbered; and to the north, at the head of the bay, the beach extends far out into shoal waters. In calm and settled weather, anchor in the entrance in 5–10m. ■

Porto to Ajaccio

Porto

42.16 N 08.41 E

Porto itself sits in the very innermost central head of the bay to which it has given its name. Its tower on the outstanding (45m high) island of rock is immediately recognisable. In front of the town there is a large sandy beach; and, contrariwise for its name, it possesses no port at all, just a tiny quay for small pleasure boats. Anchor 150m off the beach in 9–10m, noting the yellow beach marker buoys.

Golfe du Porto Nord

In the northern half of the bay, there are four anchorages. **Lignaghia** is a small rocky section below Mount Cenino just to the east of Scopa Point where you can anchor in 10–12m. There is no land access. **Gradelle**, close west to Caspio Point, is another small anchorage. The surrounds are rocky and the entrance should be on the central axis. Anchor 100m off the beach in 3–5m of good holding sand. **Caspio** is just behind its own headland, and the ground shelves gently from 10m at the entry. Anchor 100m or so off the beach in 3–5m with a sandy bottom. **Bussagna** is the last in the northern half. It is less than a mile to the north of Porto and has a good stretch of beach. The southern part of the beach has reefs up to 150m off. Anchor, tending to the northern end of the beach, in 5–10m.

Golfe de Porto Sud

In the southern half of the bay, there are four anchorages. **La Castagna** has a small quay used by small local boats; for visitors it is somewhat ineffective and potentially dangerous. There are also laid moorings, the only ones in the bay. **Ficajola** is perhaps the best choice on this side of the bay. Halfway between Porto and Cap Rosso, it offers an anchorage 100m off the beach in 6–8m. Care should be taken to avoid the rocky outfalls off the small headland to the west. **San Pellegrinu** is tucked away under the tower of Cap Rosso. It is a fine-weather spot. Approach prudently, about 500m off the very large rock. Anchor 100m off the shingle beach in 8–12m. **Sbiro** is the very last in the bay in a number of ways. The island lies directly under the spectacular Cap Rosso with its prominent tower, and is utterly dwarfed by it. Right at the end of the

bay, it is only tenable in the very best of calm and settled weather. Anchor in the north part of the beach, about 150m off in 5–10m.

Anse de Palo

42.13 N 09.34 E

Palo is immediately to the south of Cap Rosso. It is open to weather and swell. It is only suitable in calm, settled conditions. It is a quiet away-from-it-all spot compared with Bay of Porto. The anchorage is farthest east in the bay, and if you approach from a southerly aspect you will avoid the offshore rocks that are on the northern part of the tiny bay. Anchor 120–150m off in 10–15m; alternatively, you can use the section just to the north, where there is 5–10m.

Immediately next door is the anchorage known as **Porto à Leccia**. It is to the north of Tuselli Point, a quiet spot with no more than a few huts. You can anchor 100–150m off in 5–10m. If you approach from the south, it is necessary to stay well clear of Tuselli Point as a solitary rock stands some 100m or so off its point, slightly tending to the north. To the south of it is the **Anse d'Arone** where you can anchor off the beach in front of the few houses by the copses on the hill. The approach from the south is without hazard, but from the north, Tuselli Point must be well rounded. The sandy bottom shelves gently from 20m. Anchor 100–150m off the beach in 3–5m.

Baie de Chioni

42.10 N 08.35 E

There is a splendid beach here, and its situation is well protected from north and northwesterly weather by Orchino Point. This is noticeable for its small peak and, slightly inland, its Genoese tower. It marks the northerly extent of the bay. To the south the bay ends at Omignia Point, a more slender peninsula, also with a small tower. The central bay is obvious, marked by the holiday village. The 50m at the outer entrance gradually decreases to about 5m at 200m off, where there is good holding ground.

Just round the corner, between Omignia Point and Cargese Point, is another bay, the **Baie de Pero**. It is almost a twin: holiday village territory with a sandy beach between two rocky points. It lies in the shadow of the tiny town of Cargese. Landing is possible, and there is a road up to the town. Anchor some 250m off the gently shelving beach in 5–7m.

Cargese
42.08 N 08.36 E

The most eye-catching aspect of Cargese is formed by the two remarkable clock towers that stand high above the small bay. There is a small quay, but there is room for only forty boats, including local fishing boats. Maximum LOA is 12m and draught is an optimistic 2m. Reception is on the inner quay. The chances of finding a berth are small, but there is an anchorage about 1000m to the east of the port. Cargese does not have lights.

Attention must be paid to the rocks off the sea wall to the south, and to the isolated shoal patch just off to the south of the eastern rocky headland.

It is an extremely pleasant place, and there are reasonable services and facilities; but, above all, the people are charming and characterful in the best local traditions. The village itself is but a short walk up the hill.

Sagone
42.06 N 08.42 E

This miniature port/haven is situated in the north east corner of the vast Bay of Sagone. It is easily accessible, but the absence of any light makes it suitable only by day. The quay is a modest affair, carrying 2–3m, and it is not wise to count on gaining a place. It is suitable only for small craft. You can anchor to the east of the port, off the beach, in gently shelving depths from 20–5m. There are a few shops.

Baie de Liscia
42.03 N 08.44 E

At the extreme south east end of the broad Sagone Bay is this much smaller self-contained one. It possesses two anchorages: one is to the south, behind Orcine Point, and lies between the old tower and the more recent hotel. The other is to the north of the bay, about half a mile from Locca Point, and is in front of the holiday villas.

Attention should be paid to the rocks off both headlands, as well as those offshore in the centre of both anchorages. The drill is the same for each: don't approach too close to the coast, and anchor 150m off in 5–10m.

Golfe de Lava
41.59 N 08.44 E

About 3 miles from Cap Feno, this is the last bay in the sweep that is Sagone. It is usable only in calm and settled weather. To the north of the bay itself, there is an anchorage off the beach at **Port Provençal**. Attention should be paid to the rocks just offshore of the headland to the north. Anchor 150m off in 5–7m.

There is a second location, **La Figiera**, in the south west of the bay, where there is an anchorage immediately below the two peaks. Anchor 150m off in 5–10m. It is important to note and avoid the small Îlot de la Figiera to the west of the anchorage and just off the modest headland. There is no inshore passage.

Anses de Fico, de Minaccia et de San Antonio
41.36 N 08.37 E

These near twinned anchorages are the last before the Golfe d'Ajaccio. **Fico** is the smaller of the two bays, and lies just to the north of the island known as La Botte. The approach from the south is hazard free, but from the north there is the écueil de Fico to be avoided. It is a 2m shoal at 900m just to the east of north from La Botte. The anchorage is in the middle of the small bay, 100–150m from the beach in 5–7m. The two miniature heads just to the south have dangerous rocks.

Minaccia is a bigger experience: a larger bay; a more extensive beach; and many more people. The sandy bottom shelves gently and you anchor 200m off in 3–5m. There is a shoal rocky patch of 1.5m about 200m to the north west of the southern end of the bay.

San Antonio is the last. It is another tiny, sandy bay with its anchorage 100m off in 3–5m. From here, the next port of call is the completely different Ajaccio. ∎

Ajaccio to Propriano

AJACCIO
41.55 N 08.45 E

Lights					
	Grande Sanguinaire	Fl(3) 15s	98m	27M	W Square Tower
	Ecueil de Tabernacle	Fl(3)R 12s	10m	7M	R Tower
	La Guardiola	Fl R2 5s	6m	2M	R Tower
	Citadelle Shelf	Fl(4)R 15s	10m	7M	R Tower
	Capu di Muru	Oc 4s	57m	9M	W Square Tower
Mark	La Campanina	BRB Beacon			

Ajaccio, the second port of the island, is the most secure harbour on the west coast that is capable of entry in all weathers, day and night. The bay is entered between Les Îles Sanguinaires and Capu di Muru, where the opening is in excess of a mile. You then leave to port La Guardiola and the Citadelle Buoy, and then continue tending to port until the Citadelle Jetty comes into view.

Attention should be given to the third harbour in the bay: to the east, at Aspretto Point. It is a military/naval port and as such is prohibited to leisure craft. Much manoeuvring takes place in its environs, and yachtsmen should cruise prudently in the area. ■

PORT DE LA CITADELLE
41.55 N 08.45 E

Lights					
	Citadelle Light	Fl(2)WR 10s	19m	W20M/R16M	W/R Tower
	Citadelle Jetty	Oc R 4s	13m	8M	W/R Column
	Capucins Jetty	Fl RG 4s	8m	7M	G/W Base

Berths Draught is 4–10m; with 250 berths plus 63 for visitors. Maximum LOA is 50m; 15m at the pontoons.

ACCESS AND ENTRY
The harbour is available at all times, and the entrance is round the south jetty head. There are unlit mooring buoys. Reception is at O pontoon. Anchoring is permitted in the north east section of the basin. Prior permission must be obtained from the Capitainerie.

COMMENT
This is the more popular of the two harbours, because, although it is smaller and older, it is nearer to all the facilities of the town. There is much movement close by from the smallest of fishing boats up to the largest of ferries. There is a possibility of turbulence being experienced within the harbour. ■

PORT DES CANNES
41.55 N 08.45 E

Lights Jetty North Head Fl(2)R 6s   5m   6M   W/R Tower
           Jetty South Head Fl(4)Vi 15s 7m   1M   W/R Column
Berths Draught is 2–15m; with 803 berths, of which 203 are for visitors. Maximum LOA is 50m; 15m at the pontoons.

ACCESS AND ENTRY
The harbour is available at all times, and the entrance is round the north head of the outer jetty wall. Reception is immediately to port upon entry: at the foot of the light tower.

COMMENT
This is a more modern affair than the old Admiralty (Citadel) harbour. Already much bigger, it is still growing and there are many plans for development – and some works are under way. It cannot be said to match the charm of the other, but it has full services and facilities.   ∎

Anse de Sainte Barbe
41.51 N 08.46.E
Just over 4 miles south of Ajaccio, this bay is one of the most protected and also one of the prettiest on the island. Predictably, it is popular. It is found on the north face of Setta Nave Point and has tiny beaches separated by rocky promontories. The only winds that cause inconvenience are northerlies. Setta Nave has an easily recognisable wooded hill topped by a conspicuous tower. There are isolated islets and rocks to the north and these should be given good clearance: an offing of 750m clears these hazards. Anchor 200m off just round the headland in front of the bar in 5–7m.

Port de Chiavari
41.49 N 08.46 E
About 2 miles to the south east of Setta Nave, this is not a port as such, merely a haven of an anchorage. In front of the villas and pines there are anchorages provided you do not go too close in. The better part is towards the south of the beach 150m off in 3–5m.

Anse de Portigliolo
41.48 N 08.44 E
This quiet anchorage, open to the north west, is off an attractive beach at the foot of pretty hills. It is protected from south west winds by Castagna Point, but when there is weather the swell can make it uncomfortable. Local boats are moored to buoys. The approach is problem free if you make for the beach and anchor 150m off in 5–7m.

Anse de la Cacao
41.45 N 08.41 E
Near Cap Muro, this is veritably the last anchorage in the Bay of Ajaccio. It is quite a wild spot with the neighbourhood dominated by the Genoese Tower of Muro. Cap Muro itself should be rounded well off. It is best to anchor towards the south east of the bay where there is a clean zone at 150m from the beach in 8–10m.

Anse d'Orzo
41.44 N 08.42 E
This is the last protected bay before Cap Muro. It is a fine-weather anchorage. In fact, there are two: in front of the larger of the two beaches towards the east, where there is 3–5m at 150m off. Obvious rocks divide the beach area. It is not safe to venture farther in because of rocky shelving. The second is near a pretty creek fringed with sand towards the west. Anchor 100m off in 4–5m with sandy bottom. Beware of rocks each side of the entrance, but the central course is clear and plain.

Porto Pollo
41.42 N 08.48 E
This is a large bay at the north of the Golfe de Valinco. It is well protected from the north west winds by Pollo Point. Weather from the south west makes it untenable. The more popular anchorage is in front of the old village and hotel. Anchor off the buoys for small boats in 6–10m. There is an alternative spot in front of the beach at Taravo. The rocks are obvious on the small headland at the north west of the mini bay, and the anchorage is in front of the beach 100m off these rocks to the north east in 3–4m.   ∎

PORT DE PROPRIANO
41.41 N 08.54 E

Lights	Cap de Muro	Oc 4s	54m		9M	W	Square Tower
	Scogliu	Oc(3)WG12s	16m	W15M/G12M		G/W	Base
	N Jetty	Iso G 4s	11m		10M	W/G	Column
	W Breakwater	Fl(2) 6s	2m		3M	R	Structure
	E Breakwater	Fl(3)G 12s	5m		6M	G/W	Base

Berths Draught varies: 3.5–6m. There are 380 berths, of which 320 are for visitors. Maximum LOA 32m. It is permitted to anchor off, except within the zone marked by an artificial line between the marina east breakwater head and the port north jetty head.

ACCESS AND ENTRY

Upon entering the Golfe de Valinco from the north, you should stand well off the Points of Muro, Nero and Porto Pollo. The port can then be seen ahead. From the south, from well off, round the Point of Campomoro; keep well off to miss the isolated Tavaria rocks, and continue so, to avoid the rock encumbered Point Lauroso with its acclaimed beaches. From close in, it is not until this latter has been rounded that the port will be visible.

At the close approach, there are unmarked rock/shoal patches just to the north of the light tower on the Scogliu jetty; 250m clearance avoids all dangers. The white light tower at Scogliu is conspicuous, as are several white buildings in the town, especially the dominant tall hotel block.

COMMENT

Propriano is the only port of call between Ajaccio and Bonifacio for fuel, water services and shopping. There is a full range of facilities here and it is a good base for exploration. Some improvements are in hand. ∎

Portiglio
41.39 N 08.52 E

At the extreme southern end of the long and famous Tavaria beach this is an anchorage well protected from south and south west winds, but otherwise very open and suitable only in calm, settled conditions. There are rocks to be avoided off the mini headland, and 500m avoids them all. Otherwise, anchor off as you please in 5–10m.

Campomoro
41.38 N 08.49 E

This scenic and well-protected large bay is situated to the east of the extremely rock-encumbered Campomoro Point. If approaching from the north or west, you should stand well off (at least 500m) to avoid these dangers. The headland is conspicuous and has a noticeable tower. The Château Durazzo is an unmistakable landmark for the region of the anchorage. To the west of the bay, there are some moorings and a small jetty in front of the village. Anchor 100–150m off in 4–5m. There is much weed, but a little exploration will find a sandy bottom.

Anse d'Agulia
41.36 N 08.47 E

About 2 miles to the south south west of Campomoro Point is this *calanque*-like anchorage. From the Point you tend southerly towards the tower-like peak known as Palo d'Eccica, and the entrance will show. From the south, it is necessary to stand off to avoid the Île d'Eccica and the following offshore rocks; 500m does this adequately. The approach to the creek must be on its central axis, as both sides are rock strewn. There is between 8m and 10m just outside, 6m at the entrance, and the obvious central track into the narrowing creek slowly reaches 2m off the tiny beach. It is an outstandingly beautiful spot: dramatically compelling and charmingly appealing at the same time.

Calanque de Conca et Scoglio Blanco
41.34 N 08.48 E

Both these attractive settings are created and more or less dominated by the extensive Senetose Point, its conspicuous tower and its castle-like lighthouse. There are isolated rocks to be avoided all round the headland: to the south, off Aquila Point, and to the south west and west of Scoglio Blanco.

Conca is a mile or so to the north east. The approach is rocky and you should stand well off so that you can come in on a course due east towards the ruins. This will avoid the isolated shoal rocks (1.8m) to starboard. Anchor generally off the entrance in 5–8m. Further close exploration shows a gradual lessening to 2m in front of the tiny beach.

Nearby, on the north face of Senetose, there is an anchorage formed by the small peninsula of the nearly-closely joined islands. There is an unlit mooring buoy (available when not in use by the vedettes) in the west of the bay, and there are rocks to the east. Anchor near the buoy in 8–10m, or closer to the creek in 4–5m. This is a place for exploration by dinghy. A path will take the energetic to the lighthouse.

Port de Tizzano
41.32 N 08.41 E

The small jetty on the starboard hand (to the east) is all that justifies Tizzano being called a port. It is an attractive creek that shallows very quickly after the entrance into no more than 0.5m. The anchorage is more or less central in the entrance, just before the village and its jetty. The bottom is irregular and depths can be lost quickly, so it is best to venture towards the shore only in the dinghy. There are shops and cafes.

Golfe de Mortoli
41.31 N 08.52 E

The bay lies between Mortoli Point to the east and Latoniccia Point to the west. Both Points are to be well rounded: there are rocks littering Mortoli, and Latoniccia has, in addition, the small island of La Botte. Within the bay, there are two choices: the somewhat rocky Brièche, off the south face of Latoniccia, where you can anchor 100–150m off in 8–10m; and in front of the long beach, a similar distance off in 6–8m. ■

Roccapina to Bonifacio

Golfe de Roccapina
41.30 N 08.55 E

This is next door to Mortoli, separated by that headland and completed to the east by its own, rock-strewn, Point Roccapina. The whole bay is attractive, and the tower at the crest of the hills makes it unmistakable. You can anchor anywhere 100–150m off the long beach in 5–10m. In addition, there is a special open cove with an attractive small sandy beach that is quite intriguing. The close approach is tricky because of the scattered rocks that abound. To the west there are offshore rocks, so you should approach from the east. Once close to the small bay, you should enter centrally, but tending if anything to the north west. The broken reefs of rocks run parallel to the west shore. Happily, these can easily be discerned by your (obligatory) lookout. Anchor 200m off in 4–6m.

Anse de Fornello
40.30 N 09.00 E

From the west, look out for the rocky shelving off Olmeto and note the Prêtre Tower close by. Round the Olmeto headland, made noticeable by its conspicuous tower, with a wide berth. From the east, keeping well clear of the rock-encumbered coastline, head for the tower before turning to starboard into the entrance. Inside the bay, there is an isolated rock, at just over a metre, to the east. Anchor off the beach, with the miniature headland to your east, in 3–5m.

Anse d'Arbrito
41.28 N 09.01 E

Only a mile or so from Fornello, the bay can be identified by the massive Monte Milese that stands over it, and closer in by the edifice of the huge villa that rises out of the pines. The small headland to the west inside the bay is encumbered with rocks; the beach itself is fronted to seaward by an isolated rock, and immediately by a dangerous collection. Keeping your distance, at 500m from the beach, and 100m off the headland, you can anchor in 4–5m.

Anse de Capinero
41.28 N 09.02 E

Capinero is approached from the west round the îlots Bruzzi, and their associated rocks which reach out to the south and should be rounded at a good 800m. From the east, Figari Point also has its offshore rocks, to the south west. These are avoided at 500m.

Once the bay has fully opened, the central entrance course is clear and hazard free. The shore to the east is rock strewn. The safest anchorage is more or less to the centre, just past the villas on your port hand. Anchor about 200m off in 4–5m.

Baie de Figari
41.27 N 09.03 E

Rock of Ages: with its 2 miles' penetration into the surrounding hills, this is indeed a veritable cleft of a creek. Its access is not entirely problem free, due to the outlying rocks and small islands. There is no navigation light anywhere in the inlet, so a daytime arrival is a necessity.

From east and west, both small headlands must be given a clear rounding: to the east there are the St Jean rocks, while to the west there are lots off Ventilegne Point as well as the two infamous ones – the southerly Testa di Gatto and the Figari shelf to the east of the entrance. At 1000m off you will clear all hazards.

You should fully open the bay and then line up the Figari Genoese Tower with the church clock tower at Caldarello. This will give you a course just to the east of north at 008°M. It is just to port of midway between St Jean and the Figari shelf, and leads directly to the first of the anchorages. This is a fine-weather spot, where you anchor 100–150m off in a sandy bottom at 4–5m.

To proceed farther into the creek, you follow a straight track with the St Jean rocks dead astern and the gap between the Caldarello jetty straight ahead. This avoids the offshore rocks to the west and Porraja island to the east. The next anchorage is less than 1km above the tower on the port hand. It is preceded by a miniature headland, off which shoal ground reaches out for 250m.

Once past this, you anchor in the middle of the small bay in front of the big villa (with it just to the north of west) about 150m off in 2–5m.

The other two anchorages are right at the head of the creek. One is more or less central in the channel, just to the south of the small jetty, while the other is off the north east tip of the îlot du Port. The bottom shelves steeply near the pontoon, but there is 10m just beyond. Off the small island you anchor between its low head-land and the mud bank to the north, opposite an old wreck and the restaurant on the mainland. These are from 7–9m some 50m to the north east of the island.

Golfe de Ventilegne
41.26 N 09.06 E

Two miles eastward along the coast from Figari, this tiny bay offers a fine-weather anchorage in front of its small beach. Coming from the west, stand off about 150m, but from the east, it is necessary to give a wide berth to the headland, from which there are dangerous banks of rocks; 250m clears all dangers. The depths vary from 10m at the entrance to 3–5m at 100–150m from the beach.

La Tonnara et Stagnolo
41.25 N 09.06 E

Immediately to the south of Ventilegne is the group of islands known as La Tonnara. There is a small anchorage just off the inlet where there is a tiny pontoon. There is no inshore passage that can be taken in safety; therefore you approach from the north, rounding the islands and being particularly careful to pass well to the north (say 500m) of the furthermost, because of the presence of a near-drying shelf and an iso-

lated rock to its north. The anchorage is halfway between the northernmost tip of the island and the actual entrance into the Tonnara haven. Anchor 200m off the island and offshore in a sandy bottom of 3–6m.

Just a little to the south of Tonnara and the islands, there is another small, equally rocky, bay. You tend to the northerly shore to avoid the rocks (only some of which are visible) in the southern part. The best approach is from due west in 10–12m, and then you can anchor some 200–250m off the beach in 4–5m.

Cala de Paragnano
41.24 N 09.08 E

No more than a mile or so from Bonifacio is this extremely pretty creek, the last of wild majesty before the rest sets in. The contrasting colours of the cliffs make for a truly memorable experi-ence.

Except for some rocks just in front of the beach at the head of Paragnano, there is no encum-brance. The entry is problem free with depths from 25m in the entrance at large to the sandy anchorage 150–200m off in 3–5m.

Close nearby, to the south east, the tiny bay of **Fazzuolo** offers a miniature anchorage behind the islands of the same name. About 1km from Madonetta Point, there is a boating centre with facilities in 2–3m. The entrance is to the west of the islands and, apart from isolated rocks off the small headland to port, it is problem free. There is little room to manoeuvre once you are in the neighbourhood of the centre, and boats tend to stay nearer the entrance in 4–5m. It is only possible to circumnavigate the large island in a dinghy or similar shoal craft. It is a small delight.

■

Bonifacio to Porto Vecchio

BONIFACIO
41.23 N 09.09 E

Lights	Approach Lights					
	Capo de Feno	Dir Fl(4) 15s	20m	19M	W	Square Tower B Top
	and also	Fl(4)WR 15s	23m	7-4M		
	Cap Pertusato	Fl(2) 10s	100m	25M	W	Square Tower B Top
	Bonifacio Lights					
	La Madonetta	Iso R 4s	28m	7M	R	Square Tower
	L'Arenella	Oc(2)R 6s	9m	6M	W/R	Tower
	Cacavento	Fl G 4s	6m	5M	G/W	Base
	Grand Jetty	Oc G 4s	7m	7M	G/W	Base

Berths There are 400 berths, with maximum LOA 40m. Draught is 2.5–8m. In the yacht harbour, the moorings to port are fingers, while to starboard they are buoys to concrete anchors.

It is also possible to anchor within the generality of Bonifacio harbour: the Calanque d'Arenella has 1m, and the Calanque Catena has 3–6m. The authorities accept no responsibility for boats anchored here.

ACCESS AND ENTRY
The approach is problem free and Capo de Feno and Cap Pertusato are conspicuous from afar. The entry lies between Madonetta Point (to port) and Timon Point (to starboard), which with its unmistakable citadel is probably one of the finest and most dramatic sights of Corsica. The harbour is accessible at all times and in all weather.

The yacht harbour, which is completely protected, lies in the very depth of the harbour, which runs parallel to the coast in an east/west direction.

COMMENT
It is wellnigh impossible not to exaggerate the impressive beauty of the approach and the harbour itself, especially in the rays of the setting sun. The city has all the services and facilities you would expect of an international centre. Prepare to be detained – there is much to seduce. ∎

Bouches de Bonifacio
Main passage The prudent skipper who wishes to risk neither the wind nor the weather will not hesitate to take the outer circle to the south of the islands of Cavallo and Lavezzi. This takes you to the south of the islands, by Capu di u Beccu and the associated marks, rounding the headland at about 1000m for full safety, and then proceeding slowly to the north running parallel to the coasts of Lavezzi and Cavallo. The course is just to the east of north. The pass between Cavallo and Perduto is almost a mile wide and carries nearly 50m. The extremities are well marked.

SPECIAL MARK

La Pyramide de la Semillante is a remarkable, conspicuous and unmistakable skyward searching monument to those souls who perished on their way to the Crimea in 1885. The frigate was utterly destroyed. There were no survivors among the 773 on board.

Lights					
Lavezzi Island	Oc(2)WRG 6s	28m	W15/R11/G11M	Square Tower and building with R bands
Lavezzi Rock	Fl(2) 6s	18m		9M	BRB Tower
Sud Lavezzi	Q(6)+LFl 15s				YB Cardinal
Perduto Island	VQ(9) 10s	18m		11M	YBY Cardinal
Perduto Shelf	Q(3) 10s	16m		11M	BYB Cardinal

Other passages There are two choices, and they both begin in the same way. You leave the island of Saint Antoine and Cap Pertusato to port; avoid the offshore BRB marked Le Prêtre; and continue easterly past Punta de Sperono until you open the pass between Île Piana and the BY beacon marking the Tignosa di Ratino. The channel, which is just to the east of north, carries 12m. The choice comes after the beacon: to take the Passage de la Piantarella or the pass between Ratino and Poraggia. The Piantarella risks nothing, while the other, with its rocks and shallows close at each side, is perhaps best left for a calm day's exploration when there is no deadline or need to make the pass should prudence so suggest.

There are other channels, known to those who possess expert local knowledge. However, these are not for first-time visitors, the inexperienced, nor the fainthearted.

Îles Lavezzi and Cavallo

These two major islands in what is known as the Archipel des Lavezzi contain some of the most favourite summer anchorages. There is one isolated spot just to the north of Piana Island halfway in to the mainland where, just above a sandbank that reaches out to the west from the island, you can anchor in 3–5m. Otherwise, Lavezzi and Cavallo have them all – and what an all it is. Numbering around a dozen, the major ones alone offer delights for days on end. Perhaps they are best explored for the first time in calm settled weather with the dinghy at the ready. A good chart is, of course, essential.

Golfe de Santa Manza

41.25 N 09.14 E

Once past the small island of Poraggia and heading north, you are no distance at all from the vast bay of Santa Manza. The tower of Manza stands on the long peninsula that ends with Capicciolo Point. It is popular, but since it is so large there is seldom the danger of not finding room at the anchorage. The approach and wide entry are without difficulty.

Within the deep creek, there are two anchorages. The first is at the head of the main run. Anchor 200m off the beach in 3–4m. The second is within the creek that runs off to starboard. Known as the Calanque de Stentino, it is a narrow wildish spot. There is a small, private jetty at the entrance. There is usually something of a bar at the entrance, to the south east of the jetty. Generally, you can count on there being close to 2m, but it is best to approach with caution as there are shallows to both sides of this entrance channel. Once inside, there is more water, but, due to a shoaling sandbank to the north, you must follow the south side where you have 2–3m. Farther in the creek, the anchorage is in the centre (100m from each side) in 4–6m.

In the bay at large, there is another anchorage in front of the Balistro beach. This is to the north east of the Point, where you can anchor 150–200m off in 4–5m. Because of the proximity of the inland Étang de Balistro, if you propose to stay overnight you will need a mosquito watch.

Baie de Rondinara

41.28 N 09.17 E

This bay lies behind the quite unmistakable Point that bears its name. It is one of the most appealing and protected places between Bonifacio and Porto Vecchio. From north and south, the headland needs to be carefully rounded because of isolated rocks; 500m off is all that is needed. The approach and entry are broad and safe and you can anchor at will, tending to the south to avoid the isolated shallow patch (–1m) to the west of the inner promontory. Anchor 100–150m off the beach in 4–6m.

In calm and settled weather, there is an alternative anchorage to the south of Rondinara Point. There is a miniature bay where you can anchor 120–150m off in 3–5m. It is reasonably protected from weather from the north.

Baie de Porto Nuovo
41.30 N 09.16 E

This twin/split bay, at 2 miles, is midway between Rondinara and Santa Giulia. It has two pleasing anchorages, both off sandy beaches and very good for bathing. It is however open to weather from at large.

The approach and entry are easy and plain, without hazard. The easterly anchorage is completely clear and you anchor at will in 3–5m. The small headland that separates the two has small rocks off that are to be avoided. The other anchorage also has rocks close in. It is, therefore, advisable to anchor some 200m distant from the innermost part of the bay where you will have some 5–6m.

Anses d'Acciajo et La Folacca
41.33.N 09.19 E

The first anchorage is tucked well into the coast to the south of Acciajo Point. The bay is quite open and the approach from the south is plain and obvious. From the north, the headland that separates this bay from La Folacca must be well cleared to the south to avoid the many offlying rocks. They are easily visible and you should keep off at least 300m. Anchor in the centre of the bay about 200m off in 7–10m. There is a splendid view of some massive pines.

The northern part of the double bay is marked by the small Isle of Folacca. Both the northern section of the bay and the island are encumbered with rocks. The anchorage is between the island and the beach, behind which are more pines. Anchor 200m off in 5–6m.

Plage de Palombaggia
41.33 N 09.20 E

This region is known almost exclusively for the magnificence of its beach, one of the most celebrated in Corsica. You can anchor at will provided you approach no closer than 200m, after which rocks abound.

Not far to seaward are the **Îles Cerbicales**, which consist of three main groups: Pietricaggiosa, the most southerly; the largest – Piana – and its immediate rocky neighbour Maestro Maria; and the most northerly, Forana. There are possible anchorages and is best explored in calm settled weather. ∎

Porto Vecchio to Bastia

GOLFE DE PORTO VECCHIO

Lights	Chiappa	Fl(3+1) 15s	65m		24M	W	Square Tower R Top
	Pecorella	Fl(3)G 12s	12m		6M	G/W	Tower
	Ciprianu	Fl WG 4s	26m	W11/G9M		W	Square Tower B Top
	Benedetto	Fl(4)G 15s				G	Pillar
	Fozzoli	Oc(2)WRG 6s	10m	W15/R/G13M		W	Column B Top
Marks	Chiapano Rock		BRB Beacon				
	Harbour Approach Channel		Standard buoyage				

Marine d'Arghi
41.36 N 09.21 E
Tucked away on the south side of Porto Vecchio Bay, there is a small, private yacht haven project.

Access is prohibited, but there is an anchorage in front of the venture about 250m off the rocky central section of the bay in 4–6m. ∎

PORTO VECCHIO
41.35 N 09.17 E

Lights	Main Harbour	Iso.WRG 4s	9m	W11/R/G10M		W/R	Structure
	Bifurcation	QG					
	La Cioccia	Fl R 2s	3m		2M	R	Turret
	East Jetty	Fl(2)R 6s	5m		6M	W/R	Tower
	West Jetty	Fl G 4s	4m		5M	W/G	Tower

Berths There 600 berths, including 150 for visitors, for which the maximum LOA is 20m. Depths in the yacht harbour are 1–4m. Moorings in the harbour are to buoys and concrete fingers. Reception is to port after entering. Anchoring is permitted FOC in the port, outside the channels.

ACCESS AND ENTRY
The harbour is accessible at all times and in all conditions. The approach is straightforward: Cipriano Point and the Pecorella Rocks are northerly, and Chiappa Point and its associated rocks are to the south. There are wide, clear passages between Pecorella and Ciprianu and also between Ciprianu and Chiapino.

From whatever direction you arrive, the first track into the bay takes you on to the Benedetto buoy, towards Fozzoli Point. If you arrive to the south of Pecorella, the course is due west. Then you follow a south east course along the main channel until you reach the green buoy, known pedantically as Bifurcation, that marks the parting of the ways for commercial and leisure craft. Yachts then make a course for Cioccia, the red buoy that guards the shallow shelf, and so on to the yacht harbour itself.

COMMENT

Porto Vecchio is a splendid centre and possesses all services and facilities for craft as well as crew. It is an excellent base for local inland exploration. Predictably, it is always busy and usually crowded.

There are other 'ports of call' within Porto Vecchio Bay:

Îlot Ziglione

This tiny island, in the south western section of the inner bay, marks an anchorage just off the main channel. In the small bay just to the south of the island there are mooring buoys, and you can anchor outside them in the middle of the bay about 150m off in some 4–5m. There is marginally less water in the south of the bay.

Baie de Stagnolo
41.37 N 09.19 E
Away to the north of the inner bay, this small bay is the site of a holiday camp on its north east shore. There are two possible anchorages: in front of the camp, and to the west on the inside of Rossa Point.

You leave Benedetto astern and make for a central point at the entrance to the bay heading for the small rocks right in the middle. This avoids the rocks off both points. Then you take an immediate track west for Rosso, or to the east of north for the noticeable camp. In either case, keep a sharp lookout for the central hazards. Anchor 200m off the camp tending to the north or east of the rocks in 2–4m. Anchor 200m off Rosso, tending to the south west of the rocks in 2–4m.

Golfe de Saint Cyprien
41.38 N 09.22 E
Saint Cyprien is right at the north of Porto Vecchio Bay, and might be considered to be almost outside. The entrance is midway between the small islands of Cyprien and Cornuta to the north east, and the small and very rocky headland to the south west (not to be confused with Ciprianu Point, which is the main point about 1km immediately to the south).

Once inside the entrance, the anchorages are to the north and the east. More than half this bay is shallow, carrying less than 2m; but you anchor round the small headland in the east about 200m off in 4–6m, and to the north west of Cyprien island some 400m off in 4–5m.

Golfe de Pinarello
41.41 N 09.23 E
North of Porto Vecchio Bay, there are many small inlets and anchorages that can all be searched out in calm and settled weather; but Pinarello is the first and last one of any substance between Porto Vecchio and Solenzara.

The approach is problem free: well marked by the island, of the same name as the Bay, and topped at 50m by its tower. There are rocks to be avoided to the north in the main entrance, known as the ilôt Roscana. There are two anchorages: in front of the beach between the conspicuous hotel and the pines where there is 5–7m some 200m off; and tucked away behind the north face of the island, under the tower not far from the large rock much favoured by divers. Anchor 150m off in 5–7m.

In addition, just to the south of the island, there are also small anchorages in what is called the Anse de Cola. You can anchor to the north (200m off in 5–7m) near the rocks and opposite the villas, and to the south in front of the holiday camp beach (200m off in 7–10m).

En route to Solenzara, there are four more or less equally spaced, small anchorages. In north-going order, they are **Fautéa**, **Tarco**, **Favone** and **Canelle**. In the main, they must be classified as summer-season spots, suitable only in calm settled weather. Like Cola, there is a tendency for them to be busy with the camping trade. ■

SOLENZARA
41.51 N 09.24 E

Lights   There are red and green lights at the entrance to the port, of a somewhat irregular nature. Night entry is not recommended.

Berths   There are 350 berths, on floating pontoons to buoys, of which 300 are for visitors. The draught in the port varies from 1m to 3m. This is to err on the generous side, and craft of more than 2m should proceed with the greatest of caution as depths are eccentric. The maximum LOA is 25m. Reception is immediately inside, to port by the fuel jetty.

ACCESS AND ENTRY

The port is just to the south of the mouth of the Solenzara River. The offshore approach is problem free, and the entrance faces due east. It can be easily recognised by the tall blocks of flats. Access is difficult in east south east and south east winds, and in general it must be deemed to be a fine-weather port. There is a dangerous rocky area south and south west of the entrance.

COMMENT

There is little here to charm the visitor, but services and facilities are good and shopping can easily be undertaken nearby. The river is not navigable other than by shoal craft. ∎

PORT DE CAMPOLORO
42.20 N 09.32 E

Lights

Alistro	Fl(2) 10s	93m	24M		Grey Tower with B Top
East Jetty	Oc(2)WR 2s	7m	W9/R6M	W/R	Column
North Jetty	Fl G 2s	3m	2M	G/W	Tower

Berths   There are 464 berths, of which 200 are for visitors. Moorings are to pontoons and buoys. Maximum LOA is practically 20m. The reception quay lies dead ahead upon entry and is noticeably marked. Anchoring within the port is prohibited.

ACCESS AND ENTRY

The port is found 5 miles to the north of the Alistro light. It is accessible in all weather, except in strong winds from the east to north east. Approach and entry are problem free, although full recognition of the port must be delayed until less than 2 miles off. The outer port is silted up and the route to the yacht berths is buoyed.

COMMENT

Also known as Port de Taverna, this is a modern yacht harbour with comprehensive facilities for boats. Built with its self-contained social and domestic services, it is isolated from traditional town or village life of any kind. Its hinterland is well worth exploring. ∎

Bastia to Cap Corse

BASTIA
42.42 N 09.27 E

Lights	Dragon Jetty	Fl(4)WR 12s	16m	W15/R12M	Grey	Tower
	Mole Genois	Oc(2)G 6s	13m	8M	Grey/G	Tower
	Saint Nicholas	Fl G 4s	9m	9M	W/G	Tower
	Car Ferry	Q R	2m	7M	W/R	Tower

Berths There are some 300 berths, of which 40 are for visitors. The maximum LOA is given as 50m. Mooring is to pontoons and chain. Mooring to the Dragon Jetty to anchor is difficult with the wind in the east or west, and becomes untenable in strong winds from the east. Permission may be given by the Capitainerie for yachts to use the commercial Port Saint Nicholas.

ACCESS AND ENTRY

The offing is without problem; the light tower at the end of the Dragon Jetty leads the way. If coming from the north, craft must keep off until well clear of all possibility of traffic using the Port Saint Nicholas entrance, not turning west until the Mole Genois is to starboard. After that, the run in is straight. Entry is difficult when the wind is in the west. Reception is accorded at the Mole Genois or at the jetty stemming from the north quay. Silt-mud is present.

COMMENT

This is not the place for sophisticated services and facilities; for example, stand pipes are used for water. However, everything you are likely to want, for boating, socialising or just day-to-day living, can be found not far away. The moorings are overlooked by the picturesque old town. In the season, it is constantly on the go, if not indeed the Go-Go. Not really a place for a quiet night. ∎

PORT TOGA
42.43 N 09.27 E

Lights   Jetty Head   Oc R 4s   10m   5M   W/R Tower
             Jetty Head   Q G
             Leading   RWR

COMMENT

This is a new yacht harbour, just to the north of the commercial port at Bastia. The entrance, which opens to the north, is dredged to 4m. There are some 415 berths, of which 355 are private, with 150 for visitors. Maximum LOA is 25m, and the depths in the port vary from 5m to 2.2m. Reception is at the Capitainerie (recently exploded) immediately to starboard upon entry. The situation here is neither constant nor predictable. It is a good idea to call ahead of arrival: VHF 9 or Telephone: 95 32 79 79. ∎

Erbalunga
42.46 N 09.29 E

Nothing could be farther from the Bastia/Toga experience than this miniature fishing port. Just a couple of miles to the south of Cap Sagro, the cottages cling to the rocks on the tiny headland as the tower stands guardian above the entrance. It is one of the most picturesque sights on Corsica. There is room or depth in the port only for the most shoal of fishing craft, but there is an anchorage outside to the south of the tower. The tiny bay is encumbered close in with rocks, and there is an isolated patch immediately to the south of the south face. Anchor 150–200m off in 4–5m.

Marine de Sisco
42.48 N 09.30 E

This small sandy bay is just a mile to the north of Cap Sagro, 7 miles north of Bastia. There is a small rivulet with a few houses scattered along the bay. The anchorage is just to the south of the inlet's small jetties. To the north, the beach is rocky just offshore. You can anchor 100–150m off in 3–5m. It is a fine-weather anchorage.

Marine de Pietracorbara
42.50 N 09.29 E

It is impossible to miss this pleasant beach because of the presence of the conspicuous and striking Aquila Tower. To the south of the small bay there is also a noticeable hotel. The anchorage is in the middle of the bay, about 100–150m off in 3–5m. It is a fine-weather anchorage.

Porticciolo
42.52 N 09.29 E

There is a small jetty at this tiny fishing village, where the stone cottages are stacked down to the edge of the sea. The tiny port is usable only by shoal craft. The anchorage is just to the south of middle in the small bay, where at 150m off you can anchor in 3–5m. It is a fine-weather anchorage.

Marine de Luri (Santa Severa)
42.53 N 09.29 E

This is another small fishing village. Its quay is slightly larger than Porticciolo, but still only usable by local small craft, since, although there is 3m in the entrance, this quickly drops to 1m. You can anchor 100–200m to the south of the entrance in 3–4m. To the south the ground shallows and off the little port's sea wall there are dangerous shoals. It is a fine-weather anchorage.

Marine de Meria
42.56 N 09.28 E

This fine-weather anchorage is just over a mile to south of Macinaggio. Here is another pretty village with another striking tower. The anchorage is midway between the village and the small headland with tower. Anchor 120–150m off in 3–5m. ∎

MACINAGGIO
42.57 N 09.27 E

Lights Cap Corse

Île de la Giraglia	Fl 5s	85m	29M	W	Tower B Top
East Jetty	Oc(2)WR 6s	10m	W12/R8M	W	Tower R Top
North Jetty	Fl G 2s	4m	2M	G/W	Base

Berths There are 500 berths, of which 200 are for visitors. The depths in the port vary from 1.2m to 4m and access is restricted to craft under 3.4m. Maximum LOA is around 40m. Anchorage is prohibited in the port, but is pleasant in the bay immediately to the north of the entrance; here you can anchor 150m off in 3–5m. Reception is in the body of the port: along the east jetty to the south quay where there is 3m dropping to 2.5m at the end.

ACCESS AND ENTRY

The approach from the north is marked by the tower of Santa Maria and the Finocchiarola islands, the port being situated not far to the south of Cap Corse. From the south it is straightforward; however, care should be taken when coming this way not to pass too close to the sea wall which is encumbered up to 150m off. Access is straightforward by day and night: clearly open to the north. Entry is difficult in winds from the north east to south east.

COMMENT

This is the yachting/fishing port of Rogliano: the 'first and last' port on this side of the island. The modern port has all marina services and domestic and social facilities. ∎

BAIES DE TAMARONE ET ÎLES FINOCCHIAROLA
42.59 N 09.28 E

Lights

Îles Finocchiarola	VQ(3) 5s			BYB Cardinal
Île de la Giraglia	Fl 5s	85m	29M	W Tower B Top

COMMENT

Just to the south of the three small islands of Finocchiarola are two anchorages. The islands are marked by a Cardinal, a wreck to the north, and a noticeable Genoese tower on the seaward side.

The more northerly anchorage is on the south west side of the islands, about 200m offshore where you will find 4–5m. The bay is unencumbered. The other choice is in Tamarone Bay, where at 150m off you will find a mainly sandy bottom with 4–5m. ∎

Rade de Sainte Marie
42.59 N 09.27 E

This is the other side of the island experience: just to the north west of Finocchiarola. Care must be taken because of the rocky hazards in the vicinity. There are three possibilities. The most southerly is **Sainte Marie,** the traditional Patience Roads for traffic awaiting good weather for Cap Corse. The anchorage is 200m offshore in the bay itself, below the church, in 4–5m. From the south, care must be taken to avoid the rocks off the small headland. The shoals and rocks extend to some 600m.

The next is in the **Cala Genoese,** where the southern part of the small bay is free of rocks, but on the approach from Sainte Marie you should stand off a good 150m. Anchor fairly close in to the south west with 2m, or 200m off with 4–5m.

The last is the **Cala Francese,** where you anchor at will tending to the south in 2–5m. Beware of the reef to the north of the bay. ▪

INDEX